THREE VIEWS ON THE
NEW TESTAMENT
USE OF THE
OLD TESTAMENT

Books in the Counterpoints Series

Church Life

Evaluating the Church Growth Movement

Exploring the Worship Spectrum

Remarriage after Divorce in Today's Church

Understanding Four Views on Baptism

Understanding Four Views on the Lord's Supper

Who Runs the Church?

Bible and Theology

Are Miraculous Gifts for Today?

Five Views on Apologetics

Five Views on Law and Gospel

Five Views on Sanctification

Four Views on Eternal Security

Four Views on Hell

Four Views on Salvation in a Pluralistic World

Four Views on the Book of Revelation

How Jewish Is Christianity?

Show Them No Mercy

Three Views on Creation and Evolution

Three Views on Eastern Orthodoxy and Evangelicalism

Three Views on the Millennium and Beyond

Three Views on the Rapture

Two Views on Women in Ministry

THREE VIEWS ON THE
NEW TESTAMENT
USE OF THE
OLD TESTAMENT

Single Meaning, Unified Referents
Walter C. Kaiser, Jr.

Single Meaning, Multiple Contexts and Referents
Darrell L. Bock

Fuller Meaning, Single Goal
Peter Enns

Stanley N. Gundry, *series editor*
Kenneth Berding, *general editor*
Jonathan Lunde, *general editor*

ZONDERVAN.com/
AUTHORTRACKER
follow your favorite authors

We want to hear from you. Please send your comments about this book to us in care of zreview@zondervan.com. Thank you.

ZONDERVAN

Three Views on the New Testament Use of the Old Testament
Copyright © 2008 by Kenneth Berding and Jonathan Lunde

Requests for information should be addressed to:

Zondervan, *Grand Rapids, Michigan 49530*

Library of Congress Cataloging-in-Publication Data
Berding, Kenneth.
     Three views on the New Testament use of the Old Testament : general editors,
Kenneth Berding and Jonathan Lunde.
          p. cm. — (Counterpoints : bible and theology)
     Includes bibliographical references and index.
     ISBN: 978-0-310-27333-2 (softcover)
     1. Bible. N.T.—Criticism, interpretation, etc. 2. Bible. O.T.—Relation to the New
Testament. 3. Bible. N.T.—Relation to the Old Testament. I. Berding, Kenneth. II.
Lunde, Jonathan, 1960-
BS2387.T49 2008
     220.6—dc22
                                                                                    2008032.231

Interior design by Matthew Van Zomeren

Printed in the United States of America

09 10 11 12 13 14 15 16 17 18 19 20 21 22 • 23 22 21 20 19 18 17 16 15 14 13 12 11 10 9 8 7 6 5 4 3 2

CONTENTS

Editors

Stanley N. Gundry is executive vice president of the publishing group at Zondervan. With more than thirty-five years of teaching, pastoring, and publishing experience, he is the author or coauthor of numerous books and a contributor to numerous periodicals.

Kenneth Berding (PhD, Westminster Theological Seminary) is associate professor of New Testament at Talbot School of Theology of Biola University. He is the author of *What Are Spiritual Gifts?: Rethinking the Conventional View* (Kregel) and *Sing and Learn New Testament Greek* (Zondervan). Ken and his family reside in La Mirada, California.

Jonathan Lunde (PhD, Trinity Evangelical Divinity School) is associate professor of biblical studies and theology at the Talbot School of Theology of Biola University. He has contributed articles to the *Dictionary of Jesus and the Gospels* and the *New Dictionary of Biblical Theology*. Jon and his wife, Pamela, have three children and reside in Brea, California.

Contributors

Walter C. Kaiser Jr. (PhD, Brandeis University) is the Colman M. Mockler distinguished professor of Old Testament and president emeritus of Gordon-Conwell Theological Seminary in South Hamilton, Massachusetts. He has taught at Wheaton College and at Trinity Evangelical Divinity School. Dr. Kaiser has written numerous books, including *Toward an Exegetical Theology: Biblical Exegesis for Preaching and Teaching*; "Exodus" in the *Expositor's Bible Commentary*; *The Messiah in the Old Testament*; and *The Promise-Plan of God*. Dr. Kaiser and his wife, Marge, currently reside in Cedar Grove, Wisconsin.

Darrell L. Bock (PhD, University of Aberdeen) is professor of New Testament at Dallas Theological Seminary. He is the author or coauthor of numerous books including *Luke* in the NIV Application Commentary series (Zondervan) and *Luke* (2 volumes) and *Acts* in the Baker Exegetical Commentary on the New Testament series.

Dr. Peter E. Enns (PhD, Harvard University) has taught Old Testament at Westminster Theological Seminary in Philadelphia for fourteen years. He is a frequent contributor to journals and encyclopedias, and is the author of several books, including *Exodus* in the NIV Application Commentary series (Zondervan) and *Inspiration and Incarnation: Evangelicals and the Problem of the Old Testament* (Baker).

AN INTRODUCTION TO CENTRAL QUESTIONS IN THE NEW TESTAMENT USE OF THE OLD TESTAMENT

Jonathan Lunde

INTRODUCTION

"Dad, what am I supposed to do with this?" My family and I had just sat down in my parents' church at a traditional hymn sing and testimony service. When my son Trevor found the hymnal that was placed on his chair, he picked it up, looked it over for a moment, and then whispered his question into my ear. Suddenly, the experiential distance between my son and me became blatantly obvious. It had not occurred to me until that moment that my boys had grown up attending churches where the words to songs were always projected onto suspended screens rather than being arranged in musical score in songbooks stored in racks behind each pew. Thankfully, our sons were familiar with some of the hymns, since we had sung them together during bedtime prayers. But even with this partial familiarity, my wife and I spent the remainder of that service teaching our sons how to find the hymns and then to read them while they were singing.

In some ways, my sons' first encounter with a hymnal illustrates the problem that will occupy us in this volume. All of us who are acquainted with the Bible are aware that the NT authors frequently appeal to OT passages to make a theological point, to confirm a prophetic fulfillment, or to ground one ethical exhortation or another. Such basic knowledge might be comparable to my sons' familiarity with the hymns they had learned during their evening prayer times. But when we actually pick up the text and try to make sense of how the NT authors are reading the OT text, we quickly find ourselves asking, "What are we supposed to do with this?"

For instance, some of the OT passages that are "fulfilled" in the NT don't look at all like predictions in their original contexts. Others that do look like predictions often appear to have been fulfilled in events that happened or in people who lived far earlier than Jesus. In addition, theological affirmations in the OT are occasionally restated with a new and distinct reference. In sum, the meanings that the NT writers derive from the Scriptures often appear inconsistent with what their OT counterparts intended. As we encounter these tensions, what we actually are sensing is the *interpretive distance* that exists between the writers of the NT and us. This realization is sometimes so jarring that we are left with a whole new set of questions regarding the literary sensitivity of the NT authors and the nature of their approach to the OT. Issues of legitimacy and authority begin looming in the corners of our minds. "What are we supposed to do with this?"

What complicates things further is that the NT authors seem to take their cues from Jesus' own approach to the Scriptures. In the estimation of countless students of the Bible (including the two editors of this volume), one of the most tantalizing passages in the NT is Luke 24:13–35. While accompanying the two disciples on the road to Emmaus, the risen but unrecognized Jesus chastises his traveling companions for not comprehending that the prophets had pointed to the necessity of the Messiah's suffering prior to his entrance into glory (vv. 25–26). Luke then summarizes Jesus' explanation in verse 27: "And beginning with Moses and all the Prophets, he explained to them what was said in all the Scriptures concerning himself."

What did Jesus say to them? Which Scriptures did he discuss? How did the Scriptures point to the necessity of his death and glorification? What method did he use to move from the Scriptures to himself? While Luke does not preserve for us the specifics of Jesus' instruction, it is not unrealistic to assume that the apostolic writers of the NT follow Jesus' lead and that they model for us the kinds of connections that Jesus made on the Emmaus road. It is likely, therefore, that we are encountering Jesus' own hermeneutic when we study many of the OT citations and allusions in the NT.[1]

But when we examine the NT authors' use of the OT closely, rather than sharing the wonder that filled Jesus' companions on that road to Emmaus, it is sometimes difficult to avoid the impression that the NT application of OT texts is arbitrary and forced. For instance, responding to Matthew's method, S. V. Mc-Casland writes:

> Matthew's use of Isaiah 7:14 to explain the mystery of the birth of Christ ... shows ... how a misinterpreted passage might be just as influential as one correctly understood.... The interpretation of Hosea 11:1 not only illustrates how early Christians found a meaning entirely foreign to the original; it may also show how incidents in the story of Jesus have been inferred from the Old Testament.[2]

McCasland's comment points to the need to engage this topic at a deeper level than is often the case. There was a time, at least in some Christian circles, when the NT fulfillment of the OT functioned as an unassailable apologetic for the legitimacy of the NT affirmations regarding Jesus. The more one learns about the NT use of the OT, however, the more this line of argumentation needs to be nuanced. That is because the relationship between the Testaments is not as simple and straightforward as it appears at first blush. In truth, this topic can get rather complicated.

---

1. See R. T. France, *Jesus and the Old Testament: His Application of Old Testament Passages to Himself and His Mission* (Downers Grove, IL: InterVarsity Press, 1971), 172–226, esp. 225–26; C. H. Dodd, *According to the Scriptures: The Substructure of New Testament Theology* (London: Nisbet, 1952), 109–10.

2. S. V. McCasland, "Matthew Twists the Scriptures," in *The Right Doctrine from the Wrong Texts: Essays on the Use of the Old Testament in the New*, ed. G. K. Beale (Grand Rapids: Baker, 1994), 148–49. For ease of reference and accessibility to our readers, I will refer to Beale's anthology for the bibliographical information of articles and book excerpts such as this that appear there, rather than to the sources of their original publication. These will be referenced simply as *The Right Doctrine*.

Given the complexity of the issues involved, our goal in this volume is a modest one. We are seeking simply to expose our readers to a range of approaches to some of the questions posed by this issue, in the hope that their understanding will be deepened at various levels, enabling them to evaluate conclusions such as those expressed by McCasland. Though many of our readers will likely desire to delve more deeply into the issues by referring to the sources cited in these chapters, we hope that the discussions included in this volume will supply our readers with a measure of familiarity that allows them to read the "hymnal" appropriately and to know how to join in with the apostolic "choir."

THE GRAVITATIONAL CENTER AND FIVE ORBITING QUESTIONS

Anyone who has studied the use of the OT[3] in the NT knows that there are many moving parts to the issue, involving a host of related questions that orbit around and influence the whole.[4] This book could have been organized around a few of these. It is our conviction, however, that the broad issue of the relationship between the meanings intended by the OT authors in their texts and those derived from those texts by NT authors possesses the requisite density to lie at the center of gravity in this discussion. That is to say, when NT authors appeal to OT texts in order to

---

3. We recognize the appropriateness of such designations as the scholarly use of the Hebrew Bible (HB), the Tanakh, or the First Testament to refer to the same group of writings. Stamps' suggestion of the term "Jewish sacred writings" also has merit (Dennis L. Stamps, "The Use of the Old Testament in the New Testament as a Rhetorical Device: A Methodological Proposal," in *Hearing the Old Testament in the New Testament*, ed. Stanley E. Porter [Grand Rapids: Eerdmans, 2006], 10–11). In spite of its somewhat anachronistic nature in relation to the perspective of the NT writers, however, we will continue to use the "OT" in this volume, which is directed toward a more general audience.

4. For a discussion on the variety of NT uses of the OT and the resulting terminological confusion plaguing the scholarly debate, see Stanley Porter, "The Use of the Old Testament in the New Testament: A Brief Comment on Method and Terminology," in *Early Christian Interpretation of the Scriptures of Israel: Investigations and Proposals*, ed. Craig A. Evans and James A. Sanders (JSNTSup 148; Sheffield: Sheffield Academic Press, 1997), 79–96.

support or validate their arguments, the relationship between their meanings and that which was originally intended by their OT forebears is the central question.[5]

Obviously, there are many instances where these intended meanings are indistinguishable. But, as is well known, NT writers frequently use the OT in ways that at least appear to imply meanings that eclipse or diverge in some way from those of the original authors. How is the relationship between these intended meanings to be understood?[6] This is the gravitational center for the discussion contained in this book.[7]

Orbiting around this issue at varying degrees of distance are the questions to which I alluded above. I have characterized them as "orbiting questions" because they each exert a lunar-like influence on the tides of the debate, while at the same time shedding illuminating light on the issues involved. Though I will deal with each one separately, it will become obvious that four of these questions "intersect" each other's orbits, amounting at times to differing aspects of the same issue and sometimes leading to terminological confusion. While admitting this overlap, I will lay out each of these questions individually. These are our questions:

---

5. In this, we are following the many who have persisted in grounding the meaning of a given text in the intentionality of the original author. See the development and defense of this in Kevin J. Vanhoozer, *Is There a Meaning in This Text? The Bible, the Reader, and the Morality of Literary Knowledge* (Grand Rapids: Zondervan, 1998), 201–80. As such, meaning ought to be understood as "communicative action" —i.e., more as a *verb*, representing what the author *did* in the composition of the text (202). Texts are therefore to be understood as "embodied intention[s]" (253), even though our discernment of those intended meanings always includes a measure of uncertainty (207). For further justification of this approach, see Vanhoozer's discussions of the seminal views put forward by E. D. Hirsch (74–90) and John Searle (207–14).

6. It is important to affirm that there are numerous uses of the OT that do not involve an argument regarding the "meaning" of the text. Such Scriptural uses do not pose any challenge for the legitimacy of the NT use of the OT. See three categories of these uses in Douglas Moo, "The Problem of *Sensus Plenior*," in *Hermeneutics, Authority, and Canon*, ed. D. A. Carson and John D. Woodbridge (Grand Rapids: Zondervan, 1986), 188–90; cf. also the list in I. Howard Marshall, "An Assessment of Recent Developments," in *The Right Doctrine*, 204–5.

7. This issue also has ramifications for the doctrine of "inerrancy," traditionally defined. On this, see Moo, "The Problem," esp. 186–211.

1. Is *sensus plenior* an appropriate way of explaining the NT use of the OT?
2. How is *typology* best understood?
3. Do the NT writers take into account the *context* of the passages they cite?
4. Does the NT writers' use of Jewish exegetical methods explain the NT use of the OT?
5. Are we able to replicate the exegetical and hermeneutical approaches to the OT that we find in the writings of the NT?[8]

In light of our metaphor, we might depict our discussion in this way:

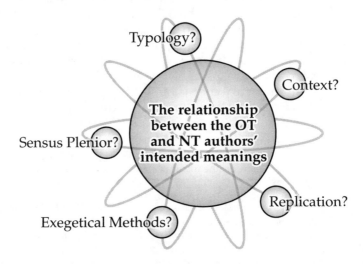

In this introductory chapter, I will briefly introduce and explain these five questions, hopefully providing readers with the necessary context in which to discern each question's importance to the debate as they read our contributors' essays. I

---

8. Another issue that far eclipses what we can do in this volume has to do with the nature and form of the texts themselves that underlie the quotations, paraphrases, and allusions preserved by the NT authors. Many of the apparent inconsistencies between the NT citations and the Masoretic Hebrew textual tradition (which

will conclude this chapter by noting the largely agreed-upon interpretive assumptions with which the NT authors approach the OT, and by surveying our classifications of the scholars who have contributed to this volume. Let us turn, then, to a brief introduction to our questions.

Orbiting Question 1: Is *Sensus Plenior* an Appropriate Way of Explaining the New Testament Use of the Old Testament?

Our first orbiting question concerns the possibility of multiple layers of meaning in the scriptural words themselves. To resolve the apparent friction between the intentions of the OT and NT authors, some appeal to a divinely-intended "fuller" meaning of Scripture that is discerned by the inspired NT authors — the so-called *sensus plenior* (lit., the "fuller sense").

The Nature of the Sensus Plenior

Though not original to him,[9] Catholic scholar Raymond Brown has done much to define this term and to develop issues pertinent

---

underlies our English translations) are explicable by appealing to the freedom in citation based oftentimes on the memory of the writer, to the variety of textual traditions that were then available (including the LXX), and to the influence of the NT writer's interpretation of the OT text. Given the complexity of this issue and space constraints, we will not be attempting to include this discussion in this volume. For bibliography on the texts and related issues, see esp. Craig A. Evans, "From Prophecy to Testament: An Introduction," in *From Prophecy to Testament: The Function of the Old Testament in the New*, ed. Craig A. Evans (Peabody, MA: Hendrickson, 2004), 1–7; cf. also Moisés Silva, "The New Testament Use of the Old Testament," in *Scripture and Truth*, ed. D. A. Carson and John D. Woodbridge (Grand Rapids: Baker, 1992), 147–65; Richard N. Longenecker, *Biblical Exegesis in the Apostolic Period* (Grand Rapids: Eerdmans, 1975), 61–66; Max Wilcox, "Text Form," in *It Is Written: Scripture Citing Scripture: Essays in Honour of Barnabas Lindars, SSF*, ed. D. A. Carson and H. G. M. Williamson (Cambridge: Cambridge Univ. Press, 1988), 193–204; Donald Hagner, "The Old Testament in the New Testament," in *Interpreting the Word of God: Festschrift in Honor of Steven Barabas*, ed. Samuel J. Schultz and Morris A. Inch (Chicago: Moody Press, 1976), 79–90; Robert H. Gundry, *The Use of the Old Testament in St. Matthew's Gospel: With Special Reference to the Messianic Hope* (NovTSup 18; Leiden: Brill, 1967), 9–185.

9. Raymond Brown, "The History and Development of the Theory of a *Sensus Plenior*," *CBQ* 15 (1953): 141.

to it.[10] As a result, Brown's influence on this debate is enormous, with scholars on all sides responding to his construal one way or another. Even so, most who utilize the term have often not maintained—or perhaps have not been able to maintain—Brown's subtle distinctions between varieties of *sensus plenior*, and between *sensus plenior* and typology. The result of this is occasional terminological confusion and a blurring of the lines between categories and issues. Consequently, though I am utilizing Brown's definition of *sensus plenior*, I acknowledge that much of what he organizes under this rubric is included in other scholars' treatments of typology.[11]

Brown defines *sensus plenior* in this way:

> The sensus plenior is that additional, deeper meaning, intended by God but not clearly intended by the human author, which is seen to exist in the words of a biblical text (or group of texts, or even a whole book) when they are studied in the light of further revelation or development in the understanding of revelation.[12]

If the "literal sense" is that which the human author *clearly* intends to communicate by his words,[13] then the *sensus plenior* is

---

10. See Raymond Brown, *The* Sensus Plenior *of Sacred Scripture* (Baltimore: St. Mary's, Univ. Press, 1955, reprinted 1960); see also his "History and Development," 141–62; and "The *Sensus Plenior* in the Last Ten Years," *CBQ* 25 (1963): 262–85.

11. For instance, one of Brown's subtle subdivisions of *sensus plenior* is what he calls the "prophetical *sensus plenior*," which pertains to prophecies that may have had temporally more proximate fulfillments, but which eventually find their ultimate fulfillment in Jesus or in the community defined by him. Many scholars understand such texts typologically. However, this is distinguished by Brown from the typical (typological) sense, since Brown assumes that the author does not see the typological future reference, whereas it is unclear to what degree the prophet discerns a more distant reference for his prophecies (*Sensus Plenior*, 108–9); see also Moo, "The Problem," 182; James M. Robinson, "Scripture and Theological Method: A Protestant Study in *Sensus Plenior*," *CBQ* 27 (1965): 8–20.

12. *Sensus Plenior*, 92 (emphasis his). Brown actually divides the "meaning" of the scriptural text into three categories: the literal, the typical, and the *sensus plenior*. We will relegate our discussion of the typical sense to our section on typology (see below). Brown does not include among the senses of Scripture either the so-called "consequent sense" or the notion of "accommodation," since the human and divine authors did not intend these meanings by the words themselves (*Sensus Plenior*, 22–27, 70; see also 121–22).

13. Brown defines the "literal sense" as "*that which both the Holy Spirit and the human author directly and proximately intended, and which the words directly convey, either*

to be understood as that meaning which goes beyond this clear and definite intention, but which is discerned in OT texts by the inspired NT writers. Still, Brown maintains that the *sensus plenior* is always to be understood as tied to the "literal sense" of the text, functioning as a "homogeneous" development of that meaning. He distinguishes the two in this way:

> ... the literal sense answers the question of what this text meant according to its author's intention as that author was inspired to compose it in his particular stage in the history of God's plan of salvation. The SP [*sensus plenior*] answers the question of what the text means in the whole context of God's plan, a meaning which God, who knew the whole plan from the start, intended from the moment He inspired the composition of the text.[14]

Since God inspired the scriptural writers, the meanings and referents he intended in the biblical text may often exceed the limited vision and understanding of the human authors, even though this divine intention retains a "homogeneous" connection to what the human authors intended. Given their subsequent location in salvation history, then, the inspired NT authors are able to discern this divine meaning, especially as it pertains to Jesus and their own day.[15]

Though Brown proceeds to subdivide *sensus plenior* into three main, yet subtle, subcategories, the most important of these for our discussion here is what he calls the "general *sensus*

---

properly or metaphorically" (*Sensus Plenior*, 4; emphasis his). Assumed in this definition is the human author's full awareness of this meaning, even though the divine author's intention might exceed it. The literal sense, then, is what is in the mind of the human author *directly* (*Sensus Plenior*, 4–6).

14. Brown, "Ten Years," 278; also 268–69. Given Brown's definition of the literal sense, the *sensus plenior* covers those senses where the writer had a vague knowledge and where he had no knowledge at all (*Sensus Plenior*, 105–7; cf. "The Last Ten Years," 265). See also Jack Weir, "Analogous Fulfillment: The Use of the Old Testament in the New Testament," *Perspectives in Religious Studies* 9 (1982): 65–66.

15. Brown does not envision a *deliberate* veiling of the divinely intended *sensus plenior* from the human author, a "*sensus occultus*," as Moo describes it ("The Problem," 206). Rather than affirming a divine concealment of this kind, Brown remains agnostic as to the extent to which the *sensus plenior* exists within the scope of the human author's knowledge (*Sensus Plenior*, 105–7).

plenior."[16] This pertains to the "enrichment" that comes to the meaning of a text once it is placed in the context of the entire Bible. Brown calls this the "historical sense" of Scripture, involving a given text's significance in the light of history's unfolding.[17] It is not the literal sense because the human author does not *clearly* intend it.[18]

The Scholarly Response to Sensus Plenior

Given its genesis and development in Catholic scholarship, it is not surprising that the term *sensus plenior* is closely associated with Catholic hermeneutics, even though not every Catholic scholar agrees on its legitimacy.[19] Other Catholic scholars seek to go beyond the limitations of *sensus plenior* itself.[20] Protestants often respond negatively to the concept because of their perception of its use by Catholic theologians to develop doctrines that go beyond the bounds of scripturally intended meanings.[21]

---

16. His two other main categories are the typical and the prophetical *sensus plenior* (Brown, *Sensus Plenior*, 2–28). I will discuss only the "general *sensus plenior*" here, leaving these other categories to emerge in our discussion of typology. An unnamed fourth subdivision, pertaining to the liturgical prayers that make use of the sapiential literature, does not contribute to our discussion (ibid., 103).

17. Ibid., 97–98.

18. Brown maintains that it is also distinct from the typological sense because this historical significance involves the *words* of the text—typology is tied solely to "things" (ibid., 98).

19. See the critiques of the notion of *sensus plenior* by the Catholic scholars Rudolph Bierberg, "Does Sacred Scripture Have a *Sensus Plenior*?" *CBQ* 10 (1948): 182–95, and Bruce Vawter, "The Fuller Sense: Some Considerations," *CBQ* 26 (1964): 85–96. See the favorable analysis in John J. O'Rourke, "Marginal Notes on the *Sensus Plenior*," *CBQ* 21 (1959): 64–71.

20. See, e.g., Sandra M. Schneiders, "Faith, Hermeneutics, and the Literal Sense of Scripture," *TS* 39 (1978): 719–36, who rejects *sensus plenior* as Brown defines it (727), but draws heavily on the work of H.-G. Gadamer (*Truth and Method* [New York: Seabury, 1975], esp. 235–341) to posit the actualization of limitless meanings as members of the believing community encounter the text, bringing with them their individual experiences and perspectives (731–32).

21. Brown advocates for the necessity of an "objective" basis to affirm *sensus plenior* readings: "This is supplied by the authority of the N.T., the Fathers, the Magisterium, the liturgy, and perhaps even a 'majority' of the theologians.... We need authority for seeing fuller meanings in the Bible; *e.g.*, the doctrines of the Immaculate

But several Protestant scholars have embraced carefully delimited versions of the concept, often agreeing with Brown's "general *sensus plenior*"—Scripture's "historical sense." Taking the dual authorship of Scripture as their point of departure, such Protestants similarly allow God's intention to exceed that of the human author, being discerned in the context of the entire canon of Scripture. While several defend a close relationship between these meanings, this "fuller sense" often involves a change of referents.[22] Some Protestant scholars, however, are not concerned to retain this close relationship, as we will see even in this volume.[23]

Sensus Plenior and the Central Issue

As it pertains to our central issue, those who appeal to a *sensus plenior* perceive no unresolvable problems created by the NT use of the Old. When NT authors utilize an OT text in ways that seem to stand in tension with the original author's intentions, adherents of *sensus plenior* simply ascribe the NT meaning to the divine author's intention. This ascription is validated

---

Conception and the Assumption *may* be contained in the fuller meaning of Bible texts, but to ascertain this we need the guidance of the Church and the Fathers" (*Sensus Plenior*, 146; cf. also Brown, "The Last Ten Years," 272–73).

22. See, e.g., Kevin Vanhoozer, *Is There a Meaning?* 263–65, 279, n. 293. Vanhoozer writes, "... to say that the Bible has a 'fuller meaning' is to focus on the (divine) author's intended meaning at the level of the *canonical* act. Better said, *the canon as a whole becomes the unified act for which the divine intention serves as the unifying principle*" (265, emphasis his). See also Robertson McQuilkin, *Understanding and Applying the Bible*, rev. ed. (Chicago: Moody, 1992), 44–46, 266–67; Douglas Oss, "Canon as Context: The Function of *Sensus Plenior* in Evangelical Hermeneutics," *Grace Theological Journal* 9 (1988): 105–27; and *Commentary on the New Testament Use of the Old Testament*, ed. G. K. Beale and D. A. Carson (Grand Rapids: Baker, 2007), xxvii. Douglas Moo's "canonical approach" also appears to be in *essential* agreement here, though Moo includes a broader notion of typology than does Brown (Moo, "The Problem," 204–9; cf. Brown, *Sensus Plenior*, 97).

23. Though they do not use the term "*sensus plenior*," see Craig A. Evans, "The Old Testament in the New," in *The Face of New Testament Studies: A Survey of Recent Research*, ed. Scot McKnight and Grant R. Osborne (Grand Rapids: Baker, 2004), 145, and James A. Sanders, "From Prophecy to Testament: An Epilogue," in *From Prophecy to Testament: The Function of the Old Testament in the New*, ed. Craig A. Evans (Peabody, MA: Hendrickson, 2004), 255–58.

by the twin assumptions of the revelatory status of the NT authors and the correctness of their convictions about Jesus as the divinely intended goal of the OT.

Orbiting Question 2: How Is Typology Best Understood?

The orbit of our second question does not take us far from the preceding discussion. It has to do with what scholars have called the "typology" of Scripture.[24] As has already been suggested above, typology is closely related to the notion of *sensus plenior*, with some scholars collapsing the two together and others seeking to draw a fine distinction between them.[25] It is important to understand from the outset, however, that a typological approach to Scripture is not an exegetical method by which the interpreter ascertains the *grammatical-historical* meaning of a given text's words. Rather, typology amounts to a perspective on history.[26]

The Nature of Typology

The words "typical" or "typological" derive from the Greek word *typos*, which means "model" or "pattern."[27] As it is used

---

24. On typology, see Leonhard Goppelt, *Typos: The Theological Interpretation of the Old Testament in the New*, trans. Donald H. Madvig (Grand Rapids: Eerdmans, 1982); Patrick Fairbairn, *The Typology of Scripture* (Grand Rapids: Zondervan, 1956); David Baker, "Typology and the Christian Use of the Old Testament," in *The Right Doctrine*, 313–30; Beale and Carson, *Commentary on the New Testament Use*, xxiii–xxviii.

25. Alternatively, Donald Hagner subsumes all typology to *sensus plenior*: "The tracing of typological correspondences is a special instance of detecting the *sensus plenior* of Old Testament material" (Hagner, "Old Testament," 94). By contrast, Raymond Brown divides typological texts into two categories, one of which he arranges under *sensus plenior* and the other he sets apart as typology proper. While Brown ties the former to the literal sense of the *words* of the text, he characterizes the latter as having to do primarily with *things* (*Sensus Plenior*, 10, 16, 100–101; idem, "Ten Years," 269–70). The reason for this, Brown contends, is that the typological sense involves a "transposition of meaning," such that the future realities to which the "things" point have nothing to do with the original, literal sense of the text (*Sensus Plenior*, 113–14, 119).

26. Baker, "Typology," 327–28. Cf. also France, *Jesus and the Old Testament*, 38–43.

27. *A Greek-English Lexicon of the New Testament and other Early Christian Literature*, 3rd ed., rev. and ed. Frederick William Danker, based on Walter Bauer,

in the scholarly discussion, it refers to events, institutions, or people that *foreshadow* future things. The earlier thing is called the "type," and the correspondingly later thing, the "antitype."

Typology is grounded in three assumptions that guide the authors of the biblical text:[28] (1) God is sovereign over history and is directing it in ways that reveal his unchanging character; (2) historical patterns that pertain to significant events, institutions, and people theologically *foreshadow* later recurrences of similar things;[29] and (3) the final historical fulfillments will *eclipse* their prior counterparts, since God's explicit expressions of his ultimate purposes outstrip what has already occurred.[30] This "eclipsing" can be a fulfillment that is more glorious than any previous fulfillment, or it can replace a previously negative occurrence with a positive one.[31]

Accordingly, events that demonstrate God's intention to bless his covenant people are held up as signposts pointing toward his future, climactic intervention on their behalf. A prime example of this is the exodus from Egypt.[32] The same is true of divine judgments of the past; the flood, the destruction of

---

Griechisch-deutsches Wörterbuch zu den Scriften des Neuen Testaments und der frühchrist-lichen Literatur, 6th ed. (Chicago: Univ. of Chicago Press, 2000), s.v. τύπος (1020). See also Baker, "Typology," 319–21.

28. I will further discuss these and other assumptions below.

29. France, *Jesus and the Old Testament*, 41; see also G. P. Hugenberger, "Introductory Notes on Typology," in *The Right Doctrine*, 331–41; esp. 340–41.

30. Francis Foulkes, "The Acts of God: A Study of the Basis of Typology in the Old Testament," in *The Right Doctrine*, 365–66; Oscar Cullmann, *Salvation in History* (New York: Harper & Row, 1967), 132–33.

31. Foulkes, "The Acts of God," 364–65; Hugenberger, "Introductory Notes," 337–38; Baker, "Typology," 325–26. Though "horizontal," historical typology is more common in the Bible, Baker notes that a "vertical," archetypical variety also exists in Scripture, identifying an analogy between heavenly and earthly realities ("Typology," 322–23). But the importance of history is what sets typology apart from allegory. Whereas the former is interested in the natural and historical sense of the context, allegory is mainly interested in the interpretation of words, which are believed to be inspired symbols (Foulkes, "The Acts of God," 367; Baker, "Typology," 24–25).

32. E.g., Isa 43:16–21; Jer 23:7–8; Hos 11:1–11; cf. Deut 7:18–19; 20:1–4; Pss 78; 114; Isa 4:2–6; 40:1–5. Cf. also Mark 1:2–3 [and par.]; Luke 9:31 (note the use of "exodus" to speak of Jesus' upcoming work); note also the deliverance of Noah as a foreshadowing of the future deliverance through Jesus in 1 Peter 3:20–23.

Sodom and Gomorrah, and the plagues on Egypt are each understood to foreshadow future devastations.[33] When these correspondences show up in history, the earlier "types" find their "fulfillments" in their "antitypes." In this way, history itself is understood to be prophetic of God's ultimate purposes, which will one day be consummated historically.[34]

Since the NT writers assume that Jesus is the Lord's Messiah, who also sums up both Israel's and humanity's roles in history, patterns in his life and ministry that correspond in some way to events, institutions, groups, and individuals in the OT are characterized as "fulfillments" of the Scriptures.[35] So prevalent is this approach to the OT that Goppelt avers that "typology is the method of interpreting Scripture that is predominant in the NT and characteristic of it."[36]

For instance, John's typological perspective enables him to state that the nonbreaking of Jesus' legs in John 19:36 "fulfills" the Scriptures pertaining to the treatment of the Passover lamb's body (Ex 12:46; Num 9:12). Similarly, Matthew can affirm that the travels of Jesus and his parents to and from Egypt

---

33. Note the use of "the flood" in Ps 29:10 and the reference to the opening of the "floodgates of the heavens" in Isa 24:18; cf. also Isa 28:2. Note the use of the destruction of Sodom and Gomorrah to foreshadow future judgments in Deut 29:22–28; Isa 13:19; Jer 49:18; 50:40; Zep 2:9; cf. Lam 4:6; Amos 4:11. Cf. also the use of the plague imagery in Deut 7:15; 28:27, 60; Amos 4:10. Note the NT use of this imagery in Matt 10:15 [par. Luke 10:12]; 11:20–24; 24:37–41; Luke 17:28–29; Rom 9:29; 2 Peter 2:5–7; Jude 7; Rev 11:8.

34. Foulkes notes that this approach to past history is grounded in the distinction they perceived between God's nature and actions from those of the capricious pagan deities ("The Acts of God," 343). See also France, *Jesus and the Old Testament*, 39–40.

35. See Dan G. McCartney, "The New Testament's Use of the Old Testament," in *Inerrancy and Hermeneutic: A Tradition, A Challenge, A Debate*, ed. Harvie M. Conn (Grand Rapids: Baker, 1988), 114.

36. Goppelt, *Typos*, 198. Paul uses the Greek word *typos* in 1 Cor 10:6 and Rom 5:14, and he utilizes the cognate adverb, *typikos*, in 1 Cor 10:11. Though he is alone among NT authors in using these words in this way, his approach to the OT is similar to that which is employed by Jesus and other NT authors. In the succeeding generations, this use of the term and its cognates quickly became firmly entrenched in Christian parlance and practice (Goppelt, *Typos*, 5, and n. 15). For an overview of the scholarly discussion, see Goppelt, *Typos*, 1–20; Baker, "Typology," 315–18; Hugenberger, "Introductory Notes," 332–36.

"fulfill" Hosea 11:1 and its description of Israel's exodus from Egypt (Matt 2:15). In Romans 9:25–26, Paul can point to the conversion of the Gentiles to faith in Jesus as the fulfillment of the promises made in Hosea 1:10 and 2:23 concerning the Northern Kingdom's return to a covenantal relationship with God after the exile to Assyria. So also does a typological perspective permit John the Baptist in John 1:23 to identify himself as the forerunner announcing the fulfillment of Isaiah's vision of the return of the Southern Kingdom from Babylon (Isa 40:3) over five centuries after its initial fulfillment. The list goes on and on.[37]

Typology and the Central Question

The important aspect of typology for our purposes has to do with the relationship between the forward-referring, typological reference and that which the human author intended. Stated in the form of a question, Is the divinely intended, *prospective* element in typology known by the original human author, or is this only ascertained *retrospectively* from the NT author's vantage point? Since most would affirm that the typological sense is not discerned by means of grammatical-historical investigation, which concerns itself with the author's clearly intended meaning, how is this additional reference to be related to the original sense of the passage? As is the case with each of our orbiting questions, there is a range of opinion here.

Some scholars contend that the human author may dimly perceive the more distant, antitypical fulfillment of the things he is describing.[38] John Sailhamer, however, is much more confident of the OT authors' knowledge of distant referents, informed by their awareness of a clearly defined messianic hope in the Pentateuch. So confident is he of this that he denies the presence of typology in places where most scholars assume it must be present.[39]

---

37. See esp. Goppelt, *Typos*, 61–237; Baker, "Typology," 328–30; Foulkes, "The Acts of God," 342–65; E. Earle Ellis, *Paul's Use of the Old Testament* (Grand Rapids: Baker, 1957), 126–35.

38. E.g., Brown, *Sensus Plenior*, 14; Moo, "The Problem," 196; cf. Baker, "Typology," 324; Foulkes, "The Acts of God," 370.

39. John Sailhamer, "Hosea 11:1 and Matthew 2:15," *WTJ* 63 (2001): 91–94.

More commonly, scholars confine the typological reference largely to the divine author, "who ordered these events in such a way that they would possess a 'prophetic' function."[40] Since it is difficult to ascertain whether or not this prophetic function was in the mind of the human author, many are more comfortable with a distinction here between the human and divine intentions.[41] But even with this disjunction, several try to defend the care with which the NT writers preserve the original *meaning* of the OT writers in their typological interpretations.[42]

Orbiting Question 3: Do the New Testament Writers Take into Account the Context of the Passages They Cite?

A third orbiting question has to do with the issue of context: When the NT writers cite an OT text, do they take into account the larger context of that citation? In his influential study, C. H. Dodd contends that when NT writers quote from particular passages, they have the larger contexts in mind—a practice similar to that of Jewish teachers who were contemporaries of the NT authors:[43]

---

40. Moo, "The Problem," 196; cf. Baker, "Typology," 324.

41. Foulkes writes, "Typology reads into Scripture a meaning which is not there in that it reads in the light of the fulfillment of the history" ("The Acts of God," 369; similarly also Barnabas Lindars, "The Place of the Old Testament in the Formation of New Testament Theology: Prolegomena," in *The Right Doctrine*, 144–45); cf. also Weir, "Analogous Fulfillment," 65–76.

42. See Baker, "Typology," 324; cf. also Foulkes, "The Acts of God," 369–70. Beale and Carson speak of the "organic links" between the OT and the NT, which allow for "a creative development or extension of the meaning of the OT text that is still in some way anchored to that text" (*Commentary on the New Testament Use*, xxvii).

43. Dodd, *According to the Scriptures*. Dodd's summary of this book was published in his brief book, *The Old Testament in the New* (Philadelphia: Fortress, 1963), now reprinted in *The Right Doctrine*, 167–81. As with the other essays included in Beale's anthology, references to this summary will be to its publication in that volume. Dodd was concerned to modify the earlier thesis by Rendel J. Harris (*Testimonies*, 2 vols. [Cambridge: Cambridge Univ. Press, 1916, 1920]), who contended these *testimonia* were in *written* form, organized according to the theological titles of Jesus. Dodd argues for an *orally* transmitted group of texts. See also Stendahl's nuanced critique of Harris's theory, appealing to practices in the synagogues to explain most

The reader is invited to study the context as a whole, and to reflect upon the "plot" there unfolded. In some way, an understanding of the plot will help him to see the significance of the strange events of the life and death of Jesus, and what followed.[44]

That is to say, once a particular OT text was recognized by the early Christians as having significance in relation to Jesus, other passages within that same context became fair game for similar appropriation and application. This contextual reference to validate the use of other texts does not, however, *directly* address the question of the impact of the context on the *meaning* that a NT writer derives from a particular citation.[45] Nevertheless, Dodd's thesis opens the door to a consideration of the latter issue, which of course is our central question.

Several scholars have sought to demonstrate that the NT authors did take into account these contexts in their discernment of the meaning of their OT citations.[46] Watts, for example, argues that Matthew's difficult use of Isaiah 7:14 (Matt 1:23) should be understood as a "programmatic statement" for the whole of his gospel, communicating the twin themes of deliverance and judgment that are derived from the use of "Immanuel" in the larger context of Isaiah 7–8.[47]

Alternatively, others argue that the NT authors appropriate the OT text "atomistically," dislodging the text from its context

---

of the textual phenomena (Kristar Stendahl, *The School of St. Matthew and Its Use of the Old Testament* [Philadelphia: Fortress, 1968], 207–17).

44. Dodd, "The Old Testament," 176.

45. Marshall, "Assessment," 202–3.

46. See, e.g., G. K. Beale, "The Old Testament Background of Reconciliation in 2 Corinthians 5–7 and Its Bearing on the Literary Problem of 2 Corinthians 6:14–7:1," in *The Right Doctrine*, 217–47; David Seccombe, "Luke and Isaiah," in *The Right Doctrine*, 248–56; G. K. Beale, "The Use of the Old Testament in Revelation," in *The Right Doctrine*, 257–76; Scott J. Hafemann, "The Glory and Veil of Moses in 2 Corinthians 3:7–14," in *The Right Doctrine*, 295–309.

47. Rikk E. Watts, "Immanuel: Virgin Birth Proof Text or Programmatic Warning of Things to Come (Isa 7:14 in Matt 1:23)?" in *From Prophecy to Testament: The Function of the Old Testament in the New*, ed. Craig A. Evans (Peabody, MA: Hendrickson, 2004), 92–113.

in a "proof-texting" manner.[48] Lindars, for instance, contends that the NT authors select and adapt proof texts from the OT in an ad hoc way to support their argumentation and proclamation.[49] He writes:

> The place of the Old Testament in the formation of New Testament theology is that of a servant, ready to run to the aid of the gospel whenever it is required ... but never acting as the master or leading the way, nor even guiding the process of thought behind the scenes.[50]

In addition, Sundberg finds only few instances of citations that need the OT text to complete the fragmentary argument in the NT context.[51]

Context and the Central Question

One's answer to this question of "context" plays an important role in answering our central question. On the one hand, if the NT writers appropriate the OT text "atomistically," neglecting the original context, they have much greater latitude in manipulating the text's meaning away from what is intended by the OT author. On the other hand, if the NT authors respect the OT context, then the NT meanings are hemmed in, at least in part, by the OT writers themselves. If this is so, the supposed gap between the meanings intended by the OT and NT writers is reduced dramatically. This perspective also helps to inform the typological approach to the Scriptures, providing the NT writers with a larger frame of reference in which to correlate aspects of the recent revelation with that which came earlier.

---

48. See Richard T. Mead, "A Dissenting Opinion about Respect for Context in Old Testament Quotations," in *The Right Doctrine*, 153–63. Mead seeks to overturn the thesis of S. L. Edgar, who contends that Jesus' use of the OT demonstrates a respect for the OT context (unlike the other NT writers), so that this element may be used as a criterion of authenticity (S. L. Edgar, "Respect for Context in Quotations from the Old Testament," *NTS* 9 [1962]: 55–62).

49. Lindars, "The Place of the Old Testament," 141–43.

50. Ibid., 145.

51. Albert C. Sundberg Jr., "Response against C. H. Dodd's View: On Testimonies," in *The Right Doctrine*, 182–94. See the critique of Sundberg's thesis by Marshall, "An Assessment," 200–203.

Orbiting Question 4: Does the New Testament Writers' Use of Jewish Exegetical Methods Explain the New Testament Use of the Old Testament?

A fourth orbiting question concerns exegetical methodology: When the NT writers appropriate the OT, do they utilize the exegetical procedures that are characteristic of the Jewish interpretive methods then in vogue?[52] In other words, does their use of Scripture resemble the ways in which Scripture was employed at Qumran, by Philo or Josephus, or in the subsequent rabbinic writings? While some of these methods amount to a common sense approach to the text and appear legitimate to modern interpreters, some of them allow substantial freedom to the interpreter in shaping and applying the text. Consequently, the answer to this question dramatically affects how we assess the relationship between the meanings intended by the OT and NT authors. Since our contributors will occasionally appeal to these methods, I will summarize the main ones here to absolve them from the responsibility of explaining what these are in their essays. Though I am keeping the overviews of our "orbiting questions" brief, this question will necessarily require a bit more explanation than the three questions already discussed.

Literalist Interpretation

The "literalist" method is the most familiar to modern interpreters of Scripture. This involves applying the text in a straightforward manner so that the "plain, simple and natural meaning of the text" is applied to the situation of the community.[53] Often,

---

52. It is important to maintain the distinction between these exegetical methods — what Moo helpfully terms, "appropriation techniques" — and the "hermeneutical axioms" or assumptions that inform them (Moo, "The Problem," 194. While the appropriation techniques used by the NT writers may be similar to the exegetical methods of Second Temple Judaism, Moo notes that the "basic convictions of [each] community about Scripture, its own identity, and the movement of God in history" are very different. Cf. also his *The Old Testament in the Gospel Passion Narratives* [Sheffield: Almond Press, 1983], 25–78). See my discussion of the NT writers' hermeneutical assumptions later in this introduction.

53. Longenecker, *Biblical Exegesis*, 28.

this results in wooden interpretations.[54] As one might expect, this method is frequently used when the NT writers appeal to the OT law, where the law's original injunction is preserved literally. This approach to the OT obviously does not present us with any difficulties with regard to our central question.

Midrashic Interpretation

Another interpretive method of the Second Temple period, the "midrashic" method, involves a much more involved attempt to explain the meaning of a given text. The word itself comes from the Hebrew word *darash*, which means "to seek, expound, interpret."[55] As such, it refers simply to "an interpretive exposition."[56] It is a method that begins with the Scriptures, but which seeks to explain any hidden, embedded meanings, delving into the spirit of the text in order to contemporize it by deriving meanings that are not immediately obvious.[57] To do this, interpreters follow agreed-upon interpretive rules, or *middoth*, which range from obvious principles to those that allow for more imaginative construals. The basic maxim of *midrash* is " 'that has relevance to this'; i.e., What is written in Scripture has relevance to our present situation."[58]

The Talmud attributes seven rules of biblical exegesis to Hillel, a rabbi who lived a generation before the NT era.[59] Several

---

54. For examples, see Longenecker, *Biblical Exegesis*, 29–32, 66–69.

55. William H. Brownlee, "Biblical Interpretation among the Sectaries of the Dead Sea Scrolls," *BA* 14 (1951): 56.

56. Longenecker, *Biblical Exegesis*, 32.

57. Ibid., 32–33. Neusner calls this form of midrash "paraphrase": "The exegete would paraphrase Scripture, imposing fresh meanings by the word choices or even by adding additional phrases or sentences and so revising the meaning of the received text" (Jacob Neusner, *What Is Midrash?* [Guides to Biblical Scholarship: NT Series; Philalephia: Fortress, 1987], 7). The meaning of the text is thereby obscured because the boundary between text and comment is dissolved.

58. Longenecker, *Biblical Exegesis*, 37.

59. See John Bowker, *Targums and Rabbinic Literature: An Introduction to Jewish Interpretations of Scripture* (Cambridge: Cambridge Univ. Press, 1969), 315–16; cf. also Longenecker, *Biblical Exegesis*, 34–35, Moo, *The Old Testament*, 25–30. These were expanded into thirteen rules by Rabbi Ishmael ben Elisha at the beginning of the second century. Probably much later, they were expanded to include thirty-two rules, attributed to Rabbi Eliezer ben Jose ha-Galili. These later rules especially

of these *middoth* are said to be evidenced in the NT authors' approach to the OT.[60]

1. "The light and the heavy" (*qal wahomer*): If a meaning is true in a less important, "light" situation, it also applies in a more important, "heavy" situation.
2. "Equivalent regulation" (*gezerah shewah*): This permits the joint exposition of texts where the same key words are present.
3. "Building a family from a single text" (*binhan a mikathub 'ehad*): When the same phrase occurs in several texts, this rule permits the application of a consideration that is found in one text to each of them.
4. "Building up a family from two texts" (*binyan ab mishene kethubim*): This involves the application of a principle to other passages when it has been established by relating two texts together.
5. "The general and the particular" (*kelal upherat*): This allows the restriction or extension of a principle when it has been either restricted or extended in another verse.
6. "As is found in another place" (*kayoze bo bemaqom 'aher*): This rule permits the resolution of a difficulty that is found in one text by comparison with another text that is generally similar, though not necessarily verbally so.
7. "A meaning established by its context" (*dabar halamed me'inyano*): This provides for the determination of the meaning of a given text by studying its context.

Pesher Interpretation

The third major exegetical method, known as *"pesher,"* is especially seen in the literature of Qumran—the Dead Sea Scrolls. The word *pesher* means "solution" or "interpretation." Given this group's conviction that they alone are the true,

---

opened the door for significant alterations in authorial intention, involving even changes in translation through the reordering of letters and vowels (Longenecker, *Biblical Exegesis*, 35–37).

60. For illustrations of these, see Longenecker, *Biblical Exegesis*, 32–38, 66–70, 114–26; see also Ellis, *Paul's Use*, 38–84, 139–47.

eschatological people of God who are awaiting the imminent in-breaking of God's kingdom, they interpret the Scriptures as finding fulfillment in their contemporary history. To do this, they assume that the eschatological meaning that has been veiled in the prophet's words has now been explicated by their Teacher of Righteousness. In this, they follow the two-stage revelatory pattern that is exemplified in Daniel, where the dream-revelation that is given to one party is explained by the interpretation given to a different party.[61] Their conviction that the text applies to their own situation is so strong that they do not appear even to admit that the text had a significant reference to an earlier context. Rather, they perceive the text as being exclusively concerned with them.[62]

Thus, rather than the midrashic assumption of "that has relevance to this," which seeks to make contemporary *application* of the text, *pesher* interpretation progresses in a "this is that" fashion—that is to say, *this* is the eschatological situation spoken of in *that* text.[63] It therefore moves from a contemporary event or person to its discovery in the heretofore mysterious prophecies of the OT.[64] Accordingly, it approaches the text from the point of view that the full sense of the text can only be perceived in a revelatory context when prophecy and interpretation are brought together.[65]

---

61. Cf. 1QpHab 7.1–5 (note that the "p" here means "*pesher*").

62. F. F. Bruce, *Biblical Exegesis in the Qumran Texts* (Grand Rapids: Eerdmans, 1959), 15–17.

63. Longenecker, *Biblical Exegesis*, 39–44; Klyne Snodgrass, "The Use of the Old Testament in the New," in *New Testament Criticism & Interpretation*, ed. David Alan Black & David S. Dockery (Grand Rapids: Zondervan, 1991), 420; see also Cecil Roth, "The Subject Matter of Qumran Exegesis," *VT* 10 (1960): 51–68.

64. For examples, see Longenecker, *Biblical Exegesis*, 38–45, 70–75, 129–32.

65. Neusner includes *pesher* under his category "Midrash as prophecy": "... the exegete would ask Scripture to explain meanings of events near at hand, and Scripture would serve as a means of prophetic reading of the contemporary world.... [This] produces the identification of a biblical statement or event with a contemporary happening" (Neusner, *What Is Midrash?* 7). See also the comments by George Brooke, "Qumran Pesher: Towards the Redefinition of Genre," *RevQ* 10 (1981): 483–503, on the loose use of the term "*pesher*" in the scholarly discussion and his contention that *pesher* exegetical methods are not distinct from midrashic exegesis. He prefers the term "Qumran midrash" over *pesher*. Cf. also the discussion in Stendahl, *School of St. Matthew*, 183–202.

Allegory[66]

The "allegorical" method extracts "a symbolic meaning from the text. It assumes that a deeper, more sophisticated interpretation is to be found beneath the obvious meaning of the passage."[67] The literal, historical sense of the text is not denied; it is simply not important to the interpreter employing this method.[68] The NT text most often thought to exhibit allegorizing tendencies is Galatians 4:21–31, where Paul uses Hagar to represent Mount Sinai and enslavement to the law characteristic of the Jews of the earthly Jerusalem, and Sarah to represent the people of the promise who belong to the heavenly Jerusalem. Paul appears not to be concerned with historical reality here—other than the historical existence of these women—but seems to utilize these women in surprising, symbolic ways to make his theological point.[69]

Exegetical Methods and Scholarly Opinion

Whether or not the NT writers utilize these Jewish methods has generated a great deal of debate. In his seminal work, *Biblical Exegesis in the Apostolic Period*, Richard Longenecker responds to this question with a resounding "Yes!" He supports this by demonstrating how both Jesus and the NT authors naturally and unconsciously appropriate the OT in ways that evince these methods.[70] Whatever tensions appear regarding the

---

66. Neusner includes allegory under the category, "Midrash as parable" (Neusner, *What Is Midrash?* 8).

67. Evans, "The Old Testament in the New," 133.

68. Dodd, "The Old Testament," 169.

69. Cf. Longenecker, *Biblical Exegesis*, 127–29. The most famous of the ancient allegorizers is the first-century Alexandrian Jew, Philo. In pursuing his interpretation of Scripture, he allegorizes anything that he finds inappropriate or nonsensical (see Longenecker, *Biblical Exegesis*, 45–48).

70. Longenecker, *Biblical Exegesis*, 28–50, 66–78. More recently, see Evans, "The Old Testament in the New," 130–45, and "The Function of the Old Testament in the New," in *Introducing New Testament Interpretation* (Guides to New Testament Exegesis; Grand Rapids: Baker, 1989), 163–93. See also Darrell L. Bock, "Use of the Old Testament in the New," in *Foundations for Biblical Interpretation: A Complete Library of Tools and Resources,* ed. David S. Dockery, Kenneth A. Mathews, and Robert B. Sloan

preservation of the OT authors' intended meanings are to be resolved by recognizing the freedom that Jews of that era had in their appropriation of Scripture. While these methods might not cohere with our modern notions of proper exegetical procedure, Longenecker suggests that we must allow the NT writers to live and work in their world and not in ours.[71] He writes:

> ... though the gospel is supra-historical in its origin and effect, it comes from a God who always incarnates his word ... and who uses current historical modes as vehicles for his grace.... Why, then, should it be thought unusual or un-Christian for early believers in Jesus to have interpreted their Scriptures by means of the hermeneutical canons then at hand? Indeed, how could they have done otherwise?[72]

Several who agree with Longenecker appeal to these methods to explain why the NT writers regularly seem to utilize OT passages in ways that may seem inappropriate. Though these practices at times render their arguments unconvincing to modern interpreters, such was likely not the case for their first-century readers, the majority of whom were probably already Christians. Given their shared presuppositional worldview regarding Jesus, their use of familiar exegetical methods actually served to *strengthen* the acceptability of their Christian apologetic in the minds of their readers. What is inappropriate for moderns was not necessarily problematic to Jews in first-century Palestine.[73]

Other scholars agree that the NT authors employed these methods, but seek to distance their use from some of the more unrestrained examples found in the Second Temple literature.[74]

(Nashville: Broadman & Holman, 1994), 97–114; Snodgrass, "The Use of the Old Testament," 409–34; Neusner, *What Is Midrash?*; E. Earle Ellis, "How the New Testament Uses the Old," in *New Testament Interpretation: Essays on Principles and Methods*, ed. I. Howard Marshall (Grand Rapids: Eerdmans, 1977), 199–219.

71. Richard Longenecker, "'Who Is the Prophet Talking About?' Some Reflections on the New Testament's Use of the Old," in *The Right Doctrine*, 385.

72. Longenecker, "'Who Is the Prophet Talking About?'" 380.

73. Cf. McCartney, "The New Testament's Use of the Old Testament," 101–16.

74. See the hesitations by Moisés Silva, "Old Testament in Paul," in *Dictionary of Paul and His Letters*, ed. Gerald F. Hawthorne and Ralph P. Martin (Downers Grove,

Conversely, some who are concerned about the implications entailed in admitting the utilization of these methods seek to deny their use altogether. What influences the positions of these groups are their assumptions regarding what the use of these methods *necessarily* entails. For instance, some have concluded that *pesher* is the primary method by which the NT authors appropriated the OT text.[75] This is easily demonstrable if what is meant by the term is any *direct* application of an OT text to a specific NT situation, grounded in a revelatory claim.

Scholars in this camp contend, however, that identifying this as *pesher* does not necessarily invalidate the exegetical conclusions deriving from it. It is only when the category of *pesher* is understood necessarily to entail an *inappropriate* reading of foreign meanings into the text that a different answer to our question might be forthcoming.[76] Accordingly, several have noted that the NT authors do not appear to use several of the exegetical devices utilized at Qumran in order to bring out the hidden eschatological meaning of the text.[77]

The same applies to *midrash*. Several have argued that there is a general absence in the NT writings of the more free-wheeling methods available to their authors.[78] Thus, while working within the exegetical world of Second Temple Judaism, the apostolic writers handled the OT in ways that are not to be considered inappropriate, even by moderns. The question

---

IL: InterVarsity Press, 1993), 634–38.

75. For examples, see Longenecker, *Biblical Exegesis*, 70–75. Notice how Paul affirms that what had been a mystery to previous generations has now been revealed to the church's apostles and prophets (Eph 3:1–6). It is said to be found, for instance, in Peter's citing of Joel 2:28–32 in Acts 2:16–21—that to which Joel had pointed all along has now arrived (cf. also Jesus' citation of Zech 13:7 in Mark 14:27; *et passim*).

76. Cf. Stendahl, *School of St. Matthew*, 191–92; Stendahl reproduces Brownlee's list of thirteen principles, derived from the study of 1QpHab, though Brownlee characterizes these as essentially "midrashic" ("Biblical Interpretation," 60–62, 76).

77. E.g., Marshall, "Assessment," 209; Lindars, "The Place of the Old Testament," in *The Right Doctrine*, 141.

78. Moo writes, "A vast gulf separates the often fantastic, purely verbal exegeses of the rabbis from the generally sober and clearly contextually oriented interpretations found in the New Testament. Indeed, it is where Jewish exegesis strays furthest from what we would consider sound principles that the New Testament differs most from it" ("The Problem," 193).

here, then, is one of *degree* rather than simply that of use or non-use.[79]

Scholars are similarly divided on whether or not the NT authors utilized "allegory" in their appropriation of the OT. Some reject this notion altogether, defending the careful preservation of the author's intended meaning by the NT authors.[80] Others admit the occasional appearance of allegory in the NT, but maintain that when it occurs the writer makes clear to his readers that this is what he is doing.[81]

Exegetical Methods and the Central Question

Interestingly, the answers that scholars give to whether or not the NT writers utilized the exegetical methods of Second Temple Judaism do not *necessarily* determine their position on our central question. One may deny the use of these so as to preserve the continuity between the meaning intended by the human author of the OT text and that which is picked up by the NT writers. Another may admit the limited use of these methods, such that *continuity* of meaning is maintained. Yet another may explain the *disjunction* between the OT and NT meanings by appealing to the use of these methods.

Orbiting Question 5: Are We Able to Replicate the Exegetical and Hermeneutical Approaches to the Old Testament That We Find in the Writings of the New Testament?

We come now to our fifth and final orbiting question: Should we be permitted to appropriate the OT in the same ways that the NT authors do? In this case, rather than influencing conclusions pertaining to the central issue, the answer we give to this fifth

---

79. For instance, Lindars notes the pervasive evidence of Jewish exegetical and hermeneutical techniques in the NT. At the same time, he distinguishes the NT uses of such methods as *pesher* and apocalyptic from their counterparts in Second Temple Judaism (Lindars, "The Place of the Old Testament," 142–43).

80. See Foulkes, "The Acts of God," 368–69, who contends most of what has occasionally been categorized as allegorical is actually typological in nature.

81. Note Paul's use of the Greek participle *allegoroumena* in Gal 4:24, from which we derive our English cognate.

question is significantly influenced *by* the answers to each of the other questions. If this fifth question is answered in the affirmative, the same issue regarding the relationship between the OT and NT authors' meanings will now pertain to the relationship between the OT authors' meanings and the ones that *we* derive from their texts. The orbit of this fifth question, therefore, is further out from the center.

One option is to exonerate the NT authors from employing the faulty exegetical methods of Second Temple Judaism and to argue that their approach is in harmony with what most consider acceptable today. That is to say, if one concludes that the NT writers used a method that is essentially the same as traditional, grammatical-historical exegesis, then there ought to be no reason to inhibit us from replicating their work.

Another option is to acknowledge the unique and authoritative role that the inspired NT writers play in their interpretation and appropriation of the OT text. Since we do not share that same authority, we should not try to follow them in the use of Second Temple exegetical procedures (e.g., *pesher*, *midrash*, or allegory) in our own interpretation and application of the OT. We can only seek to understand what they were doing with the text so as to interpret their writings correctly. When it comes to our own appropriation of the OT, however, we may only follow the NT writers in their use of the grammatical-historical method. This means that we must make a distinction between the *descriptive* and the *prescriptive*. This is the position taken by Longenecker in his response to this question:

> I suggest that we must answer both "No" and "Yes." Where that exegesis is based upon a revelatory stance, where it evidences itself to be merely cultural, or where it shows itself to be circumstantial or *ad hominem* in nature, "No." Where, however, it treats the Old Testament in more literal fashion, following the course of what we speak of today as historico-grammatical exegesis, "Yes." Our commitment as Christians is to the reproduction of the apostolic faith and doctrine, and not necessarily to the specific apostolic exegetical practices.[82]

---

82. Longenecker, *Biblical Exegesis*, 214–20 (quote on 219); see also idem, " 'Who Is the Prophet Talking about?' 375–85. Cf. Markus Barth, "The Old Testament in

To try to replicate the apostolic methodologies is to make the NT into a textbook of hermeneutics rather than to receive it in its intention—"to be a proclamation which centers in creation, fall, and redemption."[83]

Silva softens Longenecker's prohibition a bit, arguing that the gap between us and the NT authors is narrower than what Longenecker conceives it to be. At the same time, he affirms the legitimate use of the methods that are appropriate to each era. Since Second Temple methods would be acceptable and effective for the first-century readers of the NT, we must allow the apostolic authors to employ them. Therefore, while Silva backs off from drawing the same definitive line in the sand as Longenecker does, he maintains a distinction in methods, based not on the presence or absence of the inspiration of the interpreters, but on their relative acceptability to the audience. It is acknowledging this that renders imitation somewhat anachronistic:

> Well, then, if God wished to reveal something of the significance of the Old Testament through His inspired apostles, would He do so through "scientific" methods that were to take twenty centuries to develop and would therefore have been totally incomprehensible to first-century readers? Might He not rather use those very associations and interpretive clues that would awaken the intended human response? Just as the use of *imperfect* human languages like Hebrew and Greek can prove an adequate channel for conveying divine truth unmixed with error, so does prescientific apostolic exegesis serve to communicate, infallibly, the teaching of the Old Testament.[84]

We are therefore not *required* to use the same methods, but we must preserve apostolic authority. Somewhat reminiscent of Longenecker's argumentation, Silva concludes: "While we are committed to discover and *pursue* the interpretive framework that characterized apostolic interpretation, we need not suppose

Hebrews: An Essay in Biblical Hermeneutics," in *Current Issues in New Testament Interpretation: Essays in Honor of Otto A. Piper*, ed. William Klassen and Graydon F. Snyder (New York: Harper & Brothers, 1962), 76–78.

83. Longenecker, *Biblical Exegesis*, 219; Longenecker is quoting here from A. J. Bandstra, "Interpretation in 1 Corinthians 10:1–11," *CTJ* 6 (1971): 20.

84. Silva, "The New Testament Use," 164.

that such a commitment compels us to reproduce it in all its features."[85]

Replication and the Central Question

Obviously, the position taken with regard to this fifth orbiting question has significant implications regarding our central question. But here the concern is not with whether the NT authors' meanings are distinct from their OT counterparts, but whether the meanings that *we* derive from the OT are legitimate. The debate here will undoubtedly continue to be robust, as it is exemplified in the opinions of our three contributors.

INTERPRETIVE ASSUMPTIONS OF NEW TESTAMENT AUTHORS

In spite of areas of disagreement on these issues, many scholars find a wide swath of agreement on the interpretive, or hermeneutical, assumptions that guided the NT authors as they appropriated texts from the Scriptures. Knowledge of these assumptions can be useful when one is attempting to understand a particular NT use of an OT text. Passages that are initially baffling to modern readers often become clear when these fundamental presuppositions are acknowledged. It will be helpful to include a brief survey of these assumptions here since our three contributors assume familiarity with them in their essays.

It is well known that ancient Jewish groups prior to and contemporaneous with the first-century Christian Jews were perceiving fulfillments of the OT in events and people that were quite distinct from those put forward in the NT. The interpretations of Scripture found at Qumran illustrate this well. As is revealed in their writings, these sectarian Jews were convinced of their identity as the "children of light," faithful to the

---

85. Ibid. Moo ("The Problem," 206) offers a cautious, nuanced view. While we do not have the same revelatory stance, it is possible for us to perceive the theological and presuppositional stance on which the NT is based, supplying us with the same criteria as we make our interpretation. See also Foulkes, "The Acts of God," 370–71.

covenants and the rightful heirs of many scriptural prophecies concerning the last days of the age. Equipped with their herme-neutical key—which is none other than their Teacher of Righteousness—they saw in their own history the fulfillment of end time prophecies.[86] Accordingly, they unhesitatingly applied the Scriptures to their own community.

What is important to recognize is that this is analogous to what the NT authors have done in their use of the OT. Equipped with Jesus, who is their interpretive key, they appropriate the Scriptures to validate their claim that Jesus is the Messiah and to bolster their assertions concerning their own identity and destiny. Like the Qumranians, they view Scripture through the lens of their presuppositions about Jesus.[87] I will briefly discuss the most important of these here.

Jesus Is the One in Whom the Scriptures Find Fulfillment

The most seminal of these, of course, is the NT writers' assumption that Jesus is the one to whom the Scriptures point and in whom they find their fulfillment.[88] Fundamental to this is their belief in his messianic identity, identifying him as the long-awaited heir to David's covenant promises. Starting from this assumption, however, the NT writers also find many fulfillments that eclipse his role as Messiah. Naturally, they also make connections that extend to the community of his disciples.[89] This assumption is grounded in their experiences with Jesus and ultimately in his resurrection.[90] Most of the NT use of the OT that

---

86. See esp. 1QpHab 1:1–6; 2:1–2.

87. See the discussions of these in Snodgrass, "The Use of the Old Testament," 415–20; Bock, "Use of the Old Testament," 102–4; cf. also Ellis, "How the New Testament," 209–14.

88. Cf. Snodgrass, "The Use of the Old Testament," 418; Bock, "Use of the Old Testament," 104.

89. For example, note the application of OT imagery that refers to Israel to the racially mixed recipients of Peter's letter in 1 Peter 2:9–10; similarly also in Rom 9:25–26.

90. E.g., Acts 2:24–36; 4:10–12; 10:39–43; 13:32–37; 17:31; Rom 1:1–4; 1 Cor 15:3–4, 12–28. See Snodgrass, "The Use of the Old Testament," 418; Lindars, "The Place of the Old Testament," 143–45.

is distinctive from other ancient Jewish writings flows from this assumption.[91]

The Days of Fulfillment Have Come

Their second presupposition flows directly from the first: Since the Messiah has arrived and has been vindicated in a climactic way, the NT writers also assume that they are living in the days when the Scriptures are finding their fulfillment.[92] Admittedly, the Jews at Qumran also believe the last days have arrived in the events surrounding themselves and especially their Teacher of Righteousness. But the messianic age itself is merely *anticipated* by them, albeit imminently. The writers of the NT are convinced that the messianic age of kingdom blessing has already *begun*, validated dramatically by Jesus' resurrection.[93]

Corporate Solidarity or "The One in the Many"

Equipped with these first two presuppositions, the NT writers often utilize the Jewish assumption known as "corporate solidarity" or "the one in the many."[94] As we noted earlier, this assumption appears liberally in the typological relationships between the OT and the NT. This notion perceives the existence of a corporate *oneness* among the members of a group, such that "a single member of a community can represent the whole"[95] — the

---

91. See McCartney, "The New Testament's Use of the Old Testament," 107–16.

92. Snodgrass, "The Use of the Old Testament," 417; Bock, "Use of the Old Testament," 103; Lindars, "The Place of the Old Testament," 143. Note Paul's assumption of the final era's arrival in 1 Cor 10:11; cf. Luke 7:18–23.

93. Cf. Matt 26:64; Acts 2:33–35; 7:55–56; Phil 2:9; Col 3:1; Heb 1:3; Rev 5:11–13. Note Peter's assumption of the fulfillment of Joel 2:28 in Acts 2:17. Lindars points out that because of the commonality between the Christian perspective and that of such groups as the Qumranians, "the church's application of the whole range of the Old Testament to Jesus could be felt to be a plausible undertaking and find acceptance" (Lindars, "The Place of the Old Testament," 141).

94. Bock, "Use of the Old Testament," 102; cf. also Snodgrass, "The Use of the Old Testament," 415–16.

95. Bock, "Use of the Old Testament," 102.

king or priest can represent the nation,[96] an animal can bear sins representatively for all,[97] and a prophet can picture the nation's fate in his individual life.[98]

Consequently, "what is said of one figure can then be applied to another who fits within the identity of the group or who serves as its representative."[99] This assumption allows NT writers to craft arguments that pivot on relationships between Jesus and the nation or its corporate representatives.[100] It also reverberates under the surface of the titles that are applied to Jesus, such as the Son of God, the Servant, and the Son of Man. Snodgrass notes:

> [These] were all representative titles that were applied to Israel first. Jesus took on these titles because he had taken Israel's task. He was representative of Israel and in solidarity with her. God's purposes for Israel were now taken up in his ministry. If this were true, what had been used to describe Israel could legitimately be used of him.[101]

Pattern (Correspondence) in History

A close companion of corporate solidarity is the presupposition that history is expressive of God's intent and will—what we have also seen undergirding typology. Since God is sovereign over history and since he is consistently true to his character, his actions in prior history are assumed to anticipate his

---

96. Note the solidarity that the people perceive between themselves and the king in 2 Sam 5:1 and 1 Chron 11:1; cf. also Ps 118:10, where the king, representing his army, refers to himself as the one surrounded by enemies. Aaron functions as the representative of the entire nation on the Day of Atonement (Lev 16).

97. E.g., Lev 16:15–24, 34.

98. E.g., Ezek 4–5; 12.

99. Bock, "Use of the Old Testament," 102.

100. Longenecker, *Biblical Exegesis*, 94. Cf. Paul's pairing off of Jesus in relation to Adam (1 Cor 15:20–22 and Rom 5:15), grounded in Jesus' representative death for all people (2 Cor 5:14).

101. Snodgrass, "The Use of the Old Testament," 416; cf. also Dodd, "The Old Testament in the New," 179–80.

intervention in subsequent eras.[102] Accordingly, biblical authors trace "correspondences between God's activity of the past and his action in the present—between events then and events now, between persons then and persons now" or in the future.[103] As such, these are not merely historical "illustrations." Rather, they are patterns divinely intended to reveal God's will, such that "climactic events in Israel's history become the paradigms by which new events are explained."[104] This means that at times "the text is not used up by a single event,"[105] with the later event usually *eclipsing* the initial event in importance.[106]

It is clear that these four presuppositions together create the literary environment where typological interpretations can thrive.

The Inaugurated Fulfillment of the Scriptures

A final presupposition qualifies the NT authors' appraisal of the fulfillments that have come through Jesus. Although he has dramatically ushered in the kingdom, the age when God will definitively bless his people, the NT writers qualify this by affirming that the Jewish hopes have only been *inaugurated*.[107] That is to say, though the fulfillment brought by Jesus is *decisive*, it is not yet the *consummated* fulfillment—it is only the *inauguration* of what will yet come to pass. Accordingly, those fulfillments that have arrived *themselves* often point forward to their climactic culminations in the future.[108]

---

102. Note Isaiah's use of exodus motifs to describe Judah's eventual return from the Babylonian exile (Isa 43:16–19; cf. also 40:3–4). Significantly, John the Baptist picks this up again in Luke 3:4–5 (cf. Matt 3:3) to refer to what he expects soon to take place.

103. Longenecker, *Biblical Exegesis*, 94.

104. Snodgrass, "The Use of the Old Testament," 416.

105. Ibid.

106. Bock, "Use of the Old Testament," 102.

107. Ibid., 103–4.

108. Note Jesus' ominous threat to Caiaphas, acknowledging the yet future fulfillment of his destiny as the Son of Man in Matt 26:63–64; cf. also Titus 2:11–14; Rev 19:15.

PERSPECTIVES ON THE CENTRAL QUESTION

Let me conclude this introductory chapter with a brief overview of the three perspectives on our central issue that will be defended by our three contributors.

Single Meaning, Unified Referents

One possible response to the question of the relationship between the intentions of the OT and NT authors, of course, is to deny any distinction between them — what the OT author intends by his words is what the NT author intends. There is therefore a "single meaning" communicated by the text of Scripture. This extends to the referents of the text. That is to say, in addition to any prior reference, the OT writer is to be understood as ultimately having the same people or events in mind when he writes his text as the NT author does when he refers that text to Jesus and the community defined by him. This pertains even to those texts that do not appear to have any messianic significance. Walter Kaiser approaches our central issue from this general viewpoint.

Single Meaning, Multiple Contexts and Referents

A second response to this question agrees with the first view in affirming the singular nature of the meanings intended by the OT and NT authors when OT texts are cited in the NT. In spite of this essential unity in meaning, however, the words of the OT authors frequently take on new dimensions of significance and are found to apply appropriately to new referents and new situations as God's purposes unfold in the larger canonical context — referents that were often not in the minds of the OT authors when they penned their texts. Darrell Bock defends his own adaptation of this view in his essay.

Fuller Meaning, Single Goal

A third response to our central issue is to suggest that the NT writers often perceive new meanings in OT texts that are not necessarily closely related to the meanings intended by the original authors. These new meanings are legitimized by appealing to the NT authors' single-minded conviction that the Scriptures point to and are fulfilled in Christ. Advocates of this view are careful not to deny the importance of the grammatical-historical study of the OT text so as to understand the OT authors on their own terms. But since the NT writers assume that Jesus is the *goal* to which the OT story is moving, they perceive this meaning in OT texts, even when their OT authors did not have that meaning in mind when they wrote. Peter Enns articulates a version of this perspective in his essay.

These three views on our central issue of the relationship between the intended meanings of the OT and NT authors of Scripture will be fleshed out in much greater detail by our contributing scholars. We invite you to keep these general categories in mind as you look for the ways in which they answer our orbiting questions. Note that a summary and analysis of our three contributors' positions on our five controlling questions is undertaken by my coeditor, Kenneth Berding, in the conclusion of this volume.

CONCLUSION

We hope that this survey of several of the relevant aspects of this debate has prepared the reader not only to understand the essays that follow, but also to make evaluative assessments regarding them. But understanding and evaluating the range of scholarly, interpretive options are not the final goals of the contributors and editors of this volume. As I noted at the outset, our ultimate purpose goes significantly beyond this — that is, to recover the profoundly theological nature of the NT use of the OT Scriptures and thereby to appreciate more deeply the astounding glory of the revelation that has come in Jesus. It is our hope that the discussions presented here will help all of us to know what, in fact, we are to do with this, and so learn to join with the NT writers as they "sing" from the Scriptures.

Chapter One

SINGLE MEANING, UNIFIED REFERENTS

Accurate and Authoritative Citations of the Old Testament by the New Testament

Chapter One

SINGLE MEANING, UNIFIED REFERENTS

Accurate and Authoritative Citations of the Old Testament by the New Testament

Walter C. Kaiser, Jr.

One of the key debates of the past four decades has been the problem of identifying the meaning of Scripture for our day and times. Should that meaning be limited to what the human writer of Scripture obtained as a result of standing in the revelatory counsel of God, or were there additional, or even alternative, meanings to be found that God somehow quietly incorporated into the text in some mysterious way, thus hiding them from the author, or perhaps even new meanings that the audience brought to the text on their own?[1] This whole debate has been no small tempest in a teapot, for it is also tied in with several contemporary philosophical and literary movements of our own day and age, affecting the entire theological community, including, of course, many of the evangelical scholars.[2]

---

1. One of my earlier articles on this topic was, "The Single Intent of Scripture," in *Evangelical Roots: A Tribute to Wilbur Smith,* ed. Kenneth S. Kantzer (Nashville: Nelson, 1978), 123–41.

2. C. K. Barrett, "The Old Testament in the Fourth Gospel," *JTS* 48 (1947): 155–69; D. L. Bock "Evangelicals and the Use of the Old Testament in the New," *BSac* 142 (1985): 306–19; E. Earle Ellis, *Paul's Use of the Old Testament* (1957), reprint ed. (Grand Rapids: Baker, 1981); E. D. Freed, *Old Testament Quotations in the Gospel of John* (NovTSup 2; Leiden: Brill, 1965); R. H. Gundry, *The Use of the Old Testament in*

Early in my career of teaching the Bible I ran across this assessment of the problem by Bishop J. C. Ryle (1818–1900):

> I hold it to be a most dangerous mode of interpreting Scripture, to regard everything which its words may be tortured into meaning as a lawful interpretation of the words. I hold undoubtedly that there is a mighty depth in all Scripture, and that in this respect it stands alone. But I also hold that the words of Scripture were intended to have one definite sense, and that our first object should be to discover that sense, and adhere rigidly to it. I believe that, as a general rule, the words of Scripture are intended to have, like all other language, one plain definite meaning, and that to say words *do* mean a thing, merely because they *can* be tortured into meaning it, is a most dishonourable and dangerous way of handling Scripture.[3]

I could not agree more heartily; for this has become the standard by which I not only interpret the text as a biblical teacher, but it is the same view I urgently press other evangelicals to adopt.

More frequently, however, there has emerged a strong consensus running in evangelical work in this area that tends to regard the majority of the OT quotations in the NT as "hav[ing] no semblance of predictive intention."[4] Donald A. Hagner continued:

St. Matthew's Gospel (NovTSup 18; Leiden: Brill, 1967); Donald A. Hagner, "The Old Testament in the New Testament," in *Interpreting the Word of God: Festschrift in Honor of Steven Barabas*, ed. Samuel J. Schultz and Morris A. Inch (Chicago: Moody Press, 1976): 78–104; Walter C. Kaiser, Jr., *The Uses of the Old Testament in the New* (Chicago: Moody Press, 1985); Richard N. Longenecker, "Can We Reproduce the Exegesis of the New Testament?" *TynBul* 21 (1970): 3–38; I. Howard Marshall, "An Assessment of Recent Developments," in *It Is Written: Scripture Citing Scripture; Essays in Honor of Barnabas Lindars*, ed. D. A. Carson and H. G. M. Williamson (Cambridge: Cambridge Univ. Press, 1988): 9ff.; Douglas J. Moo, *The Old Testament in the Gospel Passion Narratives* (Sheffield, Almond Press, 1983); Stanley E. Porter, ed., *Hearing the Old Testament in the New Testament* (Grand Rapids: Eerdmans, 2006); Moisés Silva "Old Testament in Paul," in *Dictionary of Paul and His Letters*, ed. G. F. Hawthorne, R. P. Martin, and D. G. Reid (Downers Grove, IL: InterVarsity Press, 1993), 630–42; Bruce K. Waltke, "Is It Right to Read the New Testament into the Old?" *Christianity Today* 27 (1983): 77.

3. Bishop J. C. Ryle, *Expository Thoughts on the Gospels* (Grand Rapids: Zondervan, 1953), 2:383.

4. Hagner, "The Old Testament," 92. There are, of course, a good number of prophecies that have an undeniably predictive intention, such as Isa 9:1–2; Joel 2:28–32; Mic 5:2; Zech 9:9.

All of this leads us to the recognition of what has been called the *sensus plenior*, or "fuller sense," of the Old Testament Scripture. To be aware of *sensus plenior* is to realize that there is the possibility of more significance to an Old Testament passage than was consciously apparent to the original author, and more than can be gained by strict grammatico-historical exegesis. Such is the nature of divine inspiration that the authors of Scripture were themselves often not conscious of the fullest significance and final application of what they wrote. This fuller sense of the Old Testament can be seen only in retrospect and in the light of the New Testament fulfillment.[5]

It is this wide acceptance of various versions of *sensus plenior* among contemporary evangelicals that renders this discussion so crucial for our day.

But there are several other important issues that relate in some way to this central question—issues such as (1) the extent to which the NT authors also used ancient Jewish exegetical and interpretive methods in their use of the OT; (2) the NT authors' awareness or disregard of the larger OT context of the passages they quote; (3) the appropriate understanding of the function of typology; and (4) the question of whether contemporary interpreters may replicate the NT writers' techniques of appropriating and applying the OT Scriptures. After an initial discussion of *sensus plenior*, therefore, I will move to discuss each of these related areas in turn. I will conclude with my perspective on the legitimacy of contemporary Christians employing the same interpretive approach to the OT as was employed by first-century Christians.

CAN WE APPEAL TO *SENSUS PLENIOR*?

Father Raymond E. Brown published his dissertation in 1955,[6] in which he gave a fixed definition as to what a *sensus plenior* meaning was. Brown defined it this way:

---

5. Hagner, "The Old Testament," 92.

6. Father Brown, of course, was not the first one to speak of *sensus plenior*. That distinction belongs to F. Andre Fernandez, who coined the term in his article "Hermeneutica," *Institutiones Biblicae Scholis Accommodata,* 2nd ed. (Rome: Biblical Institute, 1927), 306.

> The *sensus plenior* is that additional, deeper meaning, intended by God, but not clearly intended by the human author, which is seen to exist in the words of a biblical text (or group of texts, or even a whole book) when they are studied in the light of further revelation or development in the understanding of revelation[7]

Later he clarified matters further by candidly instructing interpreters:

> Let us apply the term *sensus plenior* ["fuller sense"] to that meaning of his [the author's] text which by the normal rules of exegesis would not have been within his clear awareness of intention, but which by other criteria we can determine as having been intended by God.[8]

Since Brown takes it out of the hands of the human authors who stood in the counsel of God, the question is: In whose hands now does the final court of appeal rest for discovering the authoritative meaning of a biblical text? Roman Catholic scholars, of course, can fall back on the magisterium of the church, to the ecclesial tradition. But to what can Protestants appeal that matches such additional grounds of appeal?

Norbert Lohfink,[9] a Jesuit scholar, tried to find a way to get at this additional divine meaning that was free of the writer's understanding, which ordinarily was to be found in the grammar and syntax of the author's words. At first he went to the "final redactor" of Scripture, the one who had allegedly placed the books of the Bible in their present canonical shape, but then he shifted his ground to appeal to that which the whole Bible taught. Thus, above, behind, and beyond that which grammatico-historical exegesis established as the author's original meaning of the text, there was another meaning: the one that the whole Bible taught.

---

7. Raymond E. Brown, *The* Sensus Plenior *of Sacred Scripture* (Baltimore, MD: St. Mary's Univ. Press, 1955), 92. Also see idem, "The History and Development of the Theory of *Sensus Plenior*," *CBQ* 15 (1953): 141–62.

8. Raymond E. Brown, "The *Sensus Plenior* in the Last Ten Years," *CBQ* 25 (1963): 268–69.

9. Norbert Lohfink, *The Christian Meaning of the Old Testament*, trans. R. A. Wilson (Milwaukee: Bruce, 1968), 32–49.

But what was there in the whole Bible that could not be found in its individual books or in the exegesis of individual passages using the standard tools such as grammar, syntax, and the like? Trapped by his own logic, Lohfink turned, as so many evangelicals now tend to do, to the theory of *sensus plenior* in an attempt to get *beyond* the writer of Scripture. Whereas the older form of literary criticism had tried to sort out the sources that allegedly were used by the writers of Scripture in an attempt to get *behind* the biblical text, now the goal was to go *beyond* the text as it was written. God, who is viewed in this analysis as the principal author, is depicted as supplying to later interpreters of the text additional and subsequent meanings, thereby relegating the human authors of Scripture to, at best, a secondary level, if not a nuisance for getting at the really deep things of God.

But in a rather brilliant review of this theory, coming from the same Catholic side of the aisle, Bruce Vawter recognized *sensus plenior* as abandoning the old scholastic *analogy of instrumental causality*. He explained:

> ... if this fuller or deeper meaning was reserved by God to himself and did not enter into the writer's purview at all, do we not postulate a Biblical word effected outside the control of the human author's will and judgment ... and therefore not produced through a truly *human* instrumentality? If, as in scholastic definitions, Scripture is the *conscriptio* [writing together] of God and man, does not the acceptance of a *sensus plenior* deprive this alleged scriptural sense of one of its essential elements, to the extent that logically it cannot be called scriptural at all?[10]

The effect of Vawter's argument was to declare that the *sensus plenior* meaning (despite its high claims for being a deeper meaning from God himself to the interpreter) simply was not "Scripture" in the sense that it came from what was "written." That is to say, if the deeper meaning was one that was not located in the words, sentences, and paragraphs of the text, then it was not "Scripture," which in the Greek is called *graphe*, "writing" (i.e., that which stands written in the text)! Moreover, if this

---

10. Bruce Vawter, *Biblical Inspiration* (Theological Resources; Philadelphia: Westminster, 1972), 115.

"fuller sense" opened up new vistas for the interpreter, how did it also escape the sacred writers of Scripture? Could not the same process that, according to this theory, aided the interpreter likewise have aided those who were writing the words declared to be from God? As Vern S. Poythress also noted (even though he admitted his view had "certain affinities" with the idea of *sensus plenior*), this theory left "an opening for the entrance of later Church tradition,"[11] and the addition of new dogmas, rather than just the development of the biblical canon. That, of course, is precisely the point noted here thus far.

On the evangelical side of the aisle, it is interesting to see how a slipperiness in interpretation developed — one that slides from a search for "more *significance*" to eventually seeing this "significance" as one of the *meanings*, albeit a deeper one, of the text. Graeme Goldsworthy, for example, was most candid in summing up his view on this matter. He opined:

> The *sensus plenior* of an OT text, or indeed of the whole OT, cannot be found by exegesis of the texts themselves. Exegesis aims at understanding what was intended by the author, the *sensus literalis*. But there is a deeper meaning in the mind of the divine author which emerges in further revelation, usually the NT. This approach embraces typology but also addresses the question of how a text may have more than one meaning. While typology focuses upon historical events which foreshadow later events, *sensus plenior* focuses on the use of words.[12]

Such statements are confusing. If this deeper meaning cannot be found in an exegesis of the OT text, then how can it be found in the "words" vis-à-vis typology, which focuses on "events"? If the meaning of the words must await their further elaboration in the NT, then we have to answer two questions:

---

11. Vern S. Poythress, "Divine Meaning of Scripture," originally in *WTJ* 48 (1986): 241–79, but reprinted in *The Right Doctrine from the Wrong Texts? Essays on the Use of the Old Testament in the New*, ed. Greg K. Beale (Grand Rapids: Baker, 1994), 108, n. 25.

12. Graeme Goldsworthy, "The Relationship of the Old Testament and New Testament," in *New Dictionary of Biblical Theology*, ed. T. Desmond Alexander et al. (Downers Grove, IL: InterVarsity Press, 2000), 88.

(1) Were not the original audiences, to whom the OT writers addressed these words, left out of these, indeed, of *any* deeper meanings? And (2), if there is no signal from the original writers that more was stored in the words than appeared on the surface meaning, would this not be an example of what we call *eisegesis*, i.e., a reading backwards from the NT into the OT texts new meanings not discoverable by the rules of language and exegesis?

It is to be admitted that the search for the authority status of the *significance* attached to a text is a serious problem and one worthy of our best efforts and explanations. E. D. Hirsch's famous distinction between "meaning" and "significance" brought some immediate relief.[13] Hirsch declared that "meaning" was all that the human author expressed directly, indirectly, tacitly, or allusively in his own words. But "significance" named a relationship that we as readers drew as we associated what was said in the author's meaning with some other situation, person, institution, or the like. Meaning was *unchanging*, according to Hirsch; significance was *changeable* and must change since the interests and questions asked relate the texts to many new situations, persons, institutions, and scores of other relationships.

The question of the ignorance of the writers of Scripture with regard to their own meanings, which presumably permits interpreters to find "deep meanings," or different senses, than the grammar or syntax reveals, still persists. Hirsch once again addressed some of the most pressing questions:

> How can an author mean something he did not mean? The answer to that question is simple. It is not possible to mean what one does not mean, though it is very possible to mean what one is not conscious of meaning. That is the entire issue in the argument based on authorial ignorance. That a man may not be conscious of all that he means is no more remarkable than that he may not be conscious of all he does. There is a difference between meaning and consciousness of meaning, and since meaning is an affair of the consciousness, one can say more precisely that there is a difference between consciousness

---

13. E. D. Hirsch Jr., *Validity in Interpretation* (New Haven, CT: Yale Univ. Press, 1967), xi, 8.

and self-consciousness. Indeed, when an author's meaning is complicated, he cannot possibly at a given moment be paying attention to all its complexities.[14]

Even Hirsch seems to contradict himself, for he asserts that "an author cannot mean something he did not mean" and yet that same author can "mean what he is not conscious of meaning" and that about which he has no awareness. Which way does Hirsch wish to argue? Furthermore, if what the author writes is a result of a disclosure of God's revelation, how can he write what he is not conscious of writing, unless we incorrectly espouse some form of a mechanical dictation theory of divine communication to the writers of Scripture? Still, Hirsch's distinction between the unchangeable *meaning* of the original author and the various applications of this meaning's *significance* is important—a distinction to which we will return.

DOES A CANONICAL READING SUPPORT *SENSUS PLENIOR*?

It might seem that advocates of the *sensus plenior* method of interpretation are simply defending the Reformation principle that "Scripture interprets Scripture" (*scriptura scripturam interpretatur*). When we ask, "What did it mean?" Kevin Vanhoozer has observed that it all depends on what "it" refers to. His plea is for a "thick" rather than a "thin" interpretation of biblical passages that involves the whole Christian Bible. He argues:

> To interpret isolated passages of the OT as evidence of the religious or cultural history of Israel is to give "thin" descriptions only.... To read the Bible canonically is to read the Bible as a unified communicative act, that is, as a complex, multi-leveled speech act of a single divine author.... "Thin" descriptions are the result of using too narrow a context to interpret an intended action.[15]

---

14. Ibid., 22.

15. Kevin J. Vanhoozer, "Exegesis and Hermeneutics," in *New Dictionary of Biblical Theology*, ed. T. Desmond Alexander and Brian S. Rosner, et al. (Downers Grove, IL: InterVarsity Press, 2000), 61.

This comes closer to solving the problem of getting at the meaning of the text, for we must not act as if God had not given the total canon of Scripture. My only caution would be that there is a place or time in our exegesis at which we introduce the later canonical perspective; it can only come *after* exegesis has established the meaning of the OT text, *before* we go on to see how the divine revelation on this same area of teaching fills out this truth in the subsequent progress of revelation in the later books of the Bible.

In that sense, I too would warn against a premature "thin" interpretation, for I would *not* try to "thicken" my initial exegesis of the text by leap-frogging immediately over to the NT to get right into the "deep things" of God before working on the exegesis of the OT passage. Why not use first of all the divine revelation found in the books that *preceded* the selected text we are reading or studying as the context and "informing theology" that could have the first input to "thicken" the meaning? Why does the "thickening" have to stem only from the *subsequent* revelation? We need to give full weight to earlier revelation and not allow a particular understanding of later revelation to mitigate the force of God's message to early generations.

Another canonically oriented principle that may be understood by some to entail *sensus plenior* is "The Analogy of Faith." A clear explanation of the function and use of the method of the Analogy of Faith came from John F. Johnson:

> To put it tersely: *analogia* or *regula fidei* is to be understood as "the clear Scripture" itself; and this refers to articles of faith found in those passages which deal with individual doctrines expressly (*sedes doctrinae*). Individual doctrines are to be drawn from the *sedes doctrinae* [chair doctrinal-teaching-passages], and must be judged by them. Any doctrine not drawn from passages which expressly deal with the doctrine under consideration is not to be accepted as Scriptural.[16]

Since the NT testimony to Jesus is "clearer" than that which is found in the OT, one could characterize the NT authors' use of

---

16. John F. Johnson, *"Analogia Fidei* as Hermeneutical Principle," *Springfielder* 36 (1972–73): 249–59; esp. 253.

the OT as implying *sensus plenior* meanings on the grounds that these are inevitable and appropriate functions of the Analogy of Faith dictum.

However, it must also be carefully noted that when the Reformers affirmed that "Scripture interprets Scripture" along the lines of the "Analogy of Faith," they were not erecting an absolute or another external standard by which all Scripture itself had to be measured. If that had been their goal and intention in introducing these two methods of handling Scripture, that standard would have reversed the hard-fought-for and recently acquired independent authority of Scripture and returned it once again to a new set of traditions. Alternatively, it would have amounted to an appeal to a new "canon within a canon," which would act as a super-interpreter or arbitrator over competing views of the Scripture. Instead, the Reformers aimed these two methods against the tyrannical demands and stranglehold that *tradition* up to that point had exercised over the text of the Bible. As Bishop Marsh warned, "*Analogia fidei* was intended solely to deny that tradition was the interpreter of the Bible."[17]

In addition, Johnson correctly limits these two principles to teaching doctrine from "chair" passages where that doctrine was most fully developed. But neither he nor we would use either method to sanction the all-too-prevalent practice of using the NT as an "open sesame" for OT predictions or teachings. Nor should either of these principles be used as another "canon within a canon," thereby leveling the whole Bible out to what was the most recent revelation and thereby demeaning the truth unveiled and disclosed from God in its earlier forms.

ALLEGED NEW TESTAMENT TEXTUAL SUPPORT FOR *SENSUS PLENIOR*

To find further support in favor of the *sensus plenior* approach to Scripture, scholars will oftentimes appeal to NT passages that appear to affirm the ignorance of the OT human

---

17. Herbert Marsh, *A Course of Lectures Containing a Description and Systematic Arrangement of the Several Branches of Divinity* (Boston: Cummings and Hilliard, 1815), 3:16.

authors regarding the ultimate meaning and reference of their words. The following three passages illustrate these attempts.

Did the Biblical Authors Write Better Than They Knew? (1 Peter 1:10–12)

Invariably, evangelical advocates of *sensus plenior*, still desirous of finding a deeper meaning in the text of the Bible, appeal to 1 Peter 1:10–12 in order to show the possibility of some type of human ignorance on the part of the writers of Scripture as they wrote their books under the direction of God, presumably creating a divine vacuum for a possible later infilling from God. The text reads:

> Concerning this salvation, the prophets, who spoke of the grace that was to come to you, searched intently and with the greatest care, trying to find out the time and circumstances to which the Spirit of Christ in them was pointing when he predicted the sufferings of Christ and the glories that would follow. It was revealed to them that they were not serving themselves but you, when they spoke of the things that have now been told you by those who have preached the gospel to you by the Holy Spirit sent from heaven. Even angels long to look into these things.[18]

But as I have argued previously,[19] this text does not support a theory that "the authors of Scripture wrote better than

---

18. All biblical citations are from the TNIV unless otherwise stated. The RSV, NASB, and the ESV all render the Greek *eis tina e poion kairon* as "what *person* or what time [emphasis mine] the Spirit of Christ [in the OT prophets] was indicating when they spoke of the Messiah." Wayne Grudem has a long note earnestly contending for the fact that the prophets did not know the *person* they were speaking about (*1 Peter* [TNTC; Grand Rapids: Eerdmans, 1988], 74–75). He argues that *poios* could not mean "what kind of," but only meant "what?" Therefore it would be redundant to have *tina* also mean "what?" Thus, *poios* must mean "what person." That however was the point; the grammarians said it was tautological! Moreover, if Grudem is correct, why did the prophets say they knew five things about this person if they could not know him?

19. Kaiser, "Single Intent," 125.

they knew." What 1 Peter 1:10–12 does affirm is that the writers of Scripture "searched intently" for the *time* these things would take place. The Greek phrase states, *eis tina e poion kairon*, "unto what, or what manner of time" it was when these things named here in this text would be accomplished. The point is that *tina e poion* form what Greek grammarians refer to as a "tautology for emphasis,"[20] both modifying the word *kairon*, "time."

Critical to this whole argument is the way that *tina* is translated; it should *not* be rendered as "what person," as several translations have it.[21] Accordingly, this passage does *not* teach that the prophets of old were oblivious or ignorant of the exact *meaning* of what they wrote and predicted. Instead, they wished they also had knowledge of the *time* when the five things that 1 Peter 1:10–12 said these prophets announced: (1) they were predicting the coming of Messiah (v. 11); (2) they knew Messiah would need to suffer (v. 11); (3) they knew Messiah would achieve glory; (4) it would come after he had suffered (v. 11); and (5) they knew that what they wrote was not limited to the pre-Christian days, but they would have relevance for audiences beyond their day (v. 12).

Thus, it is not a case of writing better than they knew or even of writing what they were not conscious of saying. Instead, they wrote what God told them and they meant what they claimed God had said.

---

20. This view of a "tautology for emphasis" is the view held by the following grammarians and exegetes: F. Blass and A. DeBrunner, *A Greek Grammar of the New Testament*, rev. and trans. Robert W. Funk (Chicago: Univ. of Chicago Press, 1957), 155; A. T. Robertson, *A Grammar of the Greek New Testament in Light of Historical Research*, 4th ed. (Nashville: Broadman, 1923), 735–36; Walter Bauer, *A Greek-English Lexicon of the New Testament*, trans. W. F. Arndt and F. W. Gingrich (Chicago: Univ. of Chicago Press, 1957), 691; C. Briggs, *A Critical and Exegetical Commentary on 1 Peter* (ICC; Edinburgh: T & T Clark), 107–8; and E. G. Selwyn, *The First Epistle of St. Peter* (London: Macmillan, 1955), 134–38. Richard Schultz has called my attention to the same construction, though in reverse order, in Dionysius (or Longinus): *poia de kai tis aute,* "what and what manner of road is this?" (*On the Sublime*, 13.2 in The Loeb Classical Library, *Aristotle* XXIII, 199 [Cambridge, MA: Harvard Univ. Press, 1995]).

21. Cf. the translations in the RSV, NASB, ESV, Berkeley, Amplified, and the NEB footnote.

Did the Authors of Scripture Deny They Understood the Prophets or Their Own Words? (2 Peter 1:19–21)

Another text, to which some have appealed to defend a *sensus plenior* approach to Scripture, is 2 Peter 1:19–21. The text reads:

> We also have the prophetic message as something completely reliable, and you will do well to pay attention to it, as to a light shining in a dark place, until the day dawns and the morning star rises in your hearts. Above all, you must understand that no prophecy of Scripture came about by the prophet's own *interpretation* [or better: "loosing"] of things. For prophecy never had its origin in the human will, but prophets, though human, spoke from God as they were carried along by the Holy Spirit. (emphasis mine)

Some argue from this text that the prophets did not always understand, nor were they able to interpret their own words as they wrote under the inspiration of the Holy Spirit. Yet the argument made by Peter was exactly the opposite point: Peter had just claimed in verse 16 of that same context, "we did not follow cleverly devised stories," but we were "eyewitnesses" of Jesus' glory on the Mount of Transfiguration. That is why "we … have the prophetic message as something completely reliable [or secure]" found in the OT prophecies (v. 19).

Since prophecy did not originate in the free human creation of messages or by the overt will of human beings, but came as the Holy Spirit moved these ancient writers to write what they wrote, so the NT writers' "loosing" or "freeing" (Greek: *epilyseos*) of those same words was guided, not by their own wills or ideas, but by that same powerful illuminating Spirit that could bring great joy to the hearts of all who would receive it.

The substantive *epilysis* has no other examples in the NT or the Septuagint. In Classical Greek it means a "freeing" or "loosing"—a sense evinced in its cognate verbal form in Mark 4:34, where it means "to set at liberty, to let go, to loose." Only secondarily did it come to be translated "to explain, unfold, interpret." But if this secondary meaning is accepted here, it would claim too much for all parties in this debate, for it would mean that *all* prophetic writings were closed to their writers.

Moreover, it cannot mean "interpretation," as the TNIV renders it above, for how then could Peter urge his people to give heed to those same OT prophecies, which are as a "light shining in a dark place"? There would be no light on this basis. It would be as if Peter said in a contradictory manner, "give heed to the light shining in a dark place," because no prophet understood or could explain what he said or wrote, despite the fact that they were being borne along by the Holy Spirit! That "light" would have been darkness and the word would have been enigmatic.

Did Caiaphas Unwittingly Prophesy? (John 11:49–52)

In one final attempt to show that prophets can and did speak "better than they knew," appeal is made to the high priest Caiaphas in John 11:49–52, which reads this way:

> Then one of them, named Caiaphas, who was high priest that year, spoke up, "You know nothing at all! You do not realize that it is better for you that one man die for the people than that the whole nation perish."
> *He did not say this on his own, but as high priest that year he prophesied* that Jesus would die for the Jewish nation, and not only for that nation but also for the scattered children of God, to bring them together and make them one. (emphasis mine)

Caiaphas's judgment about his colleagues was most accurate: "You know nothing at all!" But as Rudolf Stier wittily noted, "What better, then, [did Caiaphas] know?"[22] His was a speech of political expediency: "It is better to let Jesus be a sacrificial lamb and let him take the rap personally for all the agitation and unrest in Jerusalem rather than having this whole thing blow up in our faces and have the wrath of Rome fall on our entire nation."

However, note carefully that it was John's inspired commentary that picked up Caiaphas's cynical remark of political correctness and who then turned it into an authoritative word from God. True, John said the high priest "prophesied," but that

---

22. Rudolf Stier, *Words of the Lord Jesus* (Edinburgh: T & T Clark, 1865), 6:56.

word must have quotes around it, for had not John picked up the words and turned them around against Caiaphas, we would never so much as heard of these words. Accordingly, these cynical and ironic words are not to be classified along with alleged examples of divinely authorized, unintentional prophecies, as Strack and Billerbeck have argued in their comments on this passage. Nor is this text a proof that the prophets of old belonged to a category proposed by Rabbi Eleazar (ca A.D. 270), who argued: "No prophets have known what they prophesied. Only Moses and Elijah knew." Or, "Samuel, the master of the prophets, did not know what he prophesied."[23]

But Caiaphas illustrates another process: one where he says in his own cool, calculated way what was politically savvy for his day, but also one in which his words were turned against him by the Holy Spirit to announce exactly what he and most of his nation had sorely misunderstood and denounced. Jesus indeed was that sacrificial Lamb of God whose blood had to be shed for the sins of the Jewish nation and for the sins of the world (John 3:16; 1 Tim 4:10). This view accorded with what John later explained: "Caiaphas was the one who had *advised* [not 'predicted' or 'prophesied'] the Jews that it would be good if one man died for the people" (John 18:14, emphasis mine).

Caiaphas's truth-intention/assertion (v. 50) is therefore to be sharply contrasted with the application and *significance* that John found (v. 51) in those hardened, bitter, and cynical words — words that were all the more newsworthy, though aimed in the wrong direction, since Caiaphas was high priest that year. Thus, John seized Caiaphas's remark from its parochial ethnocentricity and its provincialism and turned it toward the universal implications of the death of Jesus (v. 52). Rather than retaining Caiaphas's phrase that this handing Jesus over to the officials was "on behalf of the people" (v. 50), John deliberately expanded it to correspond to the purposes of Jesus' death on the cross, viz., it was now "on behalf of the nation," as well as on behalf of the "children of God scattered abroad" all over the world (v. 52). Had Caiaphas offered a prophecy in the ordinary

---

23. As cited by Edwyn C. Hoskyns, *The Fourth Gospel*, 2nd ed. (London: Faber and Faber, 1947), 412; cf. also Charles K. Barrett, *The Gospel according to St. John* (London: SPCK, 1960), 339.

sense of the word, there would have been no need for John to correct it and to expand it in his editorial comments. Caiaphas will not support the double-author theory of prophecy.

THE NEW TESTAMENT AUTHORS' RESPECT FOR THE OLD TESTAMENT CONTEXT

Again the question arises as to how far the OT writers perceived or understood the things they were writing. Is it legitimate to find a meaning that goes beyond the "authorial will" of the OT human writer, especially if that meaning exceeds the grammatico-historical process of locating that sense and if the one who exhibits that meaning is no one less than the Lord Jesus himself? And if Jesus (and later on: the apostles) did go beyond the authorial meanings, are we as interpreters allowed to follow his example? In other words, can we reproduce the exegesis of the apostles and Jesus, who are alleged to have supplied meanings not found in the texts they quote?

These additional meanings, it is usually argued, come from a Christian presupposition and are found by giving priority to the NT text over the OT text. Stephen Motyer observed:

> Many New Testament scholars maintain that the New Testament use of the Old Testament works within a closed logical circle: it depends on Christian presuppositions and reads the Old Testament in a distinctly Christian way (even if employing Jewish methods of exegesis), often doing violence to the true meaning of the Old Testament texts employed. Thus, New Testament arguments based on the Old Testament, it is held, would generally be convincing to Christians but hardly to Jews. If this is true, it will be hard to vindicate the New Testament authors from the charge of misusing the Scriptures.[24]

Precisely so! The argument that has been most persuasive for me,[25] as well, is the one that says a prediction must be seen

---

24. Stephen Motyer, "Old Testament in the New Testament," in *Evangelical Dictionary of Biblical Theology*, ed. Walter A. Elwell (Grand Rapids: Baker, 1996), 582.

25. See my defense of the same type of argument in my book, *Uses of the Old Testament*, 129–31, and in my book, *The Messiah in the Old Testament* (Grand Rapids: Zondervan, 1995), 13–35.

ahead of time and not added after an alleged fulfillment takes place.

However, Motyer later turned around and argued precisely in this way: "The New Testament authors both use the Old Testament to explain Jesus and use Jesus to explain the Old Testament—a circular process in which each is illuminated by the other."[26] He continued:

> Some basic features of the Old Testament "story" *become* prophetic in the light of Christ—that is, they are discovered to have a forward-looking predictive function in the light of Christ.... The word often used to describe this treatment of the Old Testament is "typology."[27]

Is this assessment of the function of typology correct? Surely it is proper to speak of typology in Scripture, but can this be the way to describe it? Previous generations of scholars always insisted that the key aspect of typology was the matter of *divine designation*; namely, would the fact that God providentially guided the story of the Messiah and his people be adequate also to indicate the needed divine indication that it was a type found in the text of the OT designation?[28] Let us examine this question by looking at two representative uses of the OT by NT authors.

Does John 13:18 Find a Meaning that Goes beyond the Meaning of Psalm 41:9?

The text that we will use to test these questions appears in that magnificent section in John's gospel called "The Upper Room Discourse" (John 13:1–17:26). In John 13, Jesus washes the disciples' feet to illustrate his ministry of humiliation and as a way to motivate his followers to similar humble and loving

---

26. Motyer, "Old Testament in the New Testament," 583.

27. Motyer, "Old Testament in the New Testament," 584.

28. Herbert Marsh (*A Course of Lectures*, Part III.B, Lecture XIX, 1–2) stressed that divine intent and designation of a type was most important: " ... to constitute a type, something is more requisite than a mere *resemblance* of that which is called a type.... But it is the very essence of a type to have a necessary connection with its antitype. It must have been *designated* ... from the very beginning to prefigure its antitype.... [having] a pre-ordained and inherent connection between the things themselves" (emphasis his).

acts of putting others ahead of themselves. The narrative is then interrupted by Jesus' announcement that one of the disciples will betray him: " 'I am not referring to all of you; I know those I have chosen. But this is to fulfill this passage of Scripture: "He who shared my bread has lifted up his heel against me" ' " (John 13:18 from Ps 41:9 [MT, v. 10]). In spite of his cleansing ministry toward his disciples, Jesus knows that among them lurks a betrayer (v. 10). To show that even this is the fulfillment of Scripture, Jesus cites Psalm 41.

Psalm 41 is a psalm ascribed to David. Many regard the background for this psalm to be the treachery committed against David by his son Absalom and the sudden switch of loyalty from David to Absalom by David's trusted friend and counselor Ahithophel (2 Sam 15:1–18:18).[29] Neither one is mentioned in the text, but both fit the situation described in the psalm. So wise was the counsel given by Ahithophel that the historical record regarded it as "like that of one who inquires of God" (2 Sam 16:23). With Ahithophel's advice, Absalom rebelled against his father, sending David scurrying off into the countryside to avoid being captured and sentenced by his own son. This treachery must have happened to David during a time of sickness, weakness, and suffering—perhaps some lingering illness, which however is also not otherwise mentioned in the historical books. Such treachery from his son and his best friend was certainly not to be expected, much less tolerated for one who was the king.

The flow of Psalm 41 is as follows: (1) Verses 1–3 (MT, vv. 2–4) entail a blessing from God on the person who is looking out for the helpless; (2) verses 4–9 (MT, vv. 5–10) contain a plea made at a time when David's own family and his "close friend" (Heb. lit.: "man of my peace") became his enemies; and (3) verses 10–13 (MT, vv. 11–14) conclude with a prayer for personal restoration and requital on his traitor.

David in his person and office carried the full weight of the messianic promise-plan of God. David had been given this

---

29. Franz Delitsch, *Biblical Commentary of the Psalms*, trans. Francis Bolton (Grand Rapids: Eerdmans, 1955), 2:44–46, comments that "Ps. xli belongs to the time of the persecution by Absalom.... The faithless friend is that Ahithophel whose counsels, according to 2 Sam. xvi. 23, had with David almost the appearance of being divine oracles."

knowledge in 2 Samuel 7, where the promise-plan of God that had been communicated to Abraham, Isaac, and Jacob was now being repeated and offered to him and his "seed" along with an everlasting dynastic "house," a "throne," and a "kingdom." Moreover, just as Genesis 12:3 contained the "gospel" (also see Gal 3:8) in a nutshell, so 2 Samuel 7:19 furthered the same good news by saying that what David had been given here was a "charter for all mankind" (pers. trans. of *wezo't torat ha'adam*).

Consequently, what David said about himself also extended in significant ways to the Anointed One who would one day arise from his line. Yet the psalm cannot be ascribed to Messiah in its entirety, for in Psalm 41:4, David says, "I have sinned against you." That in itself is not unusual in promises about the Davidic line, since they often include in their general purview all of David's heirs (e.g., 2 Sam 7:14–15; Ps 132:12). What is unusual here is that this psalm's referents are not restricted to David and his heirs; rather, the psalm refers also to the *enemy* of the promised line, including both David and, by extension, the Messiah. Accordingly, along with finding Messiah in the Seed promises of the OT, we also find on the flip side of the same promise-doctrine[30] a line of those opposing the promised line, such as Ahithophel, Absalom, and later Judas and the Antichrist. This too is not unique, for the same teaching occurs in John 17:12

---

30. For years now, I have been impressed with the thesis of Willis J. Beecher, *The Prophets and the Promise* (Grand Rapids: Baker, 1975). He defined the promise-plan of God this way: "God gave a promise to Abraham, and through him to mankind; a promise eternally fulfilled and fulfilling in the history of Israel; and chiefly fulfilled in Jesus Christ; he being that which is principal in the history of Israel" (178). I have refined that definition somewhat in my forthcoming *The Promise-Plan of God: A Biblical Theology of the Old and New Testaments* (Grand Rapids: Zondervan, 2008). I define the Promise in this way: "The Promise-plan is God's *word* of declaration, beginning with Eve and continuing on through history, especially in the patriarchs and the Davidic line, that God would continually *be* (in his person) and *do* (in his deeds and works) in and through Israel, and later in and through the Church, his redemptive plan as his *means* of keeping that promised word alive for Israel, and thereby for all who subsequently believed. All in that promised seed were called to act as a light for all the nations so that all the families of the earth might come to faith and to new life in the Messiah." See also my *Toward an Old Testament Theology* (Grand Rapids: Zondervan, 1978), 32–40.

and Acts 1:16–20 (the latter quotes from Pss 69:25[31] and 109:8[32]).
As S. Lewis Johnson Jr. argued:

> The logic ... found here ... is simply this: David prefigured
> the Messiah, i.e., he was a type of the Messiah.... Thus it
> is perfectly natural and justifiable to see His [sic] enemies,
> too, as prefiguring the Messiah's enemies. The unique end
> of Ahithophel by hanging, the very way by which Judas's
> life was ended, accentuates the God-designed typical rela-
> tionship and supports the validity of the use of the Old
> Testament passage. In fact, Jesus' use of an Old Testament
> type may have been the pedagogical precursor of Peter's
> similar use of the Psalms in Acts 1:16.[33]

Just as there is a royal line in the promise-plan of God, so
there is a line of evil (recall the "seed" of the serpent in Gen 3:15).
This line finds its epitome and climactic fulfillment in the final
representative of this whole line of the Antichrist.[34] Therefore,
we are not surprised that a long line of opponents to David and
his line should continue to harass that royal line all the way
up to Messiah and then to Messiah's second coming. Absalom,
then, was only one of those oppressors who sought to waylay
David, his line, and the Messiah himself, each one from his mission.[35] While agreement may be reached among interpreters on
points of the preceding argument, most will miss the key point
that Willis J. Beecher pointed out:

> Most of ... [the psalmist's predictions] should not be
> regarded as disconnected predictions, but as shoots from
> a common stem — the common stem being the body of
> connected messianic promise-history.... But even the
> instances of this kind yield more satisfactory meanings
> when examined in connection with their relations to the
> central promise.[36]

---

31. See my discussion of Psalm 69 in *The Messiah in the Old Testament*, 103–7.

32. Ibid., 107–10.

33. S. Lewis Johnson, *The Old Testament in the New: An Argument for Biblical Inspiration* (Grand Rapids: Zondervan, 1980), 77.

34. Cf. 1 John 2:18, which warned of "many antichrists" who would appear in history before the final Antichrist showed up at the consummation of history.

35. Cf. Matt 26:14–16; 26:47–56; John 13:18; 17:12; and Acts 1:16–20.

36. Beecher, *The Prophets and the Promise*, 244.

Returning to the use of Psalm 41:9 in John 13:18, note that the text calls attention to the act of betrayal by a close companion: "He who shares my bread has lifted up his heel against me." It was most appropriate to use this quote about the eating of bread while the disciples were seated at the Passover, which was the context in John 13:1–17. But it was just as significant that this breach of oriental hospitality was violated, for how could someone with good conscience go from being fed and having his feet washed by the Lord, to carrying out the treachery that Judas accomplished? So dastardly was this heinous crime that the agricultural metaphor of lifting up one's heel was all that could be said for such treachery. As a mule or a horse would give a swift kick, so Judas managed to do the same that night to the Lord, which act eventuated in the death of Jesus on the cross.

Jesus saw himself as the One spoken of in David's Seed. Therefore, the opposition that frequently came to David was a type of what would come to Christ. That is why in verse 19, the very next verse after John 13:18, Jesus asserted, "I am telling you now before it happens, so that when it does happen you will believe that I am who I am."

Does the Elder of the Church, James, Misuse Amos 9:9–15 in Acts 15:13–18 at the Jerusalem Council?

The question must be faced once again: Did the OT authors have an adequate understanding of the future meaning of their texts, as well as their present meaning, or did the NT meaning go beyond the authorial will of the human writer of the older Scripture when the apostles used materials from the OT? If it did exceed the boundaries of the original writer in the OT, would not such an exegesis be self-condemned because it had left out a theological meaning that would have come from placing each OT pericope in its own literary and biblical theological context?

We will contend that the human authors, as well as many of the original hearers and readers of the Scriptures, were more attuned to the continuing, unifying plan of God throughout history than many contemporary scholars or believers allow. Given the "generic wholeness" of the divine promise-plan of God, the prophets were divinely enabled to see "near" fulfillments, as well as some of the more "distant," climactic fulfillment of those same near fulfillments. It is this "generic"[37] quality of the promise that enables one to understand that the words contained but *one meaning* that was generically related to the collective wholeness of the fulfillment.[38]

For example, a "sharp dispute and debate" (Acts 15:2) broke out at the Council of Jerusalem with "certain individuals" (15:1), who apparently were from the party of the Pharisees, claiming, "Unless you are circumcised, according to the custom taught by Moses, you cannot be saved" (15:1). Attempts to resolve this question for the Council from an experiential point of view by the apostle Peter and his surprising experience with Cornelius (Acts 10), or Paul and Barnabas's missionary experiences in Asia Minor (present-day Turkey) among the Gentiles, did little to halt the debate. It was only after James spoke up and pointed to "the words of the prophets," by which he meant the OT prophets — especially in this case, Amos (Amos 9:11 – 12) — that a solution was in sight.[39]

But what was it in this OT passage that offered any hope for settling this ethnic controversy? Did James claim that the mission to the Gentiles was part of the divine revelation given to the prophet Amos — in any form whatever? And was James now claiming thereby that a fulfillment of Amos's prophecy had come to pass in the day of the apostles?

The subject of Amos 9:11 is the present condition of David's house or dynasty, which Amos describes as a "booth," "tent," or "hut" (*sukkah*) that is currently in a state of dilapidation, i.e., it is "falling down" (*hannopelet*). The word *sukkah* was used for the hastily constructed shelters made of branches cut from nearby

---

37. Beecher defined a generic prophecy as "one which regards an event as occurring in a series of parts, separated by intervals, and expresses itself in language that may apply indifferently to the nearest part, or to the remoter parts, or to the whole — in other words, a prediction which, in applying to the whole of a complex event, also applies to some of its parts" (*The Prophets and the Promise*, 130).

38. See my discussion of this in *Uses of the Old Testament*, 70 – 71.

39. I have examined these texts in my article "The Davidic Promise and the Inclusion of the Gentiles (Amos 9:9 – 15 and Acts 15:13 – 18): A Test Passage for Theological Systems," *JETS* 20 (1977): 97 – 111, which was reprinted for the most part in my book, *Uses of the Old Testament*, chapter 9, "Including the Gentiles in the Plan of God," 177 – 94.

trees to form temporary shelters in order to celebrate the Feast of Tabernacles (Lev 23:40, 42; Deut 16:13). Thus, what had been styled "the house of David" (2 Sam 7:5, 11)—his dynasty, with all its glorious promises of blessing—was in the state of collapsing (Hebrew Qal active participle) and looking like a makeshift booth seen at the time of the Festival of Booths. However, despite what the house of David was now or about to suffer, God promised to raise that house from its dilapidated condition in three special ways, as described by three clauses that follow in Amos 9:11b, c, d.

The three clauses and the suffixes (usually rendered neutrally as "its" or "it" in most translations) on each of the three terms in these three clauses are of special interest to the theology of this passage. These clauses are:

1. "its/of them broken places/breaches," using a feminine plural suffix
2. "its/his ruins," using a masculine singular suffix
3. "built it/her," using a feminine singular suffix

C. F. Keil was certain that the feminine plural suffix ("breaches of her [pl.]"; *pirsehen*) "can only be explained from the fact that the *sukkah* actually refers to [the healing of the split kingdoms (fem. pl.)], which [were] divided into two kingdoms,"[40] but God would reunite that breach "in that day" between the ten northern tribes and the two southern tribes of Judah and Benjamin. That, of course, is what Ezekiel 37:15–28 would later on anticipate as well. The masculine singular suffix on "its/his ruins" (*harisotayw*), however, must refer to none other than David himself, and not to the "booth of David," which is feminine. Therefore, under the new-coming-David, Christ himself, the destroyed house of David would rise from the ashes of "destruction."[41] The text, however, does not say when or how except to locate it "in that day" (9:11a).

With these two acts of reconstruction mentioned, the third clause about "rebuilding her" (*benitiha*) appears. The feminine singular refers naturally to the "fallen tent." But it is important to note that it too will be restored "as it used to be" (Amos 9:11).

---

40. C. F. Keil, *Minor Prophets* (Commentary on the Old Testament 10; Grand Rapids: Eerdmans, 1954), 1:330.

41. For this meaning of *harisa*, cf. Isah 49:19.

This surely is one of the keys to the passage, for it points back to the promise made in 2 Samuel 7:11, 12, 16, where God had promised that he would raise up David's seed after David died and God would also give David a throne and a dynasty that would "endure forever."

All of this would take place "so that they might possess the remnant of Edom, and all the nations that bear my name," taught Amos in 9:12. Linked together in this passage, then, were the reunited kingdom of Israel, a restored David, a renewed Davidic dynasty, the people of God, and a remnant from all the nations that were called by the name of the Lord.

Some think that verse 12 is even more problematic than verse 11, especially its annoying reference to "the remnant of Edom." But Edom is not referred to in a negative sense or even in a retaliatory way. Instead, Edom, along with all the other nations, is to be brought under the reign of the Davidic King who was to come, the Messiah. But there was a "remnant" that was to share in the promise made to David.

Some will object further that Amos's words in 9:12 are not the same as those found in James's citation in Acts 15:17. The differences between the two are obvious:

> Amos 9:12: "so that they may possess the remnant of Edom"
> Acts 15:17: "that the rest of humanity may seek the Lord"

However, the Hebrew word for "possess" (*yarash*) could in the ancient Hebrew script be easily mistaken for "seek" (*darash*) since the difference would only be in the length of the tail between the letters *yod* and *daleth* in that early script. Moreover, "Edom" (*'edom*) and "man/humanity" (*'adam*) are almost identical in Hebrew except for the vowels (which were not part of the original text).

It is true that the Qumran text *Florilegium* supports James's reading on this clause in Amos.[42] Therefore, there is a real possibility

---

42. J. de Waard, *A Comparative Study of the OT Text in the Dead Sea Scrolls and in the NT* (Grand Rapids, Eerdmans, 1966), 25–26. However, the phrase "after this I will return" does not appear in 4Flor or CD. Nor can this phrase be an allusion to Jeremiah 12:15, as Nestle's *Novum Testamentum Graece* suggests, since the only word common to both is *meta*. The *tauta* is missing in the LXX of Jeremiah and *epistrepso* is common only to the D text of Acts.

that the NT and Qumran readings may preserve the better text from Amos, which would make even stronger our argument for the suitability of James's appeal to this text to show that Gentiles had been in the promise-plan of God all along. But even if textual criticism is unable to verify James's reading as the preferred one, the interpretation of the present Masoretic text of Amos amounts to the same conclusion. Edom is used here and elsewhere in the OT as representing the nations of the world. Even the Edomites, then, will one day be called by the name of the Lord.

The only question left then is this: Is the remnant of mortals going to seek the Lord as a result of God's raising up the dynasty of David one more time, or is God going to fulfill his promise to David in that day so that not only the remnant of Edom may be [re-]possessed as part of the revitalization of the Davidic Covenant, but even all the Gentiles/nations over whom God will call his name may be likewise treated in the same manner? That is, are the nations called by God or do they themselves call upon God?

Gerhard Hasel pointed out that Amos employed the "remnant" theme in three ways: (1) "to refute the popular expectation which claimed all of Israel as the remnant" (Amos 3:12; 4:1–3; 5:3; 6:9–10; 9:1–4); (2) "to show there will indeed be a remnant *from* Israel" in an eschatological sense (Amos 5:4–6, 15), and (3) "to include also the 'remnant of Edom,' among and with the neighboring nations, as a recipient of the outstanding promise of the Davidic tradition" (Amos 9:12).[43]

Edom has been singled out because of her defiant hostility toward Israel. In that sense she is similar to the Amalekites, who in Exodus 17:8–16 and Deuteronomy 25:17–19 stood over against the kingdom of God as representing the kingdom of humanity.[44] Moreover, Edom's representative role is further seen in the explanatory note in Amos 9:12: "and/even all the nations/Gentiles who are called by my name." Thus, the text is not talking about the military subjugation of Edom or of the Gentiles,

---

43. Gerhard Hasel, *The Remnant: The History and Theology of the Idea of Remnant from Genesis to Isaiah* (AUSS; Berrien Springs, MI: Andrews Univ. Press, 1972), 393–94.

44. See the discussion and bibliography of M. H. Woudstra, "Edom and Israel in Ezekiel," *CTJ* 3 (1968): 21–35.

but of their spiritual incorporation into the kingdom of God. Had not God promised Abraham that would be the case in Genesis 12:3?

It would appear that the verb "to possess" in Amos 9:12 was chosen perhaps to hark back to Balaam's prophecy in Numbers 24:17–18, where a "star" and a "scepter" would rise in Israel to take possession of Edom, "but Israel will grow strong." Can there be any doubt that the "star" is a reference to our Lord's first coming and the "scepter" a reference to his second coming?

What brought this text to the mind of James, this leader of the Church in Jerusalem? Could it be his comment in Acts 15:14 where he said, "Simon has described to us how God first intervened to choose a people for his name from the Gentiles"? The usage of the clause "to choose a people for his name" placed all objects or persons so named as being under divine ownership. What God or man named, they owned and protected. This expression is also practically equivalent to the phrase in Joel 2:32 (Heb. 3:5), "everyone who calls on the name of the LORD." Accordingly, "and all the nations that bear my name" (Amos 9:12) is one of the most crucial phrases for this passage, for it teaches that the Gentiles would certainly be included in the future reign and rule of God.

Did James get it right, then, when he used this quote from Amos to quell the debate over what to do with all these Gentiles who were being saved? Did the OT text have any bearing on the problem at the Council, or was James using the OT text merely for illustrative purposes or in some kind of a spiritual way?

Two fine dispensational writers, Willard M. Aldrich and Allan MacRae, stressed the importance of the words "first" and "after this" in Acts 15:14 and 16.[45] Their argument was that "God first [*proton*] visited the Gentiles" (v. 14); "after this [*meta tauta*] [visitation he] will return ... and rebuild the tent of David" (v. 16) when God regathers Israel to her homeland and God rebuilds the house of David in events connected with the second coming of Christ.

If this interpretation is followed, then the citation of the OT reference from Amos has *no* bearing on the question the Council

---

45. W. M. Aldrich, "The Interpretation of Acts 15:13–18," *BSac* 111 (1954): 317–23, esp. p. 320; A. MacRae, "The Scientific Approach to the Old Testament," *BSac* 110 (1953): 309–20, esp. pp. 311ff.

is facing. However, the point James was making did not hinge on James's reworking the introductory words from Amos 9:11, which he recited, perhaps from memory, "after this I will return and rebuild David's fallen tent," but rather his emphasis fell on the fact that "the rest of humanity may seek the Lord, even all the Gentiles who bear my name" (Acts 15:17). Aldrich would want the words "I will return" to apply to Christ's second coming. But the Hebrew text used the words "I will raise up" (*'aqim*), not "I will return" (which would in that case have read, *'ashub*). Thus, the reference is not to the second coming, but is a reference to the historical fact that God had been saving Gentiles, to which Peter, Barnabas, and Paul testified. To obtain a dispensational view of this text, one must assume that the "first" of verse 14 signified the "first [era]" of the Gentiles (a clear interpolation) and that the second reference would then mean "after this [Gospel dispensation]" God would "come again" and restore Israel.[46] But this cannot be the meaning of this text in this context.

James's summary of Peter's testimony is surprisingly pointed, for he says, "God first intervened to choose a people [*laos*] for his name from the Gentiles [*ethnon*]" (v. 14). Accordingly, the Gentile converts were described just as Israel was, as the "people of God." It is with this fact just stated, the conversion of the Gentiles, that the writing of the prophets agreed. In fact, this is the only time in the book of Acts that an OT quotation is introduced in this manner. Moreover, there is no set formula for introducing an OT citation in the book of Acts.

There is no need to take "David's fallen tent" to mean "the tabernacle of David" and then to make that into a type of the Christian church. Instead, the rebuilding of David's tent is a brief, but direct reference to the program announced by God to David in 2 Samuel 7 and 1 Chronicles 17. Just as God had promised Abraham and his line that all mortals would be blessed through his seed (Gen 12:3; 18:18; 22:17–18; 26:3–4; 28:13–14), even so

---

46. J. E. Rosscup, "The Interpretation of Acts 15:13–18" (Th.D. diss., Dallas Theological Seminary, 1966), 148, chided Aldrich and Zimmerman ["To this Agree the Words of the Prophets," *Grace Theological Journal* 4 (1963): 28–40] for making "after these things" so strategic in their interpretations. For Rosscup noted that *meta tauta* is also used by LXX of Joel 2:28 to translate the Masoretic text, *'ahare-ken*, "afterward."

God had announced to David that the "multitude of nations" who would believe in the Seed that came from his line would be part of the "charter for all humanity" (*torat ha'adam*, 2 Sam 7:19).

The missionary consciousness of the OT reached its zenith in the eighth-century prophets like Amos and Isaiah. "The Servant," Israel, would be given to the world as a "light for the Gentiles" (Isa 42:6). Indeed, "nations you do not know will come running" to Israel (Isa 55:3–5) because the Lord was their God. Thirty-six times Isaiah linked the nations with the promise-plan of God in the last twenty-seven chapters of Isaiah.

What are we to conclude then about the Jerusalem Council? Did the ancient promise-plan of God envisage the inclusion of Gentiles in that promise? In fact, Jews and Gentiles, yes, even Edomites were to be part of the kingdom of God when they too put their trust in the coming Man of Promise. James used a plain, simple and straightforward hermeneutic when he appealed to Amos. His understanding of the term "David's tent" was replete with all the revelation of God that antedated that eighth-century revelation. What had been promised to Abraham was recommitted to David with an enlarged scope of reference: it was a veritable "charter for all humanity" (2 Sam 7:19)! As a dynasty, it symbolized God's rule and reign on into eternity.

However, the political and national aspects of that same promise could not be deleted from Amos's true intention. As the suffixes in Amos 9:11 indicate, the northern and southern kingdoms, the Davidic person, the people of Israel, and the remnant of humanity at large were all encompassed in that rebuilding of "David's tent," even though its outward fortunes would appear to sag in the immediate events of the eighth century.

DID THE NEW TESTAMENT AUTHORS USE THE JEWISH EXEGETICAL METHODS OF THEIR DAY?

Another way in which a *sensus plenior* type of approach to the NT writers' use of the OT has been defended is the contention that the apostles utilized the Jewish interpretive methods of their day, allowing them to derive meanings from OT texts that, at times, were separate and different from those in the minds of the OT authors of those texts. Admittedly, it is not uncommon to see both Jewish and early Christian interpreters support brand new meanings for devotional or meditative purposes, but one would be hard-pressed to find any convincing apologetical value for validating the messianic or doctrinal claims based on the use of such interpretive procedures as *midrash, pesher,* allegory, or even psychological impositions on the OT text. Yet the tendency in modern scholarship has been to affirm the NT authors' use of such rabbinical exegetical methods as they utilized the OT, leading to various kinds of rabbinical modifications of the meaning of the texts.[47] Frederic Gardiner (1822–89) anticipated this tendency already in 1885:

> In all quotations which are used *argumentatively* in order to establish any fact or doctrine, it is obviously necessary that the passage in question should be fairly cited according to its real interest and meaning, in order that the argument drawn from it may be valid. There has been much rash criticism … that the Apostles, and especially St. Paul, brought up in rabbinical schools of thought quoted Scriptures after a rabbinical and inconsequential fashion. A patient and careful examination of the passages themselves will remove such misapprehension (emphasis mine).[48]

I share Gardiner's convictions.

Therefore, we will look at two NT uses of the OT that are frequently submitted as illustrating the apostolic use of typical Jewish exegetical methods—one cited for the purpose of showing that what happened in the life of Jesus was in fulfillment of what had been announced long before the event came to pass, and one that applies the OT law to the life of the early church.

Is *Pesher* a Valid Category for Peter's Use of Psalm 16 in Acts 2?[49]

The challenge of the prophets to all listeners and readers was this: whereas idols and other divine pretenders claimed to

---

47. See esp. Richard Longenecker, *Biblical Exegesis in the Apostolic Period* (Grand Rapids: Eerdmans, 1975).

48. Frederic Gardiner, *The Old and New Testaments in Their Mutual Relations* (New York: James Pott, 1885), 317–18.

49. For a fuller discussion of this issue, see my article "The Promise to David in Psalm 16 and Its Application in Acts 2:25–33 and 13:32–37," *JETS* 23 (1980): 219–29. See also the chapter in *Uses of the Old Testament*, 25–41.

know the future ahead of time, it was only the God of the Bible who existed as the God who knew the future and spoke about it *before* the events came to pass. The challenges went like this:

Who then is like me? Let them proclaim it.
  Let them declare and lay out before me
what has happened …
    and what is yet to come—
    yes, let them foretell what will come.…
    Did I not proclaim this and foretell it long ago? (Isa
      44:7–8)

Declare what is to be, present it—
  let them take counsel together.
Who foretold this long ago,
  who declared it from the distant past?
Was it not I, the LORD? (Isa 45:21)

I foretold the former things long ago,
  my mouth announced them and I made them known;
  then suddenly I acted, and they came to pass.…
Therefore I told you these things long ago;
  before they happened I announced them to you
so that you could not say,
    "My images brought them about.…" (Isa 48:3, 5a-b)

The NT writers assumed this was so and therefore affirmed that God had previously announced many of the things they were witnessing. For instance, the apostle Peter boldly declared, "God fulfilled what he had foretold through all the prophets, saying that his Messiah would suffer" (Acts 3:18). In the same manner, the apostle Paul "reasoned with them [the Jewish people in the Thessalonian synagogue] from the Scriptures [i.e., the OT], explaining and proving that the Messiah had to suffer and rise from the dead" (Acts 17:2b–3a). Central to this apologetic was their appeal to the prophecy of Jesus' resurrection in Psalm 16.

Few psalms raise simultaneously as many important methodological and theological questions as does Psalm 16. Nevertheless, it has a most honored place in the early Christian church, for it serves as one of the scriptural bases for Peter's message on the day of Pentecost (Acts 2:25–31) and for Paul's address at Antioch of Pisidia (Acts 13:35–37). Both of these apostles attribute to Psalm 16 a conscious prediction of the resurrection of Jesus the Messiah from the dead. Why is it, then, that so few contemporary commentators and readers of Psalm 16 concur with the apostles, but instead feel that it was Peter and Paul who invested the old text with new meanings that can now point to Christ, based on our contemporary reading of the NT? Or is there some implicit system of interpretation that exceeds an author's known truth intentions, but which legitimizes the imposition of NT's values and meanings? Specifically, are the NT authors utilizing a *pesher* form of argument, disregarding by and large the original context and arbitrarily interpreting it as a direct prophecy of Jesus' resurrection?

If such a new imposition of meanings be allowed, we run into the warning given by Milton Terry years ago: "But the moment we admit the principle that portions of Scripture contain an occult or double sense we introduce an element of uncertainty in the sacred volume, and unsettle all scientific interpretation."[50] In the same manner, Louis Berkhof argued:

> Scripture has but a single sense, and is therefore susceptible to a scientific and logical investigation.... To accept a manifold sense ... makes any science of hermeneutics impossible and opens the door for all kinds of arbitrary interpretations.[51]

John Owen also declared, "If the Scripture has more than one meaning, it has no meaning at all."[52]

Some fear that this type of insistence will produce minimal results, but such are avoided if we take into account the OT writers' awareness of the antecedent scriptural development of words, phrases, concepts, events, and expectations. Equipped with this perspective, we will attempt to show that Psalm 16 is best understood as being messianic in its own OT context, justifying the fulfillment affirmations by both Peter and Paul, without accusing them of "reading" these into the OT text in a *pesher*-like manner.

---

50. Milton S. Terry, *Biblical Hermeneutics* (Grand Rapids: Zondervan, n.d.), 493.

51. Louis Berkhof, *Principles of Biblical Interpretation* (Grand Rapids: Baker, 1950), 57.

52. John Owen as cited by Terry, *Hermeneutics*, 493.

Many reject the messianic reference of Psalm 16, arguing that it is simply the prayer of a godly man seeking preservation from death. That is how S. R. Driver viewed it:

> The Psalm contains ... a great declaration of the faith and hope of an Old Testament saint.... But when we study it in itself, and consider it carefully in its original import, we see that v. 10 *will not support the argument which the Apostles built upon it,* and that the Psalm cannot be appealed to, in the way in which they appealed to it, as a proof of the resurrection of Christ.[53]

Peter Craigie argued similarly:

> With respect to the initial meaning of the psalm, it is probable that this concluding section should not be interpreted either messianically or in terms of personal eschatology.... Yet it is apparent that in the earliest Christian community, the psalm was given a messianic interpretation.... *This change in meaning* ... is an example of the *double meanings* which may be inherent in the text of Scripture. The new meaning imparted to the text suggests not only progress, but contrast.[54]

Nor are C. S. Lewis's comments helpful here. He opined:

> If the Old Testament is a literature thus "taken up," made a vehicle of what is more than human, *we can of course set no limits to the weight or multiplicity of meanings* which may have been laid upon it. If any writer may say more than he meant, then these writers will be especially likely to do so. And not by accident.[55]

These solutions are faulty. The first two place a heavy discontinuity between the two testaments and devalue the stock of the OT (apparently) in order to increase a high value on the NT. That does not sound like Paul's estimate that "all Scripture is

---

53. S. R. Driver, "The Method of Studying the Psalter: Psalm 16," *Expositor*, Seventh Series, 10 (1910): 37 (emphasis mine).

54. Peter C. Craigie, *Psalms 1–50* (WBC; Waco, TX: Word, 1983), 158 (emphasis mine).

55. C. S. Lewis, *Reflections of the Psalms* (New York: Harcourt & Brace, 1958), 117 (emphasis mine).

God-breathed" (2 Tim 3:16). The third begins too low by assuming that the human input must be "taken up" or "upgraded" (by the NT, apparently) so we can see all that is there in the text. But this also fails to provide for the fact that Peter claims that what the prophets wrote and said did not originate from their own wills or minds but came as a revelation from God. I will seek, therefore, to demonstrate that David had within his forward-looking purview a reference that exceeded his own experience to include that which pertained to his heirs, culminating in the Messiah.

Both because the ancient title to this psalm attributes it to David[56] and because many of the phrases in the psalm are used in the better-known psalms of David,[57] we concur with the NT attribution of this psalm to David (Acts 2:34). It is important to note that the psalm focuses first of all on David of the royal line of the Messiah.

David begins in Psalm 16:1 with a plea to God: "Keep me safe, for I have committed myself to you."[58] This is covenantal language, implying the relationship that he and his people enjoyed with the Lord. He therefore commits himself to God in the knowledge that God has measured off to him a "portion" and a "delightful inheritance" (vv. 5–6). Thus, what has been given to him are not "portions" in this world, but an "inheritance" of spiritual joys, chief of which is God himself and his presence, grace, and fellowship. It is because of this heritage that David concludes in v. 9 that his "body also will rest secure." God will not "abandon [him] to the grave, nor [will he] let [his] Holy One see decay" (v. 10).[59]

The identity of God's "Holy One" (*hasid*) is crucial to interpreting this passage correctly. The word *hasid* is a technical

---

56. The title to this psalm calls it a *miktam*, a name also used in Psalms 56, 57, and 59 — all written during David's exile and Saul's persecution and pursuit of him. However, *miktam* is probably a musical term and not one that signifies the type of its contents, for the sentiments and expressions found in Psalm 16 are much different from other psalms using the same name.

57. See the list of references in my *Uses of the Old Testament*, 30.

58. My translation. The Hebrew word *hasad*, used in a secular sense in Judg 9:15 and Isa 30:2, refers to a vassal who attached himself to a suzerain king in order to enjoy his protection.

59. My translations.

term as were the terms "Seed," "Servant of the Lord," and "Messiah" in the OT. *Hasid* is best rendered as a passive form, "one to whom God is loyal, gracious, or merciful," or "one in whom God manifests his grace or favor."[60] A key passage that connects *hasid* with David is Psalm 89:19–20 (MT 20–21):

> Then you spoke in a vision to your Holy One[61] and said: I have set the crown on a hero [a mighty man of valor], I have exalted a choice [chosen] person from the people. I have found [an election term] David my servant [a messianic term in Isaiah] with my holy oil and I have anointed [another messianic term] him. (my translation)

What else can we conclude than that in the view of Ethan the Ezrahite, writer of Psalm 89, Yahweh's *hasid*, king, servant, and anointed one, were one and the same in the person, office, and mission of David? As early as the time of Moses (Deut 33:8), there was a reference to "the man of your *hasid*, whom Israel did test at Massah" (a reference to Exodus 17, where water came from the rock). However, the only "man" who was tested and put to the test in Exodus 17:2, 7 was the Lord himself. Could this have been the background against which David began also to understand the term of himself and the Messiah who was to come through his line?

Neither are the seventeen references to *hasid* in the plural a problem for the messianic view, for the oscillation between the one and the many is exactly what we observe in parallel examples of other technical terms for Messiah: Seed, Anointed One, Servant, and Firstborn.[62] This literary technique is known as the concept of "corporate solidarity," in which the One (the

---

60. *Hasid* occurs thirty-two times and only in poetic texts, never in prose, with twenty-five examples in the Psalms. Seventeen times it is plural and eleven times it is singular and four times there are variant readings. See my defense of this meaning in *Uses of the Old Testament*, 33.

61. Many manuscripts use the singular form rather than the plural held in the MT and NIV.

62. The "seed" (Heb., *zera'*) can refer to either all the "descendants" or to the "Seed" who represents them all, just as Israel, in twelve out of the twenty references to the "Servant of the Lord" in the singular, is called the "servant" in Isaiah 41:8–10; 43:8–13; 43:14–44:5; 44:6–8, 21–23, etc., and Israel is called God's "firstborn" in Exod 4:22–23. Hebrews 12:23, however, uses the plural "firstborn ones."

Messiah) and the many (the Davidic line and those who believe in the Messiah) are embraced in a single meaning usually indicated by a collective singular, instead of it being either a simple singular or plural noun.

David, then, in Psalm 16 is God's *hasid*, his "Favored One"; yet, not David as a mere person, but David as the recipient and conveyor of God's ancient and ever-renewed promise-plan for Israel and for the world. As Beecher observed:

> The man David may die, but the *hhasidh* [*sic*] is eternal. Just as David is the Anointed One, and yet the Anointed One is eternal; just as David is the Servant, and yet the Servant is eternal; so David is the *hhasidh*, and yet the *hhasidh* is eternal. David as an individual went to his grave, and saw corruption there, but the representative of Yahaweh's [*sic*] eternal promise did not cease to exist.[63]

The fact that David is conscious and fully aware of the fact that God is his Lord and his inheritance allows him also to affirm that his "body ... will rest secure" (v. 9) as well. This confidence is grounded in his understanding of his own role. As I wrote elsewhere:

> David, as the man of promise and as God's *hasid* ("favored one"), was in his person, office, and function one of the distinctive historical fulfillments to that word that he received about his seed, dynasty, and throne. Therefore, he rested secure in the confident hope that even death itself would not prevent him from enjoying the face-to-face fellowship with his Lord even beyond death, because that ultimate *hasid* would triumph over death.[64]

David expected to arrive safely complete with all of his immaterial as well as his material being with the Lord because God had promised a future deliverance from the grave to his own *hasid*—the ultimate and final manifestation of the messianic line of which David was a part. If Messiah could be resurrected, then David's hope of being raised from the dead was just as good and just as sure.

---

63. Beecher, *The Prophets and the Promise*, 325.
64. Kaiser, *Uses of the Old Testament*, 41.

Once we have correctly understood the identity, office, and function of the "Holy One"/"Favored One" (*hasid*), it is possible for us to see that David perceived God's plan to raise up the last King in his line, so that the Messiah would not be abandoned to the "grave"/"Sheol," nor would he experience "decay" in the tomb. Instead, he would see the "path of life," a phrase Mitchell Dahood equated from the Ugaritic texts as meaning "eternal life."[65]

This interpretation is then confirmed by the way the apostles Peter and Paul used Psalm 16.[66] S. R. Driver, like so many of his day and ours, chose to conclude minimally saying:

> It is difficult not to think that the application of the words to Christ found in Acts ii. 25–31, xiii. 35–37 was facilitated by the mistranslations of the Septuagint.... But the apostles used arguments of the kind usual at the time, and such as would seem cogent both to themselves and to their contemporaries.[67]

But Driver and our contemporaries fail to note that Peter's claim is that David was a "prophet" who "spoke of the resurrection of the Messiah," because he was "seeing what was to come" (Acts 2:30–31). Acts 2:25, moreover, carefully introduces this quotation from Psalm 16:8–11 with the phrase, "David says with reference to [*eis*] him," rather than "concerning [*peri*] him" (which would have meant that the total reference was to the Messiah alone). Peter insists that his view is not a view that is novel and unique to his own style of interpreting the text (say, after the manner of the rabbis), but it was the one David offered under the inspiration of the Holy Spirit!

Neither Peter nor any other NT author invents or retrojects meaning from their setting and perspective back onto the OT text. Instead, it is precisely because the older text speaks so clearly that they are filled with confidence and hope as they announce that God has acted just as he said he would ages

---

65. Mitchell Dahood, *Psalms* (AB; Garden City, N.J.: Doubleday, 1965), 1:91. Dahood showed that Ugaritic *hayyim* was used early on in parallelism with "immortality."

66. See my explanation of Paul's use of Psalm 16 in Acts 13:35–37 in *Uses of the Old Testament*, 36–37.

67. Driver, "The Method of Studying the Psalter," 36.

beforehand. Peter's use of Psalm 16 is therefore not an example of a *pesher*-type exegesis that endows the OT text with a meaning that was not in the truth intention of the original author.

Is Allegory a Valid Category for Paul's Use of Deuteronomy 25:4 in 1 Corinthians 9:7–10?[68]

Students of Scripture have long noticed that older biblical texts are used and applied by subsequent generations of listeners and readers. But all too many argue that the biblical writers do this by departing from the literal sense of the older text. For instance, David J. A. Clines, like many postmodern interpreters, wants to give the older text a life of its own, independent of its first speaker. His case for a totally autonomous text is as follows:

> Once it is recognized that the text does not exist as a carrier of information, but has a life of its own, it becomes impossible to talk about *the* meaning of a text, as if it had only *one* proper meaning.... Meaning is seen to reside not in the text, but in what the text becomes for the reader.... Thus the original author's meaning, which is what is generally meant by *the* meaning of a text, is by no means the only meaning a text may legitimately have (or rather create). We cannot even be sure that a literary text (or a work of art) "originally" — whatever that was — meant one thing and one thing only to its author; even the author may have had multiple meanings in mind.... [Therefore] ... it is not a matter of being quite wrong or even quite right: there are only more and less appropriate interpretations ... according to how well the world of the [literary piece] comes to expression in the new situation.[69] (emphasis his)

The most effective response to this suggested solution is to apply his own hermeneutic to what he himself wrote and

---

68. See my article, "The Current Crisis in Exegesis and the Apostolic Use of Deuteronomy 25:4 in 1 Corinthians 9:8–10," *JETS* 21 (1978): 3–18 and its reproduction in *Uses of the Old Testament*, 203–20.

69. David A. Clines, *I, He, We, and They: A Literary Approach to Isaiah 53* (JSOT-Sup 1 (Sheffield: JSOT Press, 1976), 59–61. See also his "Notes for an Old Testament Hermeneutic," *Theology, News and Notes* 21 (March, 1975): 8–10.

to interpret his view exactly opposite of what Clines was try-ing to advocate: viz., we understand him to say that meaning is fixed, determinative, and singlefold as found in the author's own grammar and syntax. If Clines then objects, as he of course must, then he is left without any recourse since we will insist that that is what we got out of what he said. Who is to say other-wise, since I as an interpreter am in the driver's or the cat bird's seat? Eventually, advocacy for a plurality of meanings might drive us back to the "four senses" view found in many of the patristic and medieval exegetes.

But let us look at the Scripture found in Deuteronomy 25:4: "Do not muzzle an ox while it is treading out the grain." This is found in an OT context that sets forth a number of laws for society. For example, there is exemption from military service for those recently married (Deut 24:5), the prohibition against taking a millstone as security for a loan (24:6), the law against kidnapping (24:7), laws on leprosy (24:8–9), laws on loans (24:10–13), protection for hired hands (24:14–15), provisions for each one being accountable for his or her own sins rather than blaming the parents or children (24:16), protection for the weak and vulnerable (24:17–18), provisions for the poor to glean the edges of the harvest field (24:19–22), and limitations on the flogging of criminals (25:1–3). It is at this point that 25:4 appears. All these provisions are to raise social awareness of a caring and helping hand for those who are poor, weak, and vulnerable. God wants to see something happen in the hearts of his people — a sense of caring and a concern for moral justice and equity.

The NT context in 1 Corinthians is just as important for gaining an appreciation for how Paul uses Deuteronomy 25:4. In its setting, 1 Corinthians 8:1–13 deals with things offered to idols. The principles are announced in chapter 8 and these same principles are illustrated in chapter 9.[70]

Now with this as a background, what use does the apostle make of the text from the Mosaic law and what meaning does he derive from it before he applies it to his new situation? A good

---

70. The principles involve these points: (1) Giving to the Lord imitates the law of the harvest; (2) giving to God is a grace and not a work; and (3) some of the highest examples of giving often come from those who have the least to give.

number of scholars, such as W. Arndt,[71] have claimed that Paul uses an allegorical or mystical understanding of Deuteronomy 25:4, which, while not violating the literal meaning, is not dependent on it either! How one can do that, is not clear to me.[72] As A. T. Hanson observed, "interpreting a text in a sense which completely ignores its original meaning, or in a sense whose connection with its original meaning [is changed] is purely arbitrary."[73]

Richard Longenecker similarly defends an allegorical interpretation: Paul, he thinks, "seems to leave the primary meaning of the injunction in Deut 25:4 ... and interprets the Old Testament allegorically."[74] For Longenecker the key issue is the meaning of the word *pantos* ("it is written *pantos* for our sakes"). If *pantos* is to be translated "altogether," or "entirely," then Paul would be claiming that he thinks Moses is only concerned about the keepers of the oxen and not the oxen themselves.

But it is possible to argue that *pantos* is to be rendered "certainly" or "undoubtedly." If so, Paul is claiming that the literal principle can be applied to a new situation. Yes, oxen should be allowed to take a swipe of grain as they walked round and round, hour after hour, treading out the grain while being attached to a central post. But this ruling not only benefited the animals; it also produced a much gentler and kinder oxen owner simultaneously!

Adolf Deissmann is most caustic in his advocacy of the allegorical interpretation:

> With Philo, as also with Paul, allegorical exegesis ... was more a sign of freedom than of bondage, though it led both of them to great violence of interpretation.
>
> [Among the] instances of such violence [is] ... the application of the words about the ox, which was not

---

71. W. Arndt, "The Meaning of 1 Cor 9:9, 10," *CTM* 3 (1932): 329–35.

72. 1 Cor 9:7–10 and Gal 4:21–31 are usually regarded as the two prime examples of the Pauline use of allegory in his interpretation of Scripture.

73. A. T. Hanson, *Studies in Paul's Technique and Theology* (Grand Rapids: Eerdmans, 1974), 159. Hanson went on to argue that the original meaning had not completely disappeared. Consequently, 1 Cor 9:8–9 was only "formally" an allegory, but "not consciously to be so" (166).

74. Longenecker, *Biblical Exegesis*, 126.

to be muzzled while threshing.... Paul speaks in these strangely unpractical and feeble words as a man from the city, who does not regard animals.[75]

Others argue that this text exhibits a rabbinic type of argument called *qal wahomer*,[76] i.e., an argument from the lesser or lighter to the greater or heavier. W. Orr and J. A. Walther chose this form of interpretation in their commentary on 1 Corinthians.[77]

A third view explains that Paul expounded the passage from the Mosaic law "according to the Hellenistic Jewish principle that God's concern is with higher things," thereby allowing the literal sense to be abandoned, because it spoke of something unworthy of God.[78]

Despite these three aberrant views, our contention is that Paul has neither abandoned the literal meaning nor has he taken liberties with the Mosaic legislation in order to gain divine authorization for ministerial honoraria or salaries. Few have handled this citation from the OT better than F. Godet. He shows that the whole context in Deuteronomy was one of explaining what are the moral duties of mortals to one another and to God's created order. He explains:

> Paul does not, therefore, in the least suppress the historical and natural meaning of the precept.... He recognizes it fully, and it is precisely by starting from this sense that he rises to a higher application.... Far from arbitrary allegorizing, he applies, by a well-founded *a fortiori* [argument], to a higher relation what God had prescribed with reference to a lower relation.... The precept has not its full sense except when applied to a reasonable being.
>
> It is difficult to suppress a smile when listening to the declamations of our moderns against the allegorizing mania of the Apostle Paul.... Paul does not in the

75. Adolf Deissmann, *Paul: A Study in Social and Religious History,* trans. W. E. Wilson (New York: Harper, 1957), 102–3.

76. Also known in Latin as a *minori ad majus* type of argument.

77. W. Orr and J. Walther, *1 Corinthians* (AB; Garden City, N.J.: Doubleday, 1976), 238.

78. Hans Conzelmann, *A Commentary on the First Epistle to the Corinthians*, trans. J. W. Leitch (Hermeneia; Philadelphia: Fortress, 1975), 155 and n. 38.

least allegorize.... From the literal and natural meaning of the precept he disentangles a profound truth, a law of humanity and equity.[79]

Calvin was as insistent that Paul got it right:

> We must not make the mistake of thinking that Paul means to explain that commandment allegorically; for some empty-headed creatures make this an excuse for turning everything into allegory, so that they change dogs into men, trees into angels, and convert the whole of Scripture into an amusing game.
>
> But what Paul actually means is quite simple: though the Lord commands consideration for the oxen, He does so, not for the sake of the oxen, but rather out of regard for men, for whose benefit even the oxen were created. Therefore that humane treatment of oxen ought to be an incentive, moving us to treat each other with consideration and fairness.[80]

But what about Paul's question: "Is it about oxen that God is concerned?" (1 Cor 9:9c)? Paul answers in 9:10a: "Surely he says this for us, doesn't he?" But what would appear to be a flat Pauline denial that God has any interest in oxen is clarified by Arthur P. Stanley's reminder:

> [1 Cor 9:10 is] one of the many instances where the lesson which is regarded as subordinate is denied altogether as in Hos. vi. 6, "I will have mercy and not sacrifice," and in Ezek. xx. 25, "I gave them statutes which were not good."[81]

Therefore, while God is concerned for animals, he had spoken "mainly" or "especially" (hence a better rendering of *pantos*)

---

79. F. Godet, *Commentary of the First Epistle to the Corinthians*, trans. A. Cusin (Grand Rapids: Zondervan, 1957 reprint): 2:11, 13, 16.

80. John Calvin, *The First Epistle of Paul the Apostle to the Corinthians*, trans. J. W. Fraser (Grand Rapids: Eerdmans, 1960), 187–88. See also Philip Schaff, ed., *The Works of St. Chrysostom* in The Nicene and Post-Nicene Fathers of the Christian Church, First Series (New York: Christian Literature, 1889), 12:120–21.

81. Arthur P. Stanley, *The Epistle of St. Paul to the Corinthians*, 4th ed. (London: John Murray, 1876), 142. Further examples of the same phenomenon might be added: 1 Sam 15:22; Jer 7:21; and Matt 9:13; 12:7. Also see E. W. Bullinger, *Figures of Speech* (Grand Rapids: Baker, 1968), 24.

for people.[82] "Yes," (*gar*) Paul went on to say, "this was written for us."

Paul then introduces the rest of v. 10 by means of the Greek word *hoti*, which may be taken in one of three ways. First, it could be translated "that," carrying a declarative or explicative sense that gives the substance of the Deuteronomy command. Second, it could be understood as the equivalent of our quotation marks—in this recitative sense, it would be seen to introduce a quotation from a noncanonical source, since there is no OT equivalent to these words. Third, it could be translated as "because," communicating a causal notion that gives the reason why God gave this figurative command.

Since Paul uses the standard introductory formula of "it is written," this can only be a citation from Deuteronomy, and any apocryphal book as a source is immediately ruled out.[83] So also is the declarative sense ruled out, since Deuteronomy had no more to say on this subject than the straightforward statement. Paul wants, instead, to tell us why this command is normative for all mortals and was written for our edification. For this reason, the causal sense of *hoti* must be in Paul's mind here.

---

82. R. Jamieson, A. F. Fausett, and D. Brown, *Commentary on the Whole Bible* (Grand Rapids: Zondervan, n.d.), 2:278, follow Grotius in translating *pantos* as "mainly" or "especially," a meaning that is permissible for this word and which certainly conveys the sense in this passage.

83. In his article on "Inspiration" in the original set of *The International Standard Bible Encyclopedia*, B. B. Warfield famously argued that when "It is written" appears in the Bible, it means the same thing as "God said" (*The International Standard Bible Encyclopedia* [Grand Rapids: Eerdmans, 1952], 3:1473–83). However, Henry Preserved Smith (1880–1941) challenged Warfield's case with one exception he had noted. It was Paul's use of Job 5:13 in 1 Cor 3:19. That quotation in Job was taken from one of Eliphaz's speeches: "For it is written, He taketh the wise in their [own] craftiness" (see James Oliver Buswell Jr., *A Systematic Theology of the Christian Religion* [Grand Rapids: Zondervan, 1962], 1:208–10). Warfield did not directly answer Smith's argument, for no one held that the speeches of Job's three friends were in any sense authoritative or normative, much less from God. However, Wilbur Wallis noted that the citation Paul used in 1 Cor 3:19 was not from Job 5:13 alone, but instead God used Eliphaz's smart words back on him when, in Job 42:7–8, God told Job to pray for his three friends and for their folly. Thus, "It is written," in the NT citations of the OT, means "it is authoritatively written in the Word of God" (in Buswell, *Systematic Theology*, 1:208–10).

What then was Paul's reasoning? It was not to show that plowing and threshing were two parallel works each worthy of reward. Rather, it was that the one who had been on the job working (or in Paul's continuing agricultural metaphor, plowing the field in hope) ought to be the one who is there when the recompense for the labor is passed out (i.e., at the threshing floor when the harvest comes in). Paul has not given us a different or a secondary hidden sense from the assertion Moses would have made. Instead, he has expertly taken off the temporary wrapping and cultural setting in which the teaching was first given to show us the permanent principle that Moses and the Holy Spirit intended all along.

Herein lies a graphic illustration as to how we might begin to bridge the gap between the "then" of the text from yesterday to the "now" of today.[84] Paul's argument was grounded in the authority of Scripture found in Deuteronomy. However, he was not so taken with animal husbandry and the deuteronomic background that he had no message for later generations. It was not that Scripture has a hidden meaning that was only known by God until Paul happened to get a hold of this text.

To allow this "pastoral application" of Deuteronomy 25:4 does not mean there is something else to be found in, under, or beyond the text than the grammatical-syntactical-historical meaning. Marshall goes too far in a discussion about a different passage when he asserts, "I would be prepared to accept a 'pastoral' interpretation of John 4, even if it were not in the author's mind.... It could be that in Scripture too there is a meaning different from that intended by the author."[85] One need only to distinguish "meaning" from "significance," as E. D. Hirsch has argued all along.

It is remarkable that Paul does not appeal to Deuteronomy 24:15, which teaches: "Pay them [the hired men] their wages

---

84. Paul actually argues his case for pastoral monetary support from four separate illustrations: (1) the illustrations found in experience of the soldier, vine grower and herdsman (1 Cor 9:7); (2) the authority of Scripture found in Deut 25:4 (1 Cor 9:8–11; cf. 1 Tim 5:18 in a subsequent application of the same text of Deut); (3) as an illustration from the current practice of the church and even in pagan religions (1 Cor 9:12–13); and (4) the authoritative teachings of Jesus (1 Cor 9:14).

85. I. Howard Marshall, "The Problem of New Testament Exegesis," *JETS* 17 (1974): 67–73, esp. 72.

each day before sunset, because they are poor and are count-
ing on it. Otherwise they may cry to the LORD against you, and
you will be guilty of sin." Perhaps in the wisdom of God, the
oxen text made a better teaching tool, for it may have embar-
rassed God's reluctant people to give to the teachers/pastors
who served them well what they ordinarily would have given
to dumb animals. Moreover, this text fits nicely the illustration
from the sphere of agriculture just given in verse 7.

The apostle rightly understands that God spoke to men (not
oxen) primarily for their moral growth in generosity, fairness,
and equity. If the principle is that what was written in Scripture
was that all workers have a right to be paid for their services (be
they animal or human), then that is what Moses meant and that
is what God meant. That settles the principle.

But the original teaching can be contextualized in new situations, with new relationships, where the identical principle can
be established for the same reasons. We are taught, then, how
to move from the BC text to the twenty-first century AD, using
the same methodology that Paul illustrates in his application of
Moses' teaching to the first-century AD situation. The practical application of the Bible is not as mysterious as some would
make it to be. We need only observe the methods Paul used and
then follow them in each new situation we face in our day.

SHOULD MODERN INTERPRETERS
REPLICATE THE NEW TESTAMENT
AUTHORS' USE OF THE OLD TESTAMENT?

Modern readers and interpreters of the Bible certainly may
follow in the steps of the NT writers when they use the OT, for
those NT writers argued most carefully when they cited the OT
as an authority for apologetical or doctrinal reasons. It is only
when we begin to doubt that the NT writers were faithful to
what had been written in the OT that we begin to face problems
that are issues more for our day than they were for that day or
for most of the centuries preceding our twentieth and twenty-
first centuries.

Just because we have found midrashic, *pesher*, allegorical,
and alleged *sensus plenior* meanings in the writings of nonbibli-
cal texts surrounding the days of our Lord's earthly ministry

and of the NT writers is not a sure sign that any or all of these methods must thereby be found or consistently employed in the NT's use of the OT. For the past decades, NT scholars generally have not pursued OT studies as strenuously as they have studied extrabiblical literature, such as the rabbinic literature, the Dead Sea Scrolls, the Nag Hammadi (Gnostic) texts, and the like. Our plea, therefore, would be to let the older Testament be searched first and then the later Testament analyzed before appeal is made to extrabiblical texts for answers to the problems that beset us in interpretation. In short, specialization in one Testament along with cognate studies have forced patterns on biblical studies that do not always represent the fairest way to set the problems up in the first place.

It is the question of the divine authority of the OT that drives us to seek the authorial assertions of the meanings of their texts. It is that same quest that would make us hesitant to see the NT override what God had originally said unless he signaled in the OT text that what had been said had a built-in obsolescence and was effective as a "model" or "pattern" (*tabnit*) only until such a time as the real came (Ex 25:9, 40). Otherwise, all Scripture is inspired by God and remains useful—not always for the same thing, but in no sense is it declared to be antiquated and subject to new meanings from subsequent biblical writers or readers.

RESPONSE TO KAISER

Darrell L. Bock

Before launching into a response to "Single Meaning and Unified Referents," it is important to recall where agreement lies. All the essays agree that the Scripture comes to realization in Jesus Christ and that the plan of God centers in him. The disagreement is on how this works. So the discussion is like a discussion on which route is the best one to take on a trip.

SOME PRELIMINARY REMARKS

The key factors in this discussion include (1) the time in history when a passage is read for understanding the nature of its referents and the context into which it is placed (what we might call the temporal factor), and (2) whether the claims a person makes concerning the possible meaning of a text actually relate to the authorially intended meaning of that text and how they do so. In addition, to show that some texts can work on a single-meaning, human understanding model does not mean all such texts work this way. In some ways, Kaiser's approach has the highest burden of proof. This is because of his claim that all texts work in this manner.

Kaiser's essay begins by framing the entire issue in the following way:

> Should that meaning be limited to what the human writer of Scripture obtained as a result of standing in the revelatory counsel of God, or were there additional, or

even alternative, meanings to be found that God somehow quietly incorporated into the text in some mysterious way, thus hiding them from the author, or perhaps
even new meanings that the audience brought to the text
on their own?

The way this question is framed is prejudicial to the discussion.
Here the prophet is escorted into God's presence (standing in the
revelatory counsel of God) and any additional meaning is "mys-
teriously" supplied. Do not be moved by what is essentially a
rhetorical claim. First, the other two essays in this volume try
to remove the sense of mystery to this process by identifying
in historically sensitive ways how the themes of "additional"
meaning emerge. The process is not as mysterious as this citation suggests.

Second, Kaiser paints an exaggerated picture of the prophet
being given a clear presentation of what he is writing (as if he
had a conversation with God in the counsel room) versus being
a vessel through whom God expresses himself.

Third, Kaiser's stark manner of contrast between one meaning and additional meaning presents the issue in too much of
an either-or manner. My essay argues that the meaning that
emerges is not disconnected from the original meaning. In other
words, a key option is not even put on the table by posing the
question this way. What of the option that God begins to reveal
the promise in early texts, but develops that meaning through
time as the progress of revelation takes place, adding new pieces
to the puzzle? All of this is crucially important, because to have
a beneficial conversation about how things work, the options
need to be clearly stated.

The same definitional concern applies to the issue of *sensus
plenior*. Let me simply note that this term also has an ambiguity. When it simply means "there is more here and God did it,"
then I share Kaiser's objections. However, when it is seen how
such a sense emerges in the unfolding progress of revelation,
then the term can be useful in a limited way. Our real discussion
centers on how the progress of revelation works. Is revelation
that is antecedent to the human author the key, or is it also tied
to subsequent revelation and *how that later revelation connects to
the text in question*? It is the second option that I prefer because
it covers more ground adequately.

The handling of typology is similarly problematic. The Motyer quotation making typology strictly retrospective is not the only way to define the category. In my essay, I suggest a more nuanced approach to the issue of typology. The key to this category is how history was read as having divine "patterns" in it, which allows for both a prospective and a retrospective typology in Second Temple readings. This was so because God was seen as the designer of history no matter when the pattern was spotted.

Finally, many of Kaiser's citations that bear the burden of being authorities on this question come from a period when our knowledge of the first-century world of scriptural usage was much less than it is today. They predate the development of Second Temple period studies and the Dead Sea Scroll finds. The careful study of these sources has shown that what was seen as persuasive argument and standard practice in handling Scripture in the first century was far more varied than our very tightly defined, modern exegetical method.

These finds raise an important question. What are the rules of the game in persuading people about what a text means? Are they rules we fix today? Or did the writers play by rules they agreed on in the first century? It is a little like the difference between football and football (soccer). In one game the hands are key, but in the other they are mostly illegal. Knowing the rules of the game is required before evaluating what is or is not allowed. This is why so many of the citations Kaiser reacts against come from the more recent period. Our understanding of interpretative method has grown. Most exegetes recognize this development.

All of these factors mean that the choice is not merely between the human author's meaning and alternative added meaning, as Kaiser's essay argues. There is also the option that later revelation can complete and fill meaning that was initially, but not comprehensively, revealed in the original setting, so that once the progress of revelation emerges, the earlier passage is better and more comprehensively understood. Such a reading is not "going beyond" the original writer but working within the parameters his message introduces. (By the way, E. D. Hirsch, whom Kaiser cites, actually goes this way in his subsequent treatments of these themes, as I note in my essay).

THE CENTRAL ISSUE AND SPECIFIC PASSAGES

The key issue is whether or not the texts Kaiser cites bear all the meaning he claims for them. His claim is that earlier or antecedent revelation gives sufficient backdrop to gain a full understanding of claims made by the human author. Such a claim already ignores the fact that some writers tell us they do not understand their own prophecies. Daniel 12:8–9 indicates that this is the case for Daniel, showing that a lack of human understanding is a possibility for a prophetic text. Kaiser's assertion that 1 Peter 1:10–12 only speaks of ignorance of the time misreads the syntax of *eis tina e poion* ("what person or time") and of the analysis put forward in the Blass-Debrunner grammar. This is an important line to consider, but it is not just time that is highlighted because person and time do not belong in the same category.

The most important question is whether Kaiser has shown that the way he reads his sample passages is the best way to read these texts in their original contexts. Because of space limitations, I will discuss two examples: Amos 9 and Psalm 16.

Kaiser opens with these questions to set up this passage:

> Did the OT authors have an adequate understanding of the future meaning of their texts, as well as their present meaning, or did the NT meaning go beyond the authorial will of the human writer of the older Scripture when the apostles used materials from the OT? If it did exceed the boundaries of the original writer in the OT, would not such an exegesis be self-condemned because it had left out a theological meaning that would have come from placing each OT pericope in its own literary and biblical theological context?

My answer to this question is, "No, not if themes are brought in that fit the larger theology of the Scripture."

Our first example in Acts 15 begins with a rather unique introductory formula. It reads, "The words of the prophets are in agreement with this." James introduces his remarks by noting this is something *the prophets* (plural!) teach. The Greek verb translated "are in agreement" means "to combine." We get our word "symphony" from this verb (*symphonousin*). In other words, James cites but one text of several he might note. He cites Amos, but Isaiah 2:2–4 also comes to mind. The topic is, as Kaiser said, the dilapidated "tent" that is the Davidic dynasty. However, the context is the restoration of a unified kingship for the divided people of God, Israel. The key to understanding the text in the original context is Edom, which is seen as the archenemy of Israel, typical of her worst enemy (Ps 137:7; Isa 34:5–15; 63:1–6; Lam 4:21; Ob 1). The image in the context is that of a restored Davidic house exercising decisive power over all.

This reading is different from the LXX, which is closer to James's rendering. The LXX speaks of the hope "that the remnant of men may seek me." This turns an oracle of judgment and victory into an oracle of hope. This more positive reading does fit with other OT texts of end-time hope (Isa 66:19–24; Zech. 14:2, 9, 16). I cannot develop this in detail for lack of space, but my point here is that subsequent revelation has filled out how victory occurs. It not only is a conquering, as Amos originally detailed, but also an incorporation of the nations.

Thus, by the time of the first century—and in light of canonical considerations—the victory came to be understood as victory over and participation by the nations. This point implies, regardless of which specific view of the LXX text's origin is taken, that the LXX reflects a pre-Christian reading of Amos. In one case, we have the original, but in the other we have a reading that involves the result of connecting Amos to other expectations of what comes with deliverance. If the LXX reflects the original, then the passage moves us closer to Kaiser's claim. But since the conceptual understanding of victory still has the twofold expectation we have described, my view of canonical influence still applies.

There is one other difference to note. It appertains no matter which reading—the MT or LXX—is the original. In Amos, the restoration of the Davidic hut for a united, political Israel is in view. In the NT, the resurrection of Jesus and the presence of the exalted Messiah in a new entity is the point of the restoration. All Amos declares is the Davidic restoration and victory (the term "Messiah" is not present). The filling out of the referent in a more detailed understanding of expectation is another result of the progress of revelation, incorporating other subsequent texts, and the events tied to Jesus. Subsequent revelation and divine design are at work here. This means that the human author did not completely understand the details of the direction his words set. This kind of an outline of end-time expectation is something James's listeners and even many Jews of the period would have embraced, especially given his appeal to the prophets in general.

We turn more briefly to Psalm 16. Here we simply point out that the first person references throughout this psalm make a more natural reading to refer to the psalmist himself, who is the subject throughout. Otherwise, we must argue that one part of one verse treats a subject different from the rest of the psalm. A better way to read Psalm 16 is as a typological text. When the psalm is placed into the Psalter, it becomes a text of hope for which the experience of the psalmist is representative. As such, the psalm can ultimately be about Jesus, who is not left in death but is resurrected from it, even though Jesus' experience exceeds that of the psalmist who likely hoped for some form of deliverance from God for himself.

CONCLUSION

Although I appreciate and understand the effort to argue for a reading that is singular throughout, this view has too many hurdles to climb to be the most likely solution to the use of the OT in the NT. Being aware of the full array of options makes it more likely that NT readings are not merely exercises in exegesis in the technical, modern sense but presentations of theology taking the whole canon and theology of hope into view.

RESPONSE TO KAISER

Peter Enns

Kaiser's articulation of the NT's use of the OT is one that is well known to anyone familiar with his writings. The views he expresses in his essay do not, in my opinion, represent any real change from his previously published articles and books. I respect the work Kaiser has put into this issue and the influence he has had. Nevertheless, I am not convinced that his approach to this hermeneutical issue is helpful or accurate.

Kaiser's essay begins by addressing the general issue of "alternate" or "multiple" meanings in Scripture, but I feel that, even at the outset, we are being led down a wrong path. In fact, I disagree with the entire way in which Kaiser sets up his argument; he begins at the wrong end. He spends much effort at the beginning of his essay building a case *in the abstract* for why meaning should be located in an author's intention and why multiple levels of meaning should be avoided at all costs. This is rhetorically effective, perhaps (who would want to disagree?), but Kaiser undertakes this argument without addressing the real and difficult problems for such an approach that *are generated by the NT data themselves.*

Moreover, he sets up his own case by presenting opposing views in a negative light. Note the first series of questions at the outset of Kaiser's essay that refer to multiple meanings *"somehow quietly* incorporated into the text in some *mysterious* way, thus *hiding* from the author, or perhaps even new meanings that the audience *brought to the text on their own"* (emphasis added). This is not a helpful way of setting up the problem of the NT use of the OT, which is, for most scholars, a very real hermeneutical conundrum. Kaiser's bias is seen throughout the essay in the way he sets up arguments and employs language that leaves little room for a dispassionate view of the biblical and Second Temple evidence.

Kaiser's discussion of *sensus plenior* is likewise problematic. By citing the Roman Catholic scholar Raymond Brown, Kaiser seems to be using guilt by association to undermine *sensus plenior*. Brown is able to take meaning "out of the hands of the human authors who stood in the counsel of God" because Brown's Catholicism has an ecclesiastical tradition that allows him to treat Scripture so shabbily. I am not Catholic, but I was a bit offended by such a caricature, since Protestant scholarship owes so much to the careful and nuanced work of Roman Catholic scholars. Moreover, it is somewhat beside the point to portray Roman Catholics as manipulating the meaning of Scripture so casually. The real hermeneutical issues before us, *generated as they are by the NT evidence itself*, will not be settled by such rhetoric.

Moreover, Kaiser's treatment of *sensus plenior* is itself a caricature. It is not as if scholars are trying to find some way to wrest Scripture's meaning from the words on the page and place it in some mystical realm, and so make up the concept of *sensus plenior*. The issue, rather, is how the real difficulties of the NT use of the OT *leads* to theories such as *sensus plenior*. That, I would suggest, is the point of the three essays in this volume. But, instead of dealing head-on with the topic at hand, Kaiser mounts a pejorative case for why multiple meanings not anchored in the human author's intention are suspect, and *then* turns to the NT evidence with this conclusion firmly in hand. Kaiser should begin with the models of explanation the NT evidence allows and then offer explanations based on that analysis.

Similarly, what fuels much of Kaiser's argument is his uncritical adoption of methodologies that a study of modern hermeneutics, and especially the NT use of the OT, calls into question. It seems, in fact, that he is keen to call into question modern hermeneutical developments in general, as can be seen by his recurring citation of scholars (e.g., Bishop Ryle, Herbert Marsh, Frederic Gardiner, F. Godet) who wrote before the discoveries at Qumran. Old is *certainly* not bad, but a lot has happened in our understanding of biblical hermeneutics in the last one hundred years; it seems that particular kinds of progress in biblical studies are troubling to Kaiser, and he wishes to guard against them. To do so, however, Kaiser assumes an approach to interpretation whereby "standard tools such as grammar, syntax, and the like" or "rules of language and exegesis" are employed.

I certainly sympathize, as my own essay demonstrates, but surely Kaiser must see that such an appeal cannot alone solve the hermeneutical problem before us. For one thing, it is precisely a "grammatico-historical" exegesis of the NT that renders Kaiser's hermeneutical model unworkable (as I discuss in my essay). Secondly, Kaiser's own handling of the NT's use of the OT departs quickly from the standard of "grammar, syntax, and the like" and plunges him into hermeneutical maneuvers that are fairly midrashic.

Kaiser then turns to the question of canonical readings and whether a defense of *sensus plenior* can be found there. Predictably, the answer is no. I fully agree with Kaiser's contention that we do our OT exegesis before we see how things develop in the "subsequent progress of revelation." The "first reading," as I and others like to call it, is important. I also agree that the "thickening" of theology is a two-way street: that our understanding of the OT is augmented by seeing subsequent revelation, but that also our understanding of the NT is enriched by paying attention to the theological contours of the OT. (In this respect, Kaiser is echoing somewhat the concern of Brevard Childs and his students.)

I part company with Kaiser, however, in understanding this mutual theological "thickening" to be a function of the theological *tensions* generated by the first and second readings; that is, by reading the OT on its own terms *and then* reading how the NT authors use the OT in ways informed by Second Temple interpretive practices and a Christotelic eschatology. Moreover, it is clear that for Kaiser the theological trajectories inaugurated in the OT are *determinative* for how subsequent authors (be they later OT authors or NT authors) handle the prior revelation. In other words, subsequent authors do not stampede over the OT sense in order to read Christ willy-nilly, but are bound to the "authorial will" of prior biblical writers. Kaiser's argument here is not based so much on the behavior of biblical authors, but on Kaiser's precommitment to what kinds of hermeneutical activities inspired biblical authors—not to mention God himself—may engage in.

Continuing his argument against *sensus plenior*, Kaiser begins to engage biblical data by addressing alleged NT support for *sensus plenior*. This is ground Kaiser has covered elsewhere, and he addresses three passages: 1 Peter 1:10–12; 2 Peter 1:19–21; and John 11:49–52. I actually have large areas of agreement with Kaiser at this point. I do not think that appeal to these passages can establish *explicit* biblical support for *sensus plenior*. But more importantly, appealing to any one passage or two is not going to help the case either way. Rather than looking for a proof text or two to justify *sensus plenior*, one should pay greater attention to how the NT authors behave (a point Bock makes well) and, moreover, how they behave in the context of their hermeneutical environment (as I argue).

This is why an appeal to the passages Kaiser cites is *irrelevant* for *both* sides of the debate. They are irrelevant for pro-*sensus plenior* advocates because the hermeneutical practices of NT authors cannot be established by teasing the matter out of a couple of moderately amenable texts. But neither are these passages helpful for Kaiser. For even if it can be shown that, say, 1 Peter cannot be bent in a *sensus plenior* direction, the *fact* remains that the manner in which the NT uses the OT needs serious explaining. Kaiser, in other words, can neither appeal to abstract hermeneutical standards (as he has done thus far), nor can he appeal to the passages cited above, which supposedly establish some sort of anti–*sensus plenior* hermeneutical principle. All Kaiser has done thus far is to cast doubt on *sensus plenior* on grounds that are at best peripheral.

Rather than arguing how things ought to be or must be, Kaiser should begin his discussion inductively so that his assumptions and methodologies are more in line with the data the NT presents. As it stands, however, Kaiser's argument against *sensus plenior* that precedes his discussion of actual examples of the NT use of the OT is unpersuasive, and perhaps even misleading.

Kaiser eventually turns his attention to four examples to demonstrate that the NT authors did not go beyond the "authorial will" of the OT authors: (1) John 13:18 and Psalm 41:9; (2) Acts 15:13–18 and Amos 9:9–15; (3) the alleged use of *pesher* in the use of Psalm 16 in Acts 2; and (4) Paul's use of Deuteronomy 25:4 in 1 Corinthians 9:7–10. These are all fine examples and raise a number of important issues, such as the Jewish interpretive environment, the use of allegory, and other things. At the end of the day, however, I do not think Kaiser makes a convincing case that the NT authors have a hermeneutical commitment to respect the context of the OT authors they cite.

Space does not permit an extended discussion of the problems with Kaiser's examples, but some major issues can be mentioned.

1. He essentially ignores the Second Temple evidence (with one exception of a selective use of the Qumranian materials; see his discussion of Amos 9).
2. In attempting to demonstrate how OT meaning is determinative of its NT use, Kaiser engages in a type of exegesis of the OT that has some fairly midrashic properties. It is somewhat ironic, therefore, that Kaiser's defense of the determinative influence of "authorial will" actually demonstrates the very thing he seems so intent to guard against.
3. At significant junctures in his argument, Kaiser simply assumes the point to be proven; namely, that NT authors would never handle the OT in ways that are not tied significantly to the original OT meaning.
4. Kaiser's contention against "many contemporary scholars or believers" who are open to a flexibility of meaning in the OT does not take into account why there are in fact so many such scholars.
5. Kaiser reiterates the old argument that an ancient citation of the OT would only be persuasive if it is cited in harmony with its OT meaning. This ignores the entire issue of the use of the OT in Second Temple hermeneutics, and what would or would not be deemed persuasive *by ancient conventions*.
6. Kaiser's appeal to 2 Timothy 3:15–16 in defense of his position does not account for how *Paul himself* used the OT in creative ways. There is little here that will persuade those not already convinced of his position.

Finally, with respect to whether we can follow the NT authors in their hermeneutic, Kaiser's answer is an implied yes, provided we understand their hermeneutic the way Kaiser does. But in doing so, he claims that contemporary hermeneutical models that differ from his are caused by unfortunate academic specialization, or a failure to trust the NT authors in rendering carefully and faithfully what the OT authors had written. If the matter were that simple, however, there would be far less disagreement among evangelicals, and Kaiser would not have to spend quite so much effort in making his case. My contention is that if we *truly* allow the NT authors to lead us in our hermeneutic, we will come to a very different conclusion than the one Kaiser offers.

SINGLE MEANING, MULTIPLE CONTEXTS AND REFERENTS

The New Testament's Legitimate, Accurate, and Multifaceted Use of the Old

Darrell L. Bock

Chapter Two

SINGLE MEANING, MULTIPLE CONTEXTS AND REFERENTS

The New Testament's Legitimate, Accurate, and Multifaceted Use of the Old

Darrell L. Bock

To think about the use of the OT in the NT is to enter one of the most fascinating and complex areas of biblical study.[1] Yet even expressing the subject this way obscures a reality for the earliest Christians. Imagine someone walking up to the apostle Peter two millennia ago and asking him about Jesus' teaching on the use of the OT in the NT. He would have looked back at the questioner puzzled. For him the issue would be understanding the promises of the holy writings of old: the Law, the Psalms, and the Prophets. It is hard for us to remember that the revelation of Jesus Christ means in their context "the use of the OT in the New Era."

---

1. The first portion of this chapter is an updating and condensing of two previous articles of mine on the use of the OT in the NT. The original was in *Foundations for Biblical Interpretation*, ed. David S. Dockery, Kenneth A. Mathews, and Robert B. Sloan (Nashville: Broadman & Holman, 1994), 97–114, and in *Interpreting the New Testament Text*, ed. D. Bock and Buist M. Fanning (Wheaton: Crossway, 2006), 255–76. To this has been added a previously unpublished set of material that was read at regional meetings of the Evangelical Theological Society and Institute for Biblical Research.

Another key observation to make right at the start is the variety of ways in which the OT appears in the NT. For example, in the United Bible Societies' first edition of the *Greek New Testament*, the editors note 401 OT quotations or allusions, with only about half of these (195) having some type of introduction to indicate that the OT is being cited. In the NT, there are citations, allusions, and uses of OT ideas. The fulfillment of biblical prophecy also varies. Sometimes the OT text only looked to the future; but more often God made a promise and pictured it in a "mirror event" within contemporary history first, so that the promise presents a pattern of God's activity in history, which the fulfillment in Jesus only culminates.[2] So God's promises often work throughout history rather than merely at a moment of time. All of this means that there is more to the use of the OT in the NT than merely lining up OT texts with their NT fulfillments. There is no single way these texts are handled.

What my presentation will emphasize is that the use of the OT in the NT involves two sets of contexts: that of the OT passage, sometimes in a canonical versus a merely exegetical context, and that of the NT passage. A study of the NT context helps us appreciate how the first century conceptualization and the life of Jesus sometimes helped readers to see and appreciate the OT text more clearly than they may have before. This is why I often call this view the historical contexts view (note the plural here).

Another way to describe this view is to call it the one meaning, multiple contexts and referents view. On the one hand, I see the original context of the OT passage as playing a key role in setting the parameters of how the text is used, but it is not always the only factor. On the other hand, I do not see the NT use of many of these texts as so random that one appeals only to inspiration, even though that reading so violates the context

---

2. Klyne Snodgrass, "The Use of the Old Testament in the New," in *Interpreting the New Testament: Essays on Methods and Issues,* ed. David Alan Black and David S. Dockery (Nashville: Broadman & Holman, 2001), 209–29. For a theological consideration of the area of biblical typology, see Francis Foulkes, *The Acts of God: A Study in the Basis of Typology in the Old Testament* (London: Tyndale, 1958); and Leonard Goppelt, *Typos: The Typological Interpretation of the Old Testament in the New,* trans. Donald H. Madvig (Grand Rapids: Eerdmans, 1982).

that we could never do something like it. A careful study shows there is more to the biblical writers' method than meets the eye. In many ways, the easiest thing to do is to say as an interpreter that the rendering does not make sense, but is simply "ancient" method or "atomism" that we cannot or should not emulate. There may well be some method to what strikes us initially as seeming exegetical madness.

The key premise of this essay is that God works both in his words *and* in revelatory events that also help to elaborate his message. In other words, the use of the OT in the NT is not just about texts; it is about God's revelatory acts. The two often combine, in prediction and pattern, to show what God is doing in history through word and deed.

My initial overview considers key historical factors that impact ancient exposition. Then we articulate six first-century theological presuppositions that influenced ancient textual reading. Next, we examine issues raised because of dual authorship and the text's multiple settings. Then we consider two ways the Bible can be read today in light of progressive revelation. Finally, we treat the variety of ways in which the NT uses the OT, especially looking at the original human intent.

HISTORICAL FACTORS

Why consider historical backgrounds, especially Jewish roots, since the Christian movement ended up being so opposed to Jewish tradition? An argument against doing so is that a movement that was so opposed to Jewish tradition would certainly reject its methods of scriptural reasoning. But this is to ignore how Scripture in both the OT and NT used and accommodated itself to cultural elements to make its own, often unique, points. For example, the Leviathan image in the OT uses a popular mythological figure from ancient Near Eastern religions, but used that imagery to show that Yahweh was the God with whom all must deal.

People in those ancient centuries, especially in the period of the NT, thought about, reasoned, and argued in specific ways as they appealed to Scripture. Such thinking could lead to solid or poor arguments, but that kind of reasoning was common in discussing Scripture. We should not be surprised, then, to find the early Christian writers (most of whom were Jewish) using these common methods to make their case for Jesus. Their audiences could appreciate the argumentation. The writers used Jewish methods to show that Jesus was the Promised One of God, making their case even stronger. The difference in how Scripture was read came about not so much because of a different form or method of reading, but because Christians saw the goal of Scripture as pointing to Christ, while for Judaism the key was law or wisdom. Let's consider, then, some of the factors that must be considered as one looks at a particular text: (1) languages of the Bible, (2) midrashic technique and *pesher* technique, and (3) presuppositions about the Bible and the times.

Languages of the Bible

When we speak of the use of the OT in the NT, it is important to remember that the OT was written in Hebrew and Aramaic, while the entire NT was written in Greek. OT texts had to be translated for the Greek audiences of the NT. In addition, the dominant language used originally in many events the NT describes was Aramaic. So in the original events that are described, say, in the Gospels, the speaker likely would have cited the OT in Aramaic, not Hebrew.[3] Using the OT involved a multilingual and multicultural setting (just like our use of the English Bible).

Fortunately, the Jews already had a Greek Bible of the OT, the Septuagint (LXX). The Jews had translated different OT books, starting in about 250 B.C. The entire OT was completed before the time of Christ. Actually the LXX is a collection of translations rather than one translation, because different translation theories were applied to different books. Still, most NT quotations reflect this Greek OT version, although to differing degrees in different NT books. This version was the Bible for much of the Jewish Diaspora and was respected, since the *Letter*

---

3. For the issue of what language Jesus spoke, see Joseph A. Fitzmyer, "The Languages of Palestine in the First Century A.D.," *CBQ* 32 (1970): 501–31, reprinted in *A Wandering Aramean: Collected Aramaic Essays* (Missoula, Mont.: Scholars, 1979), 29–56. Jesus probably spoke Aramaic and Greek, and possibly Hebrew as well, but most of his public conversation would have been in Aramaic.

to Aristeas claimed that the translators agreed down to the word when they emerged with the translation of the Torah.

The translation process for the LXX was one of rendering the Bible into the language of the people for use in synagogue services. The Jews of Palestine also had the Targums, or Aramaic renderings of the OT. These ranged from very literal translation to somewhat paraphrastic renderings, if the later Targums we possess are an indication of earlier practice.[4]

---

4. On the issues associated with the nature of the Hebrew Scriptures in this period, including the issue of canon, see the article by D. Moody Smith, "The Use of the Old Testament in the New," in *The Use of the Old Testament in the New and Other Essays*, ed. James M. Efrid (Durham, NC: Duke Univ. Press, 1972), 3–13. On the nature of the Targums and their function in ancient Judaism, see Daniel Patte, *Early Jewish Hermeneutic in Palestine* (SBLDS 22; Missoula, Mont.: Scholars, 1975), 55–81; John Bowker, *The Targums and Rabbinic Literature* (Cambridge: Cambridge Univ. Press, 1969), 3–28; Anthony D. York, "The Targum in the Synagogue and in the School," *JSJ* 10 (1979): 74–86. On the diversity of usage of the OT within the NT, see Craig A. Evans, "The Function of the Old Testament in the New," in *Introducing New Testament Interpretation*, ed. Scot McKnight (Grand Rapids: Baker, 1989), 163–93; Richard N. Longenecker, *Biblical Exegesis in the Apostolic Period*, 2nd ed. (Grand Rapids: Eerdmans, 1999); and D. A. Carson and H. G. M. Williamson, eds., *It Is Written: Scripture Citing Scripture* (Cambridge: Cambridge Univ. Press, 1988). For Jesus' use of Scripture, see R. T. France, *Jesus and the Old Testament* (London: Tyndale, 1971). More historically-critical oriented treatments of the NT that are often cited in this discussion include Barnabas Lindars, *New Testament Apologetic* (Philadelphia: Fortress, 1961); and Donald Juel, *Messianic Exegesis: Christological Interpretation of the Old Testament in the New* (Philadelphia: Fortress, 1988). The last two studies overplay the differences between the OT and the NT. For an attempt to argue for certain central themes emerging from the use of the OT in the NT, with their source going back to Jesus, see C. H. Dodd, *According to the Scriptures: The Sub-Structure of New Testament Theology* (New York: Scribner, 1952). The best-known study of Paul's OT interpretation is E. Earle Ellis, *Paul's Use of the Old Testament* (Grand Rapids: Eerdmans, 1957), while a more recent treatment of allusions in Paul is Richard B. Hays, *Echoes of Scripture in the Letters of Paul* (New Haven, CT: Yale Univ. Press, 1989). His study understates the value of Jewish backgrounds to this question and overstates the differences between the OT meaning and the NT sense. The classic article on *midrash* is Renée Bloch, "Midrash," trans. Mary Howard Callaway, in *Approaches to Ancient Judaism: Theory and Practice*, ed. William Scott Green (Missoula, Mont.: Scholars, 1978), 29–50—a translation of an article written in 1957. Other treatments include Bowker, *Targums and Rabbinic Literature;* and Gary Porton, *Understanding Rabbinic Midrash* (Hoboken, NJ: KTAV, 1985). On ancient Jewish use of the Scripture, see Patte, *Early Jewish Hermeneutic.* For the wide variety of examples of *midrash*, see Jacob Neusner, *A Midrash Reader* (Minneapolis: Fortress, 1990). For a focused study on Palestinian Judaism and the NT, see Martin McNamara, *Palestinian Judaism and the New Testament* (Wilmington, DE: Glazier, 1983).

These "quotations" of the Bible often had room to engage in some freedom of rendering as the goal was to bring out the full force of a passage, sometimes in light of larger contexts, including canonical considerations from the Hebrew Scriptures. The Greek version was what the original audience of the NT would have recognized as familiar. The NT authors did not ignore this reality. Even Paul, who as a rabbi knew Hebrew and Aramaic, often chose to quote the version his audience knew (just as a pastor might know Greek and still be content to cite the English version today). So knowing these versions of the Bible is important as one studies the OT in the NT. Renderings could be somewhat interpretive and free, but often the NT writers had a larger context in view as they sought to make meaning clear or used the LXX, as already noted, to make what were often more implicit points more explicit.

Some of these MT/LXX differences reflect the fact that the text has been interpretively rendered by the translator of the text into Greek to bring out its full force (e.g., Isa 61:1–2a in Luke 4:16–20). In other instances, a summary of the larger context may be brought into the citation to compact the discussion (e.g., Ps 68 in Eph 4:7–10; Isa 42:1 and Ps 2:7 in Luke 3:22). At times, pattern is invoked (e.g., Ps 40:6–8 in Heb 10:5–10). As a result, the relationship between the meanings is often worth considering.

Midrashic Technique and *Pesher* Technique

When it comes to expounding Scripture, there were common interpretive practices among the Jews. Two Jewish techniques, *midrash* and *pesher*, are particularly relevant to the question of how the NT presents some OT texts. Since these methods have already been summarized in the introduction to this volume, they will not be repeated here.

To note this background is not to endorse Jewish technique in its every use or the conclusions made by every Jewish interpreter; but the rules do reflect how texts were read and studied during the time that the NT was being written. A careful study of Jewish interpretation in this period shows that the Jewish community had a sense of which OT texts looked to the future and the end times.[5] The rabbis just debated how to put those many

---

5. Qumran 4QFlor. [= 4Q174] is a clear example.

pieces together. Many of the texts the NT uses were already well known in Judaism, though others were not so well known.

But if elements of Jewish interpretive technique paralleled the early church, then why did many Jews reject NT expositions of the OT? To answer this question, one has to be aware of theological presuppositions. Some Christian suppositions were shared with Judaism, but the issue of how the suppositions applied is debated.

Theological Presuppositions

As discussed in the introductory chapter, there are several presuppositions that influenced the way NT authors used the OT. Of the six listed below, the first three were shared with Judaism, whereas the last three were not.[6] The six suppositions were:

1. The Bible is God's Word
2. The one in the many (corporate solidarity)
3. Pattern in history (correspondence or typology)
4. These are the days of fulfillment
5. Now and not yet (the inaugurated fulfillment of Scripture)
6. Jesus is the Christ

These suppositions have been explained in the introduction to this volume and so will not be described again here. These crucial underpinnings of how to read the OT often play a key role in interpretations that on the surface look as if they are used out of context and build bridges to the kind of biblical-theological conclusions that the use of such texts makes. This is why students of the NT use of the OT need to familiarize themselves with these presuppositions, since they are foundational to an understanding of what a given NT author might be doing when he uses an OT text in his argument.

---

6. For a discussion of Christian suppositions, see E. Earle Ellis, "How the New Testament Uses the Old," in *New Testament Interpretation,* ed. I. Howard Marshall (Grand Rapids: Eerdmans, 1978), 199–219. For a full survey of views about how the Testaments relate to one another, see David L. Baker, *Two Testaments, One Bible,* 2nd ed. (Downers Grove, IL: InterVarsity Press, 1991).

UNIQUE ISSUES ABOUT THE BIBLE AND ITS REUSE: DUAL AUTHORSHIP, *SENSUS PLENIOR*, PATTERN FULFILLMENT, LANGUAGE REFERENT, AND THE PROGRESS OF REVELATION

The issue of dual authorship raises unique problems.[7] Although God inspired the authors who wrote the books, these human authors did not understand all they had written. First Peter 1:10–12 indicates that the human authors did not understand the time or circumstances of all they predicted (also Dan 12:5–13). Some have espoused the concept of *sensus plenior* ("fuller sense") to explain the differences between the intentions of the human author and the divine.[8] God knew the fuller sense (i.e., the *sensus plenior*) of what he revealed, even if the prophet did not. God could have multiple referents and time frames in mind, even if the prophet did not.

---

7. For a full discussion of the variations of approach to this question within evangelicalism, see Darrell L. Bock, "Evangelicals and the Use of the Old Testament in the New: Parts Land 2," *BSac* 142 (1985): 209–23, 306–19. Little has changed in the character of the four basic schools since this article. However, many evangelicals have contributed an array of technical studies on specific aspects of the use of the OT in the NT that fit within the view that pays careful attention to the use of the OT in its first-century Jewish context. Among these studies are Robert H. Gundry, *The Use of the Old Testament in St. Matthew's Gospel: With Special Reference to the Messianic Hope* (NovTSup 18; Leiden: Brill, 1975); Douglas J. Moo, *The Old Testament in the Gospel Passion Narratives* (Sheffield: Almond, 1983); Darrell L. Bock, *Proclamation from Prophecy and Pattern: Lucan Old Testament Christology* (JSNTSup 12; Sheffield: Sheffield Academic Press, 1987); Mark L. Strauss, *The Davidic Messiah in Luke-Acts: The Promise and Its Fulfillment in Lukan Christology* (JSNTSup 110; Sheffield: Sheffield Academic Press, 1995); Rikki E. Watts, *Isaiah's New Exodus and Mark* (WUNT 2:88; Tübingen: Mohr Siebeck, 1997); David W. Pao, *Acts and the Isaianic New Exodus* (WUNT 2.130; Tübingen: Mohr Siebeck, 2000). Each of these studies provides a good example of method. For Pauline materials a key work is Ellis, *Paul's Use of the Old Testament*.

8. For an evangelical assessment of *sensus plenior*, see Douglas J. Moo, "The Problem of *Sensus Plenior*," in *Hermeneutics, Authority, and Canon*, ed. D. A. Carson and John D. Woodbridge (Grand Rapids: Zondervan, 1986), 179–211, 397–405. For a Catholic treatment of this theme, see Raymond E. Brown, "Hermeneutics," *Jerome Bible Commentary* (Englewood Cliffs, NJ: Prentice Hall, 1968), 605–23. For a vigorous argument against this approach, see Walter C. Kaiser, Jr., *The Uses of the Old Testament in the New* (Chicago: Moody Press, 1985), though aspects of this argument are overstated, as Moo's essay indicates.

This concept is not a bad one, provided what the human author said and whatever more God says through him have a relationship in sense to what the human author originally said. However, often *sensus plenior* avoids such detailed association. Some employ the label *sensus plenior* in such a way as to avoid any analysis of the relationship between the uses. This merely descriptive use is of little help as an interpretive concept. The question is how the *sensus plenior* actually works.

Dual authorship and the issue of a "deeper sense" raise two key, related issues about meaning: language referent relationships and the progress of revelation. Because of the presence of typological patterns in history, it is possible to address two or more events in the same utterance. The flexibility within language allows this as well, if the descriptions are kept generic enough. Let's take a closer look. Three elements that contribute to meaning (besides the context of the utterance, which is a crucial factor) are (1) symbols, (2) sense, and (3) referent. We might consider the word *paraclete* in John 14 as an example.

The *symbol*s are the alphabetic signs of a word. In our example each letter of the word *p-a-r-a-c-l-e-t-e* comprises its symbols.

The *sense* is the dictionary definition of the word, its generic meaning in the context. Here that would be "comforter" or "encourager." This sense-level meaning is likely the term one would see in a translation of a particular term from one language to another.

But most important for specific interpretation is the specific thing, person, object, or concept referred to in context. This is the *referent*. In John 14, that referent is the Holy Spirit. Jesus has a specific figure in mind when he discusses a comforter.

But what happens when a text discusses a typological pattern as opposed to one event? The sense becomes key in the text, and the referents multiply as each context is addressed. In Isaiah 40:1–11, exile can refer both to the short-term situation (Israel's rescue through Cyrus) and to the long-term one (complete salvation) at one time. This is a simple example of the language-referent process. Salvation in the short-term setting merely refers to "deliverance from exile"; but in the long-term view of the NT the referent is "salvation in Christ" or "eternal life." Such a distinction reflects biblical typology and the progress of revelation, where the event escalates in its later fulfillment.

This type of pattern fulfillment may mean that though the sense of a term is maintained at one level in all the fulfillments, the referent is heightened to a new level of realization in the later fulfillment because of the new context's escalation of scope.[9]

The mention of the progress of revelation introduces an idea that is also a special feature of the concept of dual authorship, namely, that God progressively discloses his plan throughout history. This means that the force of earlier passages in God's plan becomes clearer and more developed as more of the plan is revealed in later events and texts. This increase in clarity often involves the identification of new referents, to which the initial referents typologically point forward.

This leads naturally into the issue of two ways of reading the Bible: historical-exegetical and theological-canonical. It also brings us back in a fresh way to the topic of the progress of revelation, by pointing to possible mechanisms for how it works. But before turning to kinds of readings and the progress of revelation, one illustration of referent expansion because of the progress of revelation is needed to indicate why this discussion in combination is so central. It is important to appreciate the variety of ways in which the NT uses the OT and how sometimes the explicit meaning that the NT surfaces works within the scope of the OT meaning but does so in a surprising direction.

In Acts 4:25–27, the church prayed. They appealed to Psalm 2:1 as an example text for the nations raging and the peoples plotting against the anointed one of Israel. Every Jew reading that psalm in its OT context would have assumed that the enemies gathered against the Messiah and his Lord would be comprised only of the nations, of Gentiles. Yet when the church prayed that prayer, the enemies opposed to the Messiah included seemingly pious Jews who nevertheless had rejected Jesus alongside Gentiles like Pilate.

What produced this change in referent? It simply emerged as the psalm was read by these early Christians in a fresh con-

---

9. For a fuller treatment of this typological-prophetic category, along with numerous examples in Luke–Acts, see Bock, *Proclamation from Prophecy and Pattern*, 47–51.

text brought about by the progress of divinely orchestrated events. The central idea, or sense, of the psalm was that many people stood opposed to God and his Messiah. So whoever opposed Messiah came under the heading of enemy in the psalm, whether that person was Jew or Gentile. Here is a wonderful example where the sense of a passage is fixed, but referents shift in surprising (but scripturally anticipated) directions as a result of the progress of divine events. (This text will be looked at in more detail further in the essay.)

WAYS OF READING SCRIPTURE AND THE PROGRESS OF REVELATION

All of these issues, then, contribute to the debate that rages around the NT use of the OT. Often, this debate involves the choice between an "exegetical" reading of the text — which preserves the grammatical-historical sense of the original author's intention — and a "theological" reading of the text — which perceives the eventual significance of that text in the light of the theological-canonical development of the text's subject matter. Is one of these two to be preferred? In actual fact, a recognition of the nature of dual authorship, the progress of revelation, and the use of pattern often makes this either/or choice unnecessary, since a both/and approach often works.[10] In addition, recognizing that a text can be read in one of two legitimate ways helps solve numerous issues that initially look more daunting.

Complementary Ways to Read Individual Texts

Two ways to read a biblical text are the "historical-exegetical" reading and the "theological-canonical" reading. These terms are not altogether adequate, however. Exegesis is theological, and

---

10. The categories of discussion raised in this section are a decidedly theologically conservative way to state the question. Many critics will simply pit the historical reading of a text in the OT against the reading of the NT without trying to probe the theological relationship between the two sets of text. For another, differently stated breakdown of this question attempting to deal with the same issue, see Vern Poythress, "Divine Meaning of Scripture," *WTJ* 48 (1986): 241–79.

theology should be exegetical. Still, the terms are chosen because of what each reading emphasizes. An historical-exegetical reading is primarily concerned with discerning the original author's message to his immediate audience in its specific, historical situation. A theological-canonical reading views the text in light of subsequent revelation.

In a theological-canonical reading, the progress of revelation may "refract" on an earlier passage so that the force of the earlier passage is clarified or developed beyond what the original author could have grasped. How this is done is debated among evangelicals and divides into three broad views. (1) Some argue that the later NT meaning tells us what the original OT author meant (even though in the original OT context that meaning was not very transparent). (2) Others argue that the OT revelation determines the meaning and defines the limits of the concept and thereby fixes that meaning. (3) Others argue that the NT meaning can develop or complement what the OT meant, but not in a way that ends up denying what the OT originally affirmed.[11]

Again an illustration may suffice. In Genesis 3:15, we encounter a promise that the serpent will bruise (i.e., "nip at") the heel of the child ("seed") of Eve, while the child will crush the serpent's head. In Christian circles, this is known as the *proto-evangelium*, the first revelation of the gospel. Reading Genesis 3:15 in this way is an example of a theological-canonical reading, especially referring the "seed" to Jesus Christ and the "serpent" to Satan. When Genesis was written, the human author could not have named Jesus. That understanding is "refracted" by the progress of revelation.

But is there more here? In the context of Genesis, and reading historically-exegetically, one could argue that the major thrust is

---

11. The author prefers this third option as being most consistent with how language works and with a belief that Scripture is designed to have a clear sense from the time it is given. Historically, the three options often reflect the difference between a Reformed amillennial approach (view 1), a traditional dispensational approach (view 2), and a progressive dispensational approach, which some historic premillenarians might also share (view 3).

that enmity is introduced within the creation.[12] The near context is certainly one emphasizing the judgment God brings into the creation because of Adam's disobedience. Nature and humanity are now at odds with one another, where previously harmony had existed. The snake is condemned to the ground (Gen. 3:14) and a battle between a man and a snake (enmity) takes place (v. 15a), with the now-grounded snake lunging at the man's most vulnerable target within its reach—the heel. The point of this text in simply its Genesis 3 context is that, after sin, the creation becomes more hostile to humankind. This certainly is a central point in Genesis 3.

However, *we do not have to force a choice* between the interpretations about Jesus as the seed of Eve and the introduction of hostility into the creation because of Adam's sin. Both are legitimate readings of the text. It is simply a matter of which type of reading and how much context is being drawn into the reading that allows one to make either point. Subsequent revelation makes it clear that Jesus is a son of Adam (Luke 3:38), even the Second Adam (Rom. 5:12–21), and compares Satan to one crushed by God through Jesus (16:20). The key in thinking through interpretations related to the use of the OT in the NT is understanding how the NT text is reading the OT text. Which of the two levels of reading is being applied? It is not always the case that a reading of the OT was or is limited to its exegetical level. It is often the case that the NT is reading these OT texts more canonically than exegetically.

The benefit of understanding the possibility of a dual reading is that a text has a full range of meaning, depending on the contextual limits placed upon the reading. Usually there is more in the text than we look for at any one level of reading. Some short-circuit the short-term message by leaping immediately to its larger, canonical significance. Others cut short God's development of the imagery by limiting themselves only to the short-term, historical context. The exegete of the Bible should be aware of the possibilities and be sensitive to both readings as the text is studied. The point is that the text can yield meaning

---

12. Josephus (*Ant.* 1.1.4.40–51) reads the text this way. He is one of the earliest commentators on this text.

at either level, and the meaning of the two readings are inter-related, as my illustrations below will seek to show.

Types of Usage

We now turn our attention to specific types of usage.[13] The use of the OT extends beyond fulfillment about Jesus. The first few categories deal with prophetic fulfillment; we then move to more illustrative and explanatory categories.

Prophetic fulfillment. Some texts reflect *directly prophetic* fulfillments. In such cases, the human author and the divine author share the expectation, and only one event or series of related events is in view. The NT fulfillment of Daniel 7:13–14 is an example of this (among many such uses, see Luke 21:27). The text pictures the granting of authority to "one like a son of man" by "the Ancient of Days" (God), pointing to the vice-regent and representative authority that the Son of Man has for God's people. The concept of the "one and the many" applies as well, since Daniel 7:27 associates the Son of Man with the vindication of the saints. Jesus picked up this image and used it of himself as his favorite self-designation (Mark 14:62; Luke 22:69). He chose it because it beautifully weaves together his divinely bestowed authority with his representative role on be-half of God's people. In this case what the NT sees as fulfilled is all that was in view—the decisive vindication of God's people through a representative authority figure.

Typological-prophetic. Other texts are *typological-prophetic* in their fulfillment. This means that pattern and promise are present, so that a short-term event pictures (or "patterns") a long-term fulfillment. This category is common for Christologi-cal readings. It is often debated whether this is a prophetic cat-egory in the strict sense of the term since often the pattern is not identifiable until the ultimate fulfillment is seen. In light of this observation about realization, it is best to distinguish two types of typological-prophetic fulfillment.

---

13. Moo, "Problem of *Sensus Plenior*," 179–211, is right to make the point that there are a variety of ways the NT uses the OT. His article contains numerous helpful references to periodical discussions on this theme.

The first is *typological-PROPHETIC* fulfillment. In these texts, there is a short-term historical referent, and yet the promise's initial fulfillment is such that an expectation remains that more of the pattern needs "filling up" to be completely fulfilled. The passage begs for and demands additional fulfillment (because God's Word is true). In fact, such expectation usually already existed among Jewish readers of these texts. A nonchristological example is Isaiah 65–66, where the descriptions of victory over the enemies are so idyllically portrayed as a new creation that the expectation arose of a greater, ultimate fulfillment than merely the return from the Babylonian exile. This fulfillment looked for total restoration, a type of "golden age." Although this is expressed most explicitly in Revelation 21–22, the expectation was a part of Jewish thinking about the end times as well (*1 Enoch* 6–36; 90).

Another way in which OT passages might be fulfilled in this way is for a promise to be only *partially* realized in the short term, so that the expectation of its *completion* is anticipated in the future. The image of the "day of the Lord" fits here. Although "day of the Lord imagery" is fulfilled in certain events within the OT (e.g., parts of Joel 2), the incomplete nature of that fulfillment anticipates the decisive period of such fulfillment (the "day *par excellence*").

Perhaps the best Christological example of this category is the servant figure of Isaiah (Isa 42:1–9; 49:1–13; 50:4–11; 52:13–53:12). In Isaiah 49:3, this figure is explicitly called "Israel." Now Jewish hope saw a future for a glorified servant figure, viewed in terms of the nation; but Judaism did not know how to integrate the servant's suffering into the image nor did it cope well with the individuality of the expression in Isaiah 52–53. The issue of pattern and "one in the many" was not sufficiently taken into account. It is the decidedly individual nature of the language in Isaiah 52–53 that serves as the major clue that both pattern and "one in the many" are invoked. Other OT texts that belong in this category include Ps 110:1 and 118.

The second typological-prophetic category is better labeled *TYPOLOGICAL-prophetic*. Here the pattern is not anticipated by the language, but is seen once the decisive pattern (or fulfillment pattern) occurs. Only then does the connection become clear. It is still a prophetic category because God designed the correspondence. But it works differently from the previous category in that the pattern is not anticipated or looked for until the fulfillment makes the pattern apparent.

Perhaps the outstanding illustration here is the use of Hosea 11:1 in Matthew 2:15 ("Out of Egypt I called my son."). In Hosea, when the book is read historically-exegetically, this remark applies to Israel as she was called out in the exodus. Everything about Hosea 11:1–4 looks to the past, although it is important to observe that Hosea 11:8–11 does not give up hope for Israel. It is possible that this larger context was in play along with the "one in the many" idea. Jesus' reenactment of the nation's exodus experience invokes the pattern of God working for his people again. So, the TYPOLOGICAL-*prophetic* connection can be made when one recognizes that the exodus itself is a "pattern" image for salvation and that Jesus as King (and as the "one in the many") is able to represent (and thus recapitulate) the nation's history.

Numerous righteous-sufferer psalms and other regal psalms applied to Jesus also belong to this class of usage (Pss 16; 22; 45; 69). These righteous-sufferer texts are used in the Passion accounts. In their historical-exegetical use, they described the plight of an innocent sufferer who is persecuted for identifying with God. But they are uniquely true of Jesus Christ. So when the NT points to their fulfillment in him, they emphasize the uniqueness of the way he fulfills them.

Psalm 45 is a beautiful illustration, since it is a wedding psalm, complete with reference to the queen who is marrying the king. Jesus never married a queen, but the "regal" tie allows the connection. What is said of the king's position before God is also true of the subsequent and decisive King, Jesus (Heb 1:8–9, with the heightened sense). Another possible example in this category is the use of Jeremiah 31:15 in Matthew 2:18, where the pattern of suffering and the "one in the many" connects Jesus and the nation.

Authoritative illustration. A final category that appeals to pattern or analogy can be called *authoritative illustration*, or what might be called *simple typology*. The term itself is reflected in the example of the exodus used by Paul in 1 Corinthians 10:1–13, where Paul explicitly speaks of exodus events as "types" (v. 6; the Greek term is *typos*; in many translations the term is translated "examples"). Here the goal is *not* prophetic but exhortation. The Corinthians are to learn from a past example about behavior to avoid. The use simply points to past lessons. This makes it distinct from the variety of typological-prophetic categories we mentioned earlier, where a forward looking element is embedded in the pattern. The problem is that typology in my mind involves a spectrum of usage, some of which is prophetic and some of which is not, so it is not a defining characteristic of the category as a whole, but comes to us in distinct ways. This illustrative use of the OT is common.

Principle. In a variation on such usage, the OT presents a *principle* of spiritual life. The text states a truth to be applied to living or appeals to an event to contemplate for its ethical significance. Jesus' multiple use of Deuteronomy during his temptation is a good example (cf. also Deut 5:16 in Eph 6:2–3, and Abraham and Rahab in Jas 2:20–26).

Allegory. This usage is rare. It appears in Paul's use of Hagar and Sarah in Galatians 4. Paul tells us that this is what he is doing here. The usage may well be polemical, working from examples that his opposition may well have provided. Allegory is a kind of rhetorical argument and is less rooted to historical context than other forms, but it is driven by a historical basis reread in light of newer revelatory realities, as in Galatians 4.

OT ideas, language, or summaries. Another use of the OT simply appeals to the use of ideas or summaries. The teaching of the OT is summarized (Luke 24:44–47). No texts are cited explicitly, but one senses that all the texts Luke uses in Luke–Acts stand behind the remark. A variation of this last use is the appeal to OT language, where no specific passage or context is in view, just the use of an OT image. So, for example, 1 Corinthians 4:6 appeals to the general OT teaching about pride.

SOME DETAILED EXAMPLES AND THE ISSUES OF MEANING AND INTENT

A Few Personal and Hermeneutical Comments

I have worked in this area personally for over thirty years. My introduction came in a biblical introduction class as a first year student at Dallas Theological Seminary. The professor was

S. Lewis Johnson, who introduced me to the reality that OT citations in the NT often followed the LXX rather than the MT. It was the first of many surprises that have come my way as I have examined actual texts where the OT is used in the NT. However, the reality of the frequent use of the LXX was my first warning that generalizations in the study of Scripture, even though they might seem logical, just might not square with the text. The simplest surface solution might not match the details. Nuancing in theology is not necessarily a bad thing, especially when it attempts to carefully consider the text.

Dr. Johnson, along with many of the professors at Dallas, followed the hermeneutical approach of E. D. Hirsch as advocated in *Validity in Interpretation*, a work that became a cornerstone for many in defending the integrity of meaning in hermeneutics.[14] Simply put, the goal of exegesis/interpretation involved pursuing the intention of the author, who is solely responsible for a text's meaning. That meaning, to have merit and stability, needed to be determinate and determinable, or else texts could mean anything. This Hirschian view was taught as an interpretive principle that should be embraced and passed on. (My theological education came in the midst of the inerrancy battles of the 1970s.) I was a willing student and embraced the belief.

One other value has molded my theological perspective, namely, the value of appealing to specific biblical examples in formulating beliefs about what the Bible does. This I also inherited from my time at Dallas. This commitment and the initial example of surprise I have already noted left an impression on me that doctrines or hermeneutical expectations formulated logically or strictly philosophically may not turn out to be biblical, even though they might make internal, perfect sense. I came to believe that it was imperative to check my instincts and logic (as well as my tradition) against the text.

I still hold to authorial intent, as I hope to show. I still cling to the belief that biblical examples should count for a great deal. But these three factors—respect for authorial intent, importance of biblical examples, and the surprises textual study has shown

---

14. E. D. Hirsch, Jr., *Validity in Interpretation* (New Haven: Yale Univ. Press, 1967).

me—have made me more cautious in the use of bold general-izations about how meaning works in the case of reused and future-oriented texts. Whereas I would have years ago answered the question about whether meaning changes with an unquali-fied no, I now want to answer with a combination of "no and yes," with each sphere of the answer more carefully defined. Such an answer, though it might appear self-contradictory, in fact, is not. If asked what changed my thinking about meaning, nothing says it better than a twist on a little refrain I learned in Sunday school: "the Bible shows me so."

This section presents three OT in the NT examples that explain my caution—one each from Acts, Romans, and 2 Co-rinthians. I would claim these readings reflect good exegeti-cal, historical-grammatical method. (By the way, in the interim Hirsch himself has also become more nuanced because of some of the same factors I hope to illustrate).[15] The resulting quali-fication, I believe, has better potential to defend the stability of meaning to which evangelicals are so committed as a basis for biblical authority. However, this approach also avoids de-fining the issue more narrowly than Scripture itself does. Such open-endedness leaves the door open for the development of meaning in line with an original intent, which still constrains meaning and prevents the text from meaning anything we want it to mean.

Before I turn to my examples, I wish to define two terms just introduced. They are "reused" texts and "future-oriented" texts. By "reused" texts, I am referring to the early church's

---

15. Two articles of his show this refinement; see E. D. Hirsch, "Meaning and Significance Reinterpreted," *Critical Inquiry* 11 (1984): 202–24; "Transhistorical In-tentions and the Persistence of Allegory," *New Literary History* 25 (1994): 549–67. It is important to note that what Hirsch means by allegory, theologians often refer to as typology, a point about which I have corresponded with Hirsch through email. These articles represent an adjustment of the older Hirschian perspective, a fine-tuning. They have not received as much attention as his original proposal and some reaction has been guarded. I think his adjustments are significant and have much merit. I plan to go in a similar direction with my remarks here. Of course, there is sig-nificant background to the debate involving Hirsch, who was reacting to important points made by Gadamer in his *Truth and Method* (New York: Seabury, 1975; trans. of 1960 German work). In particular, Gadamer convinced Hirsch that the line between meaning and application was not as clear as Hirsch originally suggested.

appeal to texts or language from the Jewish Scripture to make a theological point about Christian teaching or practice.[16] "Re-used" texts *possess an implicit, if not explicit, claim of divine design*, which tells us that meaning is discussed with application. By "future-oriented" texts, I refer to a temporal open-endedness to the future that is inherent in the original setting of many reused Jewish Scripture texts.

The main point is this: Any freshness of meaning that emerges in such texts is a function of the development of that meaning in line with the text's inherent "futureness" and in line with, but not necessarily a reproduction of, the text's original meaning. In addition, that "freshness" is informed by the presence of new factors in the progress of revelation within the movement of the history of salvation, factors not obvious at the time of the original production of the text. It is such factors that keep us from reading in "flat" or "one dimensional" ways. It is also these factors that make a text capable of being read at different exegetical or canonical levels or from different theological perspectives. It might be well to speak of a meaning in the original setting and the meaning of a text in its reuse. My thesis will be that the meanings are connected and fundamentally one, but not always exactly the same. This is why I often refer to this approach as the historical contexts view.

Interpreters express these factors in various ways. They might speak of a text operating at a biblical theological level, allude to the "progress of revelation," appeal to application alone, or argue for the presence of typology to try and maintain the unity of meaning. All of these explanations can be legitimate. No matter which of the above explanations we give, my point is that the resultant reading emerges from factors that were often implicit in the earlier text, but hardly explicit at the time of its original composition. In other words, those factors became evident as a result of the text finally beginning to enter the very futurity to which the text ultimately was aimed.

I do not argue that this is true of every future-oriented text. To spot this factor and understand it is important, because it

---

16. I refer to Jewish Scripture deliberately in these examples. When the works we refer to as NT were written, there was no sense of an "Old" Testament. They merely were the Scriptures that Jews used.

recognizes how temporality impacts a text's interpretive history. It also can explain how a text can "deepen" in meaning *without departing from its inherent sense*. This factor suggests that meaning remains unchanged at one level and fresh at another.[17]

Three Examples of Complex OT/NT Use

Psalm 2:1–2 in Acts 4:25–26

The use of Psalm 2:1–2 is fascinating, as Acts 4:25–26 is the only place in the NT that appeals to these verses. The text of the psalm reads, "Why do the nations rage (perfect tense), and the peoples are imagining (imperfect tense) a vain thing? The kings of the earth set themselves (perfect tense) and the rulers are taking counsel (imperfect tense) together, against the Lord and his anointed ..." (pers. trans.).

There is virtually no controversy over the psalm's meaning, though its setting is much discussed. The psalm warns the gathered and conspiring nations that opposition to God and his anointed is futile. Rather, one should give homage to the son as Yahweh's representative. The anointed's sonship is affirmed in line with promises made to David in 2 Samuel 7. The nations are warned about God's wrath and are called to honor the son with a submissive kiss of respect in vv. 10–12. Anyone reading this psalm would see that it discusses how the nations (*goyim*, v. 2) are gathered against the king whom God has set "upon Zion, my holy mountain." The kings of the nations are addressed throughout (vv. 2, 10), so we are not looking at internal opponents of the king within Israel. In the psalm, the nations and the peoples gathered against the king of Israel stand duly warned.[18]

---

17. "Future orientedness" is a factor that I believe evangelicals have largely ignored. Sensitivity to the temporal perspective of a text appreciates a dimension of perspectivalism that modern hermeneutics and its key figures such as Heidegger, Gadamer, and Ricoeur discuss in some detail. It also allows one to recognize such factors and yet not succumb to the relativism that total perspectivalism often embraces. Works that treat this area have been noted in n. 15.

18. Peoples stands in parallelism to the nations, which is a reference to non-Israelites (Ps 44:2, 14). The kings of vv. 2 and 10 stand in contrast to the king of Israel in v. 6 (Ps 76:12; 89:27; 102:15; 138:4; 148:11; Is 24:21). Kings and peoples are in parallel in Ps 148:11. On rulers, see Isa 40:23; Hab 1:10; Judges 5:3.

The fact that this psalm appears as the second psalm should also not be lost. It is the national counterpart to the first psalm. Here is God's commitment to his people. Its placement at this prominent location in the Psalter tells us that the expression of this call and warning was part of Israel's worship. As we will see, its prominence was not lost on Jews who continued to look for its full realization.

Far more contentious is the question of the psalm's original setting.[19] Though some have proposed David (2 Sam 5 or 10), Solomon (1 Kings 11:21), or Ahaz, it is generally recognized that no single, clear setting emerges. Even more contentious is the question of whether it was part of a coronation setting or simply part of a declaration of Davidic sovereignty. Either way, the text's point is its declaration of Yahweh's support for his regent-king.

The lack of background for Psalm 2 has led some to suggest the passage is strictly prophetic and messianic about the future (so no immediate referent to a near kingship). This reading argues that we have a unique text, with only one referent, the future Messiah. Perhaps this might be the way to see the passage, but I think a better explanation exists. The reference to the nations and the text's placement at the front of the Psalter tell us this is a fundamental text about the regal rights that David's line possessed because of God.

Now, the Israelites could direct their hopes toward a future ideal Davidic ruler because of commitments God had made to Israel about national *shalom* in the land, commitments dating

---

19. For a survey of options, see A. F. Kirkpatrick, *The Book of Psalms* (Cambridge Bible for Schools and Colleges; Cambridge: Cambridge Univ. Press, 1891), 5–6, and J. J. Stewart Perowne, *The Book of Psalms*, Vol. 1: *Psalms 1–72* (Grand Rapids: Zondervan, 1976 printing of 1878 ed.), 113. More recently it has been common to argue that a specific event is less important to the understanding of the psalm because the passage expresses kingship in terms of its ideal. Kirkpatrick (6–7) says that "as successive kings of David's line failed to realize their high destiny, men were taught to look for the coming of One who should fulfill the Divine words of promise, giving them a meaning and reality beyond hope and imagination." Peter Craigie, *Psalms 1–50* (WBC; Waco, TX: Word, 1983), 66, argues that "the psalmist is not necessarily referring to any particular event in history.... The language reflects primarily all—or any nation—that do not acknowledge the primacy of Israel's God, and therefore, of Israel's king."

back to Abraham and repeated to David. This created a kingship expectation, what Caird has called a "situation vacant" promise.[20] Here each applicant, as he comes on the scene to assume David's throne, might be the ideal one. In one sense, the hope is eschatological; in another sense, it already resides in the kingship through God's promise that points to that future hope. One day, all that God promised about regal sonship will be realized.

Perhaps Perowne summarizes best: "But though the poem was occasioned by some national event, we must not confine its application to that event, nor need we even suppose that the singer himself did not feel his words went beyond their first occasion."[21] What motivated the original expression of the psalm was a commitment God had made that explained who this king was. Psalm 2 was intended as a declaration of God's commitment to this kingship and as an open-ended warning about the authority of the one God chose to represent him. One day God will give judgment on behalf of this figure and his line.

Submission to the king is advised, because one day God will judge and vindicate his authority. Here is the stable point of meaning for the psalm. However, it must be noticed that anyone originally reading this psalm would have naturally placed the discussion in the context of Israel among the nations, as that setting is expressed in the original referents of Psalm 2:1–2. In other words, the opposition the psalm most naturally calls for in its original setting is an opposition coming from Gentiles and those outside of Israel. This is the crucial observation for the hermeneutics of the use of Psalm 2 in Acts 4 and the question of a change of meaning.

Before treating Acts 4, let me simply note how consistently Jews read the psalm in this "Gentile" manner. In *Psalms of Solomon* 17:21–25, probably in reaction to Pompey of Rome in 63 B.C., there is expressed the hope that one day a military Messiah would arise, who would crush the nations:

> See, Lord, and raise up for them a king, the son of David,
> to rule over your servant Israel in the time known to you,

---

20. George B. Caird, *The Language and Imagery of the Bible* (Philadelphia: Westminster, 1980), 57–58.

21. Perowne, *The Book of Psalms*, 1:113.

> O God. Undergird him with the strength to destroy the
> unrighteous rulers, to purge Jerusalem from gentiles,
> who trample her to destruction; in wisdom and righ-
> teousness to drive out the sinner from the inheritance; to
> smash the arrogance of sinners like a potter's jar; to shat-
> ter their substance with an iron rod [Ps 2:9!]; to destroy
> the unlawful nations with the word of his mouth; at his
> warning the nations will flee from his presence; and he
> will condemn sinners by the thoughts of their hearts.[22]

That the language of the psalm is applied to the nations
is obvious from just reading the text. Similar may be the use at
Qumran (4QFlor 1:18–2:2), which also cites and explains Psalm
2:1–2.[23] The fragmentary nature of the text makes matters less
than clear, but it appears that the nations-versus-Israel context is
likely intended on the basis of what visible fragments of the passage show. The later *midrash* to Psalm 2 sees a timeless principle
true for Israel from the start of her history. Various figures are
the "opposition." Pharoah, Sisera, Sennacherib, Nebuchadnez-
zar, and the generation after the flood are named. In the end,
Gog and Magog will also stand as the last opponents to oppose
God and his anointed.[24] My survey of Jewish readings shows
that in three different periods and contexts, the nation saw expressed in Psalm 2 the hope of victory against the nations. The
midrash is a clear example of what we have called an ancient
"pattern" (typological) reading. What is true in one era also belongs to another period.

With this background both to Psalm 2 and its reading in
Judaism, let us consider this psalm in Acts 4. The introductory
formula should not be ignored. God is the master, the One who
made the heavens and the earth and the sea and all that is in
them. Thus, it is the sovereign, creator God who is addressed
in this prayer. The language recalls texts like 2 Kings 19:15 and
Isaiah 37:16, where God is called "you, the one having made the
heavens and the earth" (see LXX version), as well as Nehemiah

---

22. Citation is from James H. Charlesworth, *Old Testament Pseudepigrapha* (New York: Doubleday, 1985), 2:667.

23. The text is also known as 4Q174.

24. For the citation of the full text, see William Braude, *The Midrash on the Psalms*, 2 vols. (Yale Judaica Series; New Haven: Yale Univ. Press, 1959), 35–37.

9:6 (see also 2 Esd 9:6 LXX). The first two texts picture God with his cherubim. The cry in 2 Kings and Isaiah is for Hezekiah's vindication in the face of Sennacherib's threats. It is the nation's opposition to the king that is at issue. Nehemiah's context is Israel's confession of the need of forgiveness and a cry for God not to abandon the people he has defended over the ages. Their distressful situation in exile needs his strong hand. They are there because of their sin. The point of the formula is that the sovereign God has always defended his faithful people and is needed again.

It only takes one reading to see the surprise here. As is common practice in the early church's use of Scripture, key Greek terms in the psalm show up in the following exposition and thereby show where the conceptual links are and how the text is being read. This is a practice often referred to as *gezerah shewa*, or equivalent regulation (see a fuller explanation of this in the introduction to this volume). The link terms include "gathered against" (*synechthesan* vv. 26, 27) the holy servant whom God anointed, Jesus; Herod, together with (note the emphatic *te kai* with *syn*) Pontius Pilate, standing together with the nations (forms of *ethnos* in vv. 25, 27) and the peoples (plural forms of *laos* in vv. 25, 27), meaning Israel (!).

The plural "peoples" may see Israel made up of various parts. Everything fits the pattern of how the text might be read and has been read in Israel until we get to "peoples" and "Israel." In verse 28, as the early church confesses and submits to the sovereign design of the ruler God (note God as *despota* in v. 24), the gathered disciples name Israel as a co-conspirator against the Messiah. Israel is now numbered among the enemies described in Psalm 2. Her opposition makes her a referent. Even though the plural (*ethne laoi*) is unusual, it is likely that the plural is retained to show the explicit connection to the psalm. The addition of the explanatory *laois Israel* is designed to make the identification clear, just as the mention of Herod and Pilate does. (Note also how Israel is part of "all the peoples" mentioned in Luke 2:29–32.)

It is time for our hermeneutical question. Has the meaning of Psalm 2 changed? I say, "No, in terms of sense, and yes, in terms of referents." The key to the early church's reading of this psalm still rests in the meaning that there exist nations and peoples who gather against the Lord and his Messiah. The battle in which the early church found itself was one that was playing out a conflict described long ago in Scripture. That text had expressed a principle about how the world had related to God's plan and those he had chosen. It also expressed a hope that one day God would show One to be all that was promised and hoped for.

But now something had changed. Now a detail existed that did not exist previously. God had identified the Anointed One in the resurrection-exaltation-vindication. Once the Messiah became known, then the identity of the opponents gathered against him became clear. The situation, once vacant, had now become identified, at least in part. *As a result, the scope of the referents, which appeared to be limited to the kings and rulers of nations, appears to expand, yet within linguistic boundaries of the language used in the psalm's conceptual core.* Any who join in the "conspiracy" that surrounds the Anointed One, now identified in God's vindicating action as Jesus, come under the scope of the text's meaning. If you asked those who prayed in Acts 4 if they were "applying" the text's significance or indicating what they thought it meant in their circumstance, I believe they would have looked back at you cross-eyed. In this case, application and meaning merge as the combination of application and meaning is the core of the psalm.

There is a major qualification to what I have just said. The expansion is one of "appearance." My point is that the expansion emerged against the expectations that the text generated when it was read before the details of the plan were completed. More revelation made for more clarity. Neither a story nor a promise is done until the last chapter is written and the one who made the promise either stops talking or acting. One making an open-ended promise can always develop or elaborate on it as time passes. In doing so, earlier commitments become clearer in their import.

Note also that no referents were lost in the expansion. The Gentile nations still gather against Jesus. In fact, one could suggest that the setting has opened up the psalm's meaning, not by changing it but by revealing its depth of meaning. There are no actual "kings" mentioned in the passage; rather there are only rulers, namely, prefects and tetrarchs, who represent kings and nations. First-century political Israel is kingless, yet still opposes, largely on the basis of what her religious leaders (rulers?) have done.

The use of this text cautions us against being overly literal. The meaning has "changed" (read "has expanded and been clarified") even as it has remained the same. As events became clear by aspects of realization of the future hope anticipated by the text, its meaning also was clarified. I think this passage is exceedingly instructive to us hermeneutically. Note also that it takes both historical contexts to appreciate the full reading. *In addition, the resultant reading does not cancel or deny the earlier reading, but complements it.*

I know of only two attempts to explain this psalm in other ways than to acknowledge an expansion of referent here. One argues that the placement of Psalm 2 after Psalm 1 in the Psalter shows that enemies can come from within the nation, from the wicked within the nation. I would suggest, however, that this theological synthetic reading is not an exegesis of Psalm 2 alone in its context, but a theological deduction related to its canonical-compositional locale. We already suggested that this reading denies the internal referents in verses 2 and 10 that are addressed to other kings and to whom they represent. In addition, there is some evidence that these two psalms were read as one by some Jewish and Christian interpreters.[25] However, even if one sees them in this light, most recognize that the psalms were originally separate and were only combined later into a unit.

Seen in this way, this first attempt merely makes my point a different way. It sees another, outside text impacting how this text should be read. Rather than placing the shift in a NT context, it argues that the door to the expansion is already possible in the setting that placed Psalm 1 next to Psalm 2. This kind of canonical argument is not the one I would prefer to make, but in terms of hermeneutical approach, it also attempts to engage the text beyond its original setting into its recast role, and

---

25. Craigie, *Psalms 1–50*, 59–60. See *b. Ber.* 9b and the Western tradition of Acts 13:33 as reflected in D and the *itala*, which cites Psalm 2:7 as part of the first psalm. On their distinct messages, see Perowne, *The Book of Psalms*, 107–8. It may be that the first psalm was seen as a prologue and the second psalm was treated as the first psalm.

as such reaffirms the hermeneutical tack we are taking. Such a reading just places an expanded referent earlier in the historical sequence at a point where the psalms were collected.

The second attempt argues that the original psalm is about the Gentiles alone and that the Acts 4 reference to Israel does not identify Israel with the "peoples," but that "peoples" is merely a parallel reference to nations with Israel operating as a "genitive of relationship," so we have peoples who are related to Israel in their opposition to God's people. Thus, there is no meaning change to the original psalm. Israel is simply seen in her position as suffering in exile under submission to the nations.

Two problems plague this view. First, an allusion to Israel in exile in this context is extremely subtle. Why mention exile in a contextual discussion where Herod and Pilate and Gentiles and especially the people (Luke 23!) have recently been responsible for Jesus' death? This leads to the second objection. The driving force of the opposition to Jesus in the Lucan narrative is the Jewish leadership and the people of the nation (Luke 23). The Jews in *this* story are not victims under the Gentile thumb, but instigators. They are responsible for the most recent opposition, the arrest of the apostles.

Thus, the attempt to claim that the meaning of Psalm 2 and the new setting are precisely the same fails. So, does meaning change? I say this example tells us, "No and yes." The hermeneutical key in describing the use is to pay careful attention to each historical context and a range of meaning that the original utterance can tolerate at the level of its sense.

Deuteronomy 30:12–14 in Romans 10:6–8

One hesitates to discuss this Romans passage since it is an exegetical minefield.[26] For our hermeneutical concerns, most of these exegetical questions are not important. We focus only on those key hermeneutical issues.

Deuteronomy 30:12–14, the passage to which Paul appeals in Romans 10:6–8, follows a section of Deuteronomy (30:1–10)

---

26. For a thorough treatment of the text, see Mark A. Seifrid, "Paul's Approach to the Old Testament in Rom 10:6–8," *Trin J* n.s. 6 (1985): 3–37.

where God has presented his response to the predicted prospect of Israel's unfaithfulness. That passage anticipates that the nation will experience the curses of covenant unfaithfulness for her actions. It is part of a larger context, starting with Deuteronomy 28, where the blessing and cursing of covenant are set forth. In a real sense Deuteronomy 30:5–10 takes on a prophetic air as it looks to a time of restoration and return when the nation, scattered among the nations, calls to mind what is said, returns to God, and obeys him (30:2–3). As God regathers them, he will bring them back to the land, and prosper and multiply them more than their fathers (30:4–5). In fact, God will circumcise their hearts to love God that they may live (30:6).[27] Curses will fall on their enemies and obedience will return to the people (30:7–8). Prosperity will follow, *if* they obey the Lord (30:9–10).

At this point the exhortation turns back to the present and issues a call for obedience in Deuteronomy 30:11: "Now what I am commanding you today is not too difficult for you or beyond your reach." The key question is, "What is the commandment in the original context of Deuteronomy?" Either of the primary candidates involves an allusion to the law that God has just revealed and is renewing. Thompson and Von Rad argue that the commandment is "the whole of the divine will as set forth in Deuteronomy."[28] Craigie speaks of the renewal teaching at Moab, to the "law of the covenant."[29] This second option seems correct. It fits the historical setting and stands in contrast to the remark coming before the chapter in Deuteronomy 29:29, that "the secret things belong to the LORD our God, but the things revealed belong to us and to our children forever, that we may follow all the words of this law." Just as 30:12–14 emphasizes that the law need not be searched for, since God has made it

---

27. This circumcision sounds like Deuteronomy 10:16, but there are major differences. Where earlier God had called for circumcised hearts, in Deuteronomy 30 God will provide such a heart. The language is like Jeremiah 4:4; 31:31–35; 32:39–41 and Ezekiel 36:24–27 in its emphasis on spiritual renewal. See Gerhard von Rad, *Deuteronomy* (OTL; London: SCM, 1966), 183.

28. Von Rad, *Deuteronomy*, 183; J. A. Thompson, *Deuteronomy* (London: Inter-Varsity Press, 1974), 286.

29. Peter Craigie, *The Book of Deuteronomy* (NICOT; Grand Rapids: Eerdmans, 1976), 364.

known and brought it near, so the last verse of Deuteronomy 29 makes the same point. The law is not a mystery. It is present and comprehensible. There is only the need to respond to it.

In Deuteronomy 30:12–14 comes the affirmation that the commandment is neither inaccessible nor unattainable. So the response is possible. One need not think that understanding the law is unattainable because it is hidden away in heaven, nor is it inaccessible because it is tucked away behind an insuperable barrier "beyond the sea." There is no need to send someone "to get it and proclaim it to us so we may obey it." Deuteronomy 30:14 gives the explanation, "No, the word [the commandment of v. 11] is very near you; it is in your mouth and in your heart so you may obey it." The covenant being renewed by the nation has been clearly revealed; its message is clear. It represents a choice between two ways: life and prosperity versus death and adversity (vv. 15–16). A warning follows concerning the peril of turning away from what is set forth. Should they turn away, they will then perish (vv. 17–18). Heaven and earth serve as witnesses (v. 19a). So they should choose life by loving the Lord, obeying his voice, and holding fast to him that they might live in the land (vv. 19–20).

Here is an exhortation to respond to God's grace and experience blessing. In its original setting, the point of Deuteronomy is about the accessibility of life as it relates to the presentation of the law. It reinforces a point made both at the start and the end of the book (Deut 4:6–8; 29:29).

It should come as no surprise that for some within Judaism these verses and images became almost proverbial in force. They were related to the law or to wisdom, which is what the law contained. Only one text that we have is certain to predate Paul's use. First Baruch 3:24–37 (c. 100–150 BC) adapts the image in describing wisdom as that which God has. He "gave her [wisdom] to his servant Jacob and to Israel, whom he loved" (3:36 NRSV).[30] In 4:1, this wisdom is identified, "She is the book of the commandments of God, the law that endures forever. All who hold her fast will live, and those who forsake her will die." The relevant use of Deuteronomy is in Baruch 3:29–30 and reads, "Who has gone

---

30. For this date range for Baruch, see C. A. Evans, *Ancient Texts for New Testament Study* (Peabody, MA: Hendrickson, 2005), 17 (c. 100 BC); Howard Clark Kee, *NRSV Cambridge Annotated Study Apocrypha* (Cambridge: Cambridge Univ. Press, 1994), xxii (c. 150 BC).

up into heaven, and taken her, and brought her down from the clouds? Who has gone over the sea, and found her, and will buy her for pure gold?" Other later Jewish texts speak of heaven being emptied of Torah or of its being so near that one is accountable for the lack of knowledge about it (*Midrash Deuteronomy* 8.6–7; *Tanchuma* 27b). These also allude to the law as the referent.

So we come to Romans 10:6–8. We quote the text, so the difference in Paul's reading is immediately obvious.

> But the righteousness that is by faith says: "Do not say in your heart [see Deut 9:4 LXX], 'Who will ascend into heaven?'" (*that is*, to bring Christ down) "or 'Who will descend into the deep?'" (*that is*, to bring Christ up from the dead). But what does it say? "The word is near you; it is in your mouth and in your heart," *that is*, the message concerning faith that we proclaim. (emphasis added)

As difficult as Paul's reading is, we can be grateful that at least Paul tells us what his referents are in the three explanatory *tout' estin* clauses (see italics above): Christ in light of his ascension, Christ in light of his death, and the word of faith preached by Paul and others. One suspects that Paul has inserted the explanatory remarks because he is aware of what the normal reading is. Seifrid states the problem most clearly:

> Paul uses a citation which in its original context served as an exhortation to maintain (by obedience!) the stipulations of covenant made in Moab, as a depiction of "the righteousness by faith"; and he clearly employs the passage in a manner which conceives a close relationship between the text of Deut 30:11–14 and the apostolic message.[31]

---

31. Seifrid, "Paul's Approach," 27. Matthew Black, "The Christological Use of the Old Testament in the New Testament, *NTS* 18 (1971): 8–9, finds the textual reading so transformed that he says that it is "an interpretation which can only be described, from the modern point of view, as a drastic and unwarrantable allegorizing." Perhaps the major point that makes it seem so is how Paul has separated the text from a tie to the law. However, Paul does attempt to justify this and the resulting distinction he makes of two ways to pursue righteousness in 10:3–4. If Paul's temporal/telic premise about the relationship of law to Jesus is correct, then the move is neither allegorizing nor arbitrary.

The hermeneutical question is: How does Paul take a text about law and make it a text about Jesus? Or has the text's meaning changed?

As radical as Paul's reading seems to be, it can be defended with the same "no and yes" answer as our example from Acts 4. Attention to both the deuteronomistic context and to Paul's own explanation in Romans provides major clues as to Paul's reading. The meaning of Deuteronomy 30 is stable. Meaning has not changed in that Paul sees Deuteronomy affirming the accessibility of the word that God reveals for his people. When God reveals his word, it is neither inaccessible nor unattainable. He makes it quite visible.

Still another factor may make the Pauline reading appropriate. Deuteronomy 30:1–11, the passage that precedes the one Paul cites, looks to a day when God will restore people to an obedient walk. God through a new act will enable his people to respond to his will. For Paul, the "circumcised heart" that God promised he would provide (Deut 30:6) came in the work of the exalted Christ (Phil 3:3).

Thus, built within the original regiving of the law to which Israel was to respond was the hope that God would one day remedy that which the law from the outside could not do. That hope was expressed in the larger OT context. What was missing in Deuteronomy is *how and through whom* this internal work would come. The anticipated work was both connected to the law and distinct from it, as the later new covenant idea shows. With the coming of Jesus, new, more specific referents emerged. Details that the original setting of Deuteronomy lacked were now present. The meaning of what Deuteronomy proclaimed could be deepened, *not because Deuteronomy 30:11–14 is a prophetic text*, but because of how the law itself would come to meet its realization in Christ.[32] This is what Paul preached.

---

32. I make this point, because some reject such an appeal on the correct basis that Deuteronomy 30:11–14 is not a prophetic text. For such a rejection, see Douglas Moo, *The Epistle to the Romans* (NICNT; Grand Rapids: Eerdmans, 1996), 652. My point in appealing to 30:1–10 is more nuanced. It is that within what God calls for in responding to the law in 30:11–20 is an expectation how one day that hope can be realized. Frank Thielman, *Paul and the Law: A Contextual Approach* (Downers Grove, IL: InterVarsity Press, 1994), 208–10, takes a similar approach on Deuteronomy 30:1–10.

Paul has already explained in Romans 6–8 how it is that Jesus brings the promise of the life-giving Spirit, so the apostle need not mention it here (see also Rom 2:29). In other words, the Spirit's presence through Jesus had already been explained in the letter as part of "his word of preaching" about salvation and Jesus. This provides the theological backdrop for Paul's fresh move.

However, this is not all. Romans 10:3b–4 declares how Paul could justify this reading. Paul works up to this argument, beginning in Romans 9:30–31, by stating the failure of most of Israel. There he notes that Gentiles obtained righteousness, the one by faith, whereas Israel failed, because she sought a law of righteousness and thus failed to attain that toward which the law was aimed. Though Paul does not name what the law aimed at, in all likelihood it is life or righteousness that is meant. They failed, he tells us in 9:32–33, because they stumbled over the stumbling stone laid in Zion, a reference to Jesus. The reference to believing in him in 10:12–13 reveals this identification as it picks up the thought given from 9:32–33. So they did not subject themselves to the righteousness that comes from God (by faith through Christ's gift of life and the Spirit, part of the riches of 10:12 as described in chapters 6–8).

In Romans 10:4, Paul makes his key hermeneutical move. He declares that Christ is the *telos* of the law for righteousness to everyone who believes. There is a library of debate around whether *telos* means "end," "goal," or both. I tend to agree with Seifrid that it is both.[33] The imagery of attaining a goal in pursuit of something is present in 9:31, yet Paul's normal handling of the issue of law suggests "end" (Gal 3). Such a subtle double entendre fits this former rabbi.

Fortunately, no matter which meaning exists, it does not alter the hermeneutical point. For whether Paul meant end, goal, or both, the point is that the law has a relationship to Jesus that makes him a turning point for the law. What could be said of the law could be said of him. He was the key revelation of God's will now, just as the law had been.[34] As such, to make him the

---

33. Seifrid, "Paul's Approach," 6–10.

34. Paul takes up the other alternative in Romans 10:5, where he states that one who pursues life by a law of righteousness is required to obey completely to find life. That is the way he argues that Israel has wrongly chosen to seek life. By not

subject of Deuteronomy 30:11–14, though a fresh reading, is not a violation of the text—that is, once the passage is put into the appropriate temporal perspective.

Once again, meaning has remained the same (in terms of basic sense) and changed (with regard to referent, given the effect of revelation's progress). What is the same sense is the imagery: one need not search high and low for God's revelation. What is new is that God has made revelation clear in Jesus' exalted position and death, not in the law.[35] So Paul preaches a message that is to be heeded, a message as visible and available as the law was. So Israel's failure to respond to such a manifest demonstration of God's presence and report can only be the result of their being "a disobedient and obstinate people." This disobedience is what Romans 10:21 stresses with Paul's citation of Isaiah 65:2. Hermeneutically, Paul reads the imagery of revelation now in terms of the revelation God has brought in Christ. Once again, has meaning changed? The answer is "No—in terms of sense" and "Yes—in terms of referents."

---

choosing faith but their own righteousness through law, they have left themselves a standard they cannot meet, as Romans 1–3 had already shown. So Paul's contrast is not law–gospel, or two competing views of law within the law, but righteousness sought on our own attainment on the basis of law versus a righteousness that God now has provided and had promised when the law was given.

35. The one major change in the imagery is the shift from Deuteronomy's "beyond the sea" to Paul's "into the abyss." This alteration is not as dramatic as it first may appear. First, the sea and the abyss were often associated in Judaism, though admittedly often with the term *tehom*, not *yam* as appears in Deuteronomy (Jonah 2:3–10; Sir 1:3; 16:18: 24:5, 9). In Jonah, the imagery is also tied to the image of a grave. Second, all the change does is to alter the direction of the image, not its real point. What was a horizontal image (beyond the sea) has become a more balanced vertical image (in relation to the previous mention of heaven). The association of sea and depth allows the move to be an easy one to conceive (see Ps 107:26; sea is often contrasted to heaven, e.g., Pss 33:7; 77:16–17). Finally, there may be precedent for reading the text this way in Judaism. *Targum Neofiti on Deuteronomy* 30:12–13 reads, "The Law is not in heaven that one may say, 'Would that we had one like the prophet Moses who would ascend into heaven and fetch it for us and make us hear the commandments that we might do them.' Neither is the Law beyond the Great Sea that one may say, 'Would that we had one like the prophet Jonah who would descend into the depths of the Great Sea and bring it up for us and make us hear the commandments that we might do them." Note how both the horizontal and vertical images are mixed in the sea reference here, though there is no explicit mention of abyss.

One final point remains. Is Paul's usage an application or is it the meaning of the text now that the new era has come? Once again, I believe a distinction here is hard to maintain. I think the proper response to this question is that it is both an application (in light of the fresh setting) and the meaning, at least now that the new era has come (in light of the new meaning's connection to the old stable sense). I cannot accept the judgment of Fitzmyer that Paul is merely applying the text here.[36] Too many uses of the OT in this context are being piled up to make a combined and powerful textual argument for Paul. Moo sums up my point well:

> Because Christ, rather than the law, is now the focus of God's revelatory word (see 10:4), Paul can "replace" the commandment of 30:11–14 with Christ. Paul's application of Deut 30:12–14, then, is of course not a straightforward exegesis of the passage. But it is a valid application of the principle of that passage in the context of the development of salvation history.[37]

Let me make one qualifying observation about this citation from Moo. When Moo refuses to call this Romans text a straightforward exegesis of Deuteronomy 30, I think he means that Paul is not simply employing the original context in order to affirm the original sense. With that point I would agree. My hermeneutical point here more closely ties meaning and application together than Moo does.

This represents a major point in all the test cases in this essay. Fresh meaning has emerged in light of the presence of new details in the plan that "refract back" on earlier texts, deepening them with a more complex understanding than what the original human author intended. Later revelatory acts of God explain earlier texts of hope and give them more detail. Sensitivity to the temporal progress of Scripture results in a more sensitive awareness of how the message develops as well as how it now should be understood. What God had said about the law is now just as true about Christ. Paul makes his application in part because he now sees it as the meaning of God's actions. This

---

36. Joseph A. Fitzmyer, *Romans* (AB; New York: Doubleday, 1993), 590.
37. Moo, *Romans*, 653.

realization helps him to appreciate in a fresh way what Scripture teaches and affirms. To simply call this application, I believe, understates Paul's theological claim. Paul is showing how Jesus fulfills promise and God's revealed plan, even as the nation rejects him as Messiah and Lord. For Paul, that promise and plan, expressed in old inspired texts, finds its ultimate meaning in Christ (Rom 1:1–4; 16:25–27). In this sense the ultimate reading of such texts is Christocentric.

Leviticus 26 and 2 Samuel 7:14 in 2 Corinthians 6:16–18

The last test case is more complex, because many OT texts appear. So what is expressed may be influenced in part by the juxtaposition of texts present. But this does not alter my fundamental point: the early church read older texts in light of developments of these old themes within the OT and through the impact of Christ, including his death and exaltation. In fact, such examples indicate that readings of an OT passage are impacted by the triangulation of texts and events. Sometimes what we are getting is not exegesis but a biblical theology of divine events.

In addition, these texts appear in an exhortation that itself is combining OT language from texts involving command or promise. Nonetheless, in another sense, this example is more startling, because a key citation in 2 Corinthians 6:18 is clearly the language of 2 Samuel 7:14, as is noted by virtually any commentator on this passage.[38] As to the influence of another text on the wording of the verse 18 about sons and daughters, two candidates are mentioned: Isaiah 43:6 and Deuteronomy 32:19. The impact of one of these texts is surely there, but the point is *that either way the combination* has produced a new reading of the earlier text and a fresh resultant theological point rooted in a scriptural claim.[39] Finally, there is an allusion to God the Al-

---

38. Just to list a sampling, the commentaries of Barrett, Bellville, Furnish, Héring, and Plummer note its presence.

39. Isaiah is the most popular choice to explain the presence of "my sons and my daughters" in 2 Corinthians 6:18. All the commentators named in the previous note mention it. Deuteronomy is argued for by John Olley, "A Precursor of the NRSV? 'Sons and Daughters' in 2 Cor 6.18," *NTS* 44 (1998): 204–12. His case, which is possible, argues that contextually it treats the issues of false worship and idols

mighty, which most connect to 2 Samuel 7:8, given that 2 Samuel 7 is already present in the Corinthian context.

So what of the use made of Leviticus 26 in 2 Corinthians 6:16 and the use of 2 Samuel 7 in 2 Corinthians 6:18? The Leviticus 26 text is impacted by the likely presence of Ezekiel 37:27 in the 2 Corinthians 6:16 context, producing a fused text like the one involving 2 Samuel 7 and either Isaiah 43:6 or Deuteronomy 32:19.[40] Most see Leviticus 26 as the key text in this 2 Corinthians 6:16 citation, while others suggest that Ezekiel 37 is the main text.

The problem here is that an OT theme is at work in both texts, namely, the idea that God will dwell among his people, so that "I will be their God, and they will be my people." The third person pronouns in 2 Corinthians fit Ezekiel, while the idea of "walking among them [*emperipateso*]" comes only from Leviticus 26. What makes the 2 Corinthians text difficult is that the phrase "I will live with them [*enoikeso*]" is not found in the LXX or the MT. We may be treating an OT idea here and a fused quote with a resultant new sense. If so, then Leviticus is developed in light of the Ezekiel 37 context of new covenant or eschatological hope.

My contention is that the movement of a text through its scriptural, temporal development of salvation history must always be kept in mind as we work with meaning in the early church citation. Again the point is that *the combination* of OT texts has opened the door for a development of theological meaning. To try and show the point, I will start with the original contexts of these passages from Leviticus 26 and 2 Samuel 7.

---

as the 2 Corinthians text does. For my hermeneutical point it makes no difference which text provides the influence. *The outcome is still that the earlier text is expanded by the combination of references, resulting in clear biblical theological development of the original context.*

40. For the textual details, see William J. Webb, *Returning Home: New Covenant and Second Exodus as the Context for 2 Corinthians 6.14–7.1* (JSNTSup 85; Sheffield: Sheffield Academic Press, 1993), 32–58, esp. 33–40, where he argues Ezekiel is the key text in contrast to Hans Dieter Betz, "2 Cor 6:14–7:1: An Anti-Pauline Fragment?" *JBL* 92 (1973): 93–95, who treats Leviticus as the key text. The possibility that Paul may be using an OT idea and synthesis may make the need to make a choice unnecessary.

Leviticus 26:11–12 is part of a larger section beginning in 26:1, where the nation of Israel is told not to make idols. The nation is to keep the Sabbath. In being obedient, blessings of rain, fruitfulness, and peace in the land will follow, as enemies are successfully expelled (vv. 2–10). So God commits to "tabernacle" among them (v. 12: "I will walk among you and be your God, and you will be my people"). So the text affirms the promise of the Mosaic covenant that God's people are part of a special relationship with him, as they hold him to be the only God. The LXX in translating the text uses the term *laos* to identify the beneficiaries of the promise. It is a term that identifies the nation in covenant relationship to God, the covenant people.

Second Samuel 7:14 is the Davidic covenant text. David is promised a dynastic line that has the honor of a unique, intimate relationship with God identified as one between a father and a son. The promise, in its original setting, is individualized to that line of kings with the promise extending initially to Solomon. So this text is a specific promise made to a specified and limited group, the Davidic line.

In 2 Corinthians, what is amazing is that in the midst of a catena of citations that include, at the least, Leviticus 26:11–12 and Isaiah 52:11, a reference to the Davidic promise from 2 Samuel 7 appears and is applied to all the Corinthians, who not only are not kings, but are mostly Gentiles! Even if other ancient texts contribute to the wording, as was noted above is likely, it is the echo of this text that is the most prominent, leaving the question of how Paul could string this text together with the others in a way that leaves it with this fresh, even radical, sense. Beyond the use of 2 Samuel 7, there stands the citation of Leviticus, which also extends its former sense to include those very Gentiles as part of the people of God. Three questions cry out for consideration. How could Paul so radically reread the Bible of Israel? Can we explain what is happening hermeneutically? Are there clues from within those Scriptures themselves that these readings could be made?

The texts as a group support the claim that God has made a living temple of his people. This act, in turn, means that they should live in holiness and integrity. This involves a lifestyle and purity of worship in the midst of the pagan world. So Paul uses Leviticus 26 to identify the church as God's people, his covenant family. There is no mere analogy here based on a past precedent involving Israel, as the theological ground for the exhortation is based on what God *is* saying to them, according to 2 Corinthians 6:16b ("We *are* the temple of the living God," emphasis added). He makes this exhortation in 7:1 by emphasizing (lit.), "therefore having these promises" (*tautas oun echontes* [present participle!] *tas epangelias*). The key term *laos* ("people")appears as the last word of 6:16 to make their special identity abundantly clear, even though Paul is addressing a predominantly Gentile audience. The citation of 2 Samuel 7 in 2 Corinthians 6:18 will elaborate this point and this relationship.

Leviticus 26:11–12 involves a promise given to establish the type of relationship God has with those who are his. The familial nature of the relationship serves as the text's stable meaning. Paul can apply it to the Corinthians because they have, by God's grace, entered into the blessing in which all the promises of God have become "yes" in Jesus. This blessing binds Paul and the Corinthians together in a relationship sealed by God's promised eschatological Spirit. The indwelling Spirit makes them a living temple (2 Cor 1:20–22; chs. 3–4; 5:5, 17; 6:16). I do speak of application here, because once again Paul is not trying to take us back into the original setting alone, but has now, yet again, read the text and "updated" it in light of the realities that (1) additional revelation has come since the time of Leviticus, and (2) Jesus has brought that era of realization. These new temporal revelatory factors develop the meaning.

Has the meaning of Leviticus changed? Once again my answer is, "No—in terms of basic meaning" and "Yes—in terms of referents." The relationship God has to his people is still one of a "family." But, for Paul, Christ's work has extended that family. Paul exhorts the Corinthians in 2 Corinthians 7:1 that they have these promises as the ground for his exhortation to be clean from all defilement of flesh and spirit. They are to perfect holiness in the fear of God and distance themselves from the defilement of old because of the benefits they now possess as God's blessed family members. They should live like it. The blessings of the new era complete what the old era stood for. In fact, the language of Leviticus 26 is repeated in the eschatological context of Ezekiel 37:27, showing how one era will merge into the other. Ezekiel announces that in an era to come God will redeem his people, reunite them, and revive them with his Spirit and blessing in the land (Ezek 37:1–23, esp. v. 14). They will no longer defile themselves and "they will be my people, and I will be their God" (v. 23; also v. 27). The basic language of Leviticus reappears in Ezekiel, only in a decidedly eschatological context. The theme's development sets the stage for the meaning's development.

There seems to be one more addition to the "meaning." Not only are Gentiles included, because of their connection to Jesus, but God's dwelling with them has become God's dwelling *with* them (i.e., in them — in other words, with an added intensity the original recipients of Leviticus could not have yet appreciated). The introduction to this Leviticus 26 and Ezekiel 37 fused citation refers in 2 Corinthians 6:16 to the Corinthians and Paul as the living temple of God. One cannot be absolutely sure of this sense carrying over — Paul makes no elaboration of his remarks here, but one can be suspicious it is there. The introduction to this catena and his use of the imagery in 1 Corinthians 3:16–17, where the corporate nature of the community as temple is stressed, seem to point in this direction.

Another reason for my suspicion is the reuse of Ezekiel imagery in NT settings (note, for example, the use of this imagery behind John 3:1–14 and 4:1–14, as well as 7:37–39). God is not only among them, as in the past. He is in them, working from the inside out. That is what makes them a "living" temple. So once again we see a meaning that is stable, and yet at the same time the passage takes on fresh nuance and detail because of what Jesus has brought in the era of realization.

In 2 Corinthians 6:17, the exhortation to come out and be separate makes the exhortation explicit, also using scriptural language from Isaiah 52:11. It anticipates Paul's closing exhortation in 2 Corinthians 7:1, so we have an A (people)-B (cleanse) — A (people)-B (cleanse) pattern in 6:16–7:1. It is intriguing to consider that the Isaiah passage comes just before the redemptive Servant Song of Isaiah 52:13–53:12. Redemption, the work of reconciliation between God and people, stands in the backdrop to this text, as 2 Corinthians 5:21 suggests.

So we come to 2 Corinthians 6:18. What I will say here should not be surprising in light of where we have been. How do we get from the "regal son" of 2 Samuel 7:14 to "my sons and my daughters" in 2 Corinthians 6:18? It really is not so complex. What is promised to David is realized in Jesus. His sonship is the basis for our sonship, a point Paul elaborates in detail in other contexts, when he speaks of our adoption (Rom 8:1–17; Gal 3–4). What Jesus the Christ has received, he passes on to us. His position can become our position. It is why in Romans 8:17 Paul speaks of us as "co-heirs" with Christ, or in Ephesians 2:6, of our being "seated … with him in the heavenly realms."

But this is not all. Once again, in the background, there may be precedent for the move Paul makes from the OT, something that spurred him to go in this direction. In Isaiah 55:3, there is a text that "democratizes" the Davidic promise (see also 1 Peter 4:13–14 and its democratized use of Isaiah 11:2). So what is for the Davidic house in Samuel is for all of Israel in Isaiah. Interestingly enough, this Isaiah 55 text is cited by Paul in a speech in Pisidian Antioch in Acts 13:34. It reads, "I will give you [read a good old southern plural y'all!] the holy and sure blessings promised to David." What God offered in relationship to David and his sons is now passed on to those related to Jesus, who is *the* Davidic Son. In addition, these benefits are identified with more specificity as they now include being declared righteous through him on the basis of forgiveness of sins.

What Paul does with the language in 2 Corinthians he also preached in the Jewish synagogue. In 2 Corinthians, language that once applied only to the king in Samuel was passed on to the people. This is another example of the extension and expansion of God's grace in promise tied to the One who receives and distributes the benefits of salvation. Not only that, but now the people are clearly said to be "my sons and my daughters," an explicit gender inclusiveness to make sure there is no gender discrimination in the preaching and teaching about who participates in salvation.

It is important to note that the entire catena is introduced with the introductory formula, "as God has said." Paul is pointing to divine language as the ground of this exhortation. Paul says the text *means* this now in light of Christ.

This reading honors the original meaning on the one hand, while deepening it on the other. Has the meaning of the OT changed here? Again, I think the answer is, "No—in its basic sense" and "Yes—in its referents." There is an intimacy that the

Father promised would reside in the regal Son. Such an intimacy is the basis for the extension of God's promise, as beneficiaries of this promise are articulated throughout the progress of revelation. When Paul in 2 Corinthians 6:15 juxtaposes Christ and Belial and then immediately follows it with believer and unbeliever, he shows us the conceptual link and the contextual basis for the move. The Davidic Son is the Christ. The believer is now the child of God. The relationship privilege of the Son becomes that of those related to him as he has brought them from darkness and lawlessness into light and righteousness (6:14–15). So Paul extends the scope of the promise in light of his awareness of the broader theology that informs 2 Samuel 7 and impacts its sweep.

Conclusion on the Examples

The sample texts we surveyed have come from a variety of settings to illustrate that the variation is not a function of a single theme's presence. It seems what we are seeing is evidence of a fundamental hermeneutical way the early church read the Jewish Scripture.

So we sum up. *There is a sense (a basic principle or subject matter) in which meaning is stable. There is a fundamental meaning to the text. Such meaning can be clearly stated. What can shift is that to which the meaning applies. Linguistically this shift of meaning is associated with what is called the referent, since a new context often means fresh referents. However, in that later application of meaning, the original meaning is still at work and it is still developing. What is more, once the additional meaning becomes clear, that later meaning can refract in a way on the earlier text to give it fresh understanding. All of this development is the function of multiple contexts being at work with the meaning, a factor that impacts the theological force and application of the textual meaning, giving that meaning additional depth.*

So, for example, we can suggest that room exists for the *protoevangelium* being about Jesus in Genesis 3:15, when Moses did not know Jesus' name when he described the conflict between the seed of the woman and the serpent in that passage. The line between meaning and significance is not as clean as we might have thought. Rather than always being completely separate boxes, sometimes, in reused texts, it is like an overlapping Venn diagram. Some of the categories related to promise are in temporal, historical, and referential flux as texts aim at the future and are developing, and the divine author of promise continues to speak and act as we move through the OT era and enter the era of realization in Christ. God commits himself to what he will do in promises that are stable for those to whom they were originally given. However, such stability does not mean that he cannot come on the scene later and expand the scope of his commitments and blessings.

This has implications for how we read the OT now that the NT has come. What I am arguing is that *reading from both contexts is legitimate. Reading is not singular, but multiple, depending on which context is in view.* Obviously the reading emerging out of the NT is more comprehensive, but the OT meanings remain relevant except where the NT completes the meaning by making a complete replacement clear. In addition, although major moves are made Christologically between the Testaments, other structures are not radically redefined at the expense of earlier structures.

CAN WE DO WHAT THE APOSTLES DID?

One other question remains: Can we do what the apostles did? My argument is that we do it even when we claim we do not. Our theological structures are built off of how we put the texts together theologically as a whole unit, much like the theological-canonical reading I have been defending. As long as this is done within the framework of the theological grid the Scriptures give us, this is legitimate. It is why certain texts that are initially ambiguous can be reread legitimately in light of the whole of Scripture. So Joseph can be a type of Christ. The "us" of Genesis 1 may well allude to the Trinity. Details of realization can be developed from Isaiah 53 that are not explicitly developed within the NT. This completed reading is something Jesus does in Luke 24:44–48, for which the apostles are the witnesses and become our hermeneutical guides.

I believe each example I have shown has revealed a movement within a stable meaning. In each case the question about whether meaning has changed is to be answered, "No—in its sense" and "Yes—in its referents." The key point here is that there is both a relationship and connection to the original meaning even while there is development of it. These associations are not arbitrary, nor are they merely randomly made for convenience sake. They are thought through.

The implication of this hermeneutic for our reading of the Testaments is also significant. It appears that there are some cases where the use of the Jewish Scripture by the early church is not just a "contextual" reading in the original context. Rather, it is a synthetic one, where themes developed by Scripture or raised by the life of Jesus have impacted how the text is read.

In saying this, I am not arguing that the original context is irrelevant, for that original context is a base from which the developed meaning works. The "no" change or lack of change within the meaning is as important as any developments in it.

Neither should one think that this approach is "reading back" into the text what was not there. Where Jesus' life is influencing the reading, we often are working on thematic developments that have already been raised by the progress of revelation within the Jewish canon. It is God advancing his story as the author of the whole of Scripture. As the author he can develop the story by giving fresh revelation that provides details that enhance what has already been revealed.

This is why the new covenant theme as connected to issues of law or promise is so central. So the early church preaches scriptural themes about (1) the true, believing people, (2) the enemies now seen in fresh ways, (3) the Abrahamic hope that the seed would bring blessing to the world (Gentiles!), and (4) the temple seen now in the Spirit-indwelt community as a result of new covenant realization. These are biblical, synthetic claims about promise. They are built on more than a contextual reading of individual texts. They often represent a reading where old texts have been linked to younger ones with both expansion and stability in meaning.[41]

---

41. In conservative circles, there is good precedent for this type of reading. Some texts where the church has claimed Trinitarian implications also surface as a result of this kind of theological synthetic refraction. For some eschatological views, OT texts that are called millennial can only be so described in light of the refractive influence of a later text from Revelation 20. These "millennial" texts in their original setting are really only promised kingdom texts.

In addition, the appeal to historical pattern, what is often called typology, is something with which Jews would have identified. The earlier example of the *midrash* on Psalm 2 shows such a "pattern across time" reading. Sometimes the early church makes scriptural points from such a reading, though we did not trace in detail any specific examples in this study. The point of typology is the design of God, which works itself into repeated patterns of action (Hos 11 in Matt 2; Isa 7:14 in Matt 1). Jews read history in such patterns. Perceiving God as acting in patterns designed in days of old but renewed today points to his fresh activity.

The presence of pattern fulfillment has good precedent in images associated with the exodus or new creation from within the Jewish Scripture, even though such a view tends to elude an analytical Western mind. Thus, pattern fulfillment (which in Christ is usually accompanied by escalation) represents yet another type of synthetic, thematic reading of text and history that has roots in the Scripture of old.

In sum, one can urge that we adopt a fully historical reading of the Jewish Scripture that is sensitive to the temporal flow of the development of promise through Scripture on the basis of its key themes. One can also urge that we be sensitive to the patterns that Scripture and event bring to our attention as evidence of God's new work. These readings are grounded in the open-endedness of the hope expressed in these texts. Reused texts simply make use of the futurity already built into revelation, a futurity of expressed hope and repeated action. Such a reading also opens up the possibility for a theologically unified reading of the text that a strictly original contextual reading fails to provide. In fact, narrowly contextual readings show themselves inadequate for making sense of Scripture as a whole. It is the interconnectedness of Scripture as it moves into its future of realization that makes a unity of its message. Thus the reading is one of "historical contexts," not merely one historical context.

The early church's use of the OT is *not* a reading of a narrow passage left merely to its own original context (as many conservative readers tend to claim). *The NT reading is not a mere exegetical treatment of a passage from the OT as we are used to doing.* Conversely, neither is a text read only in light of its contemporary context without regard to the original context or biblical-theological development (as many nonconservatives claim). *Neither is the text read in an atomistic way as still others claim.* Rather, when the reading gets complex, as it often does, it is the product of a kind of grand synthetic reading, drawing on the language of venerated Scripture and elaborating it in light of the progress of revelation. That progress itself comes from a combination of other passages from the sacred text as well as from the events of Jesus' life.

This is the impact of multiple contexts, reflection on the whole and in their inner relationships, as well as a full understanding of the key revelatory context that is in Jesus. We often view the reading as arbitrary because we have not done the hard work in Scripture or have failed to appreciate how much Jesus' coming helped to open up those old texts in fresh directions. He fills in the missing pieces that make sense of the promise of Scripture, giving it a unified and unifying message of hope and reconciliation that is at the core of the gospel about Christ.

Both conservatives and liberals err here. Conservatives often read the text as if the full meaning should have been transparent from the beginning rather than honoring revelatory progress, a progress that Jesus' appeal back to such texts also takes into account when he rebukes Jewish readers for not understanding those original texts. In trying to freeze meaning in the original setting, conservatives either read back into the original context or fail to see how the reading of some early texts has been impacted by the refraction of later texts and events.

Liberals, interestingly enough, often get stuck in the past as well, even as they affirm that the church has merely read the text arbitrarily in light of the church's present. They fail to see how texts thematically are often future oriented, not locked into the original context alone. They also fail to appreciate the fact that the Scripture does move progressively into the future, propelled in a unified direction as it does so. Their divisive bibliology gets them off track, as they often see and affirm only a group of disparate, individual books within the Bible, each expressing individualized or even competing theologies. Any push for unity is condemned under the hermeneutically judicial sentence of being a dreaded and illegitimate (read "harmonizing" or "dogmatic theological") reading.

In other words, early church exegesis was not like much modern exegesis in simply trying to go back to the original historical context with its referents and stopping there. The early church focused on texts that opened up to the future, that sat in contexts next to such future-oriented texts, that treated themes that Scripture would later develop more, or that were expressed in recognizable patterns of divine activity. Such texts were read in the early church in light of those later texts and/or in light of the new temporal realities that had surfaced in Christ. Such readings are not atomistic but holistic. They are readings with a singular core meaning developed through multiple contexts and the final context's resultant referents. This kind of "depth" reading honors the fact that behind Scripture ultimately stands a single grand, unifying Author. It honors the fact that when Jesus appeared, he truly was the Word.

CONCLUSION

The use of the OT in the NT involves a complex interaction between hermeneutics, the time of the reading, history, and developing theological-canonical concerns. It is a rich area of study and reflection. If one pays careful attention to the historical contexts, one just might be able to make more sense out of how it all fits together.

RESPONSE TO BOCK

Walter C. Kaiser, Jr.

The best part of Darrell Bock's argument is that he sees "the original context of the OT passage as playing a key role in setting the parameters of how the text is used, [even though, he quickly adds correctly] ... it is not always the only factor." In that regard, the two of us are in agreement. To be sure, "there is no single way these [OT] texts are handled [by NT authors]."[1] Not every citation of the OT by the NT is intended to argue doctrinally or apologetically from the OT. In these cases, what we need to be especially sensitive to is the issue of truth claims and the *sensus literalis*.

HISTORICAL FACTORS

Why, asks Bock, should Jewish interpretive roots be given such high interpretive value, "since the Christian movement ended up being so opposed to Jewish tradition"? Though Bock does put stock into Jewish interpretive traditions, the question he asks at this point in his essay should have been inscribed in gold. Was not the specific point of our Lord's disapproval of many of his Jewish contemporaries specifically in the method by which they interpreted Scripture? For example, in the Sermon on the

---

1. See my discussion of these matters in Walter C. Kaiser, Jr. and Moisés Silva, *Introduction to Biblical Hermeneutics: The Search for Meaning*, rev. ed. (Grand Rapids: Zondervan, 2007), 95–105, 262–64.

Mount, the point at tension was "You have heard it *said*," over against what was clearly written in the Law and the Prophets.

Bock specifically lists midrashic and *pesher* techniques as illustrations of what Christian and Jewish interpreters held in common. But why not appeal instead to Rabbi Hillel's "seven rules [*middot*]," which, as David Daube points out,[2] reflect the same logic and methods found in Hellenistic grammar and logic, and which are similar to what are today regarded as "modern" methods of analyzing a text? Why should the Christian imitation of the Jewish methods of interpretation stop with midrashic and *pesher* techniques of interpretation and not also include *gematria* (the computation of numerical values of letters in order to gain deeper meanings), *notrikon* (the breaking up of a word into two or more words, or reconstructing a word by using the initial letters of all the words in a sentence), *temura* or *cabalistic readings* (the permutation of letters by using three Cabalistic alphabets), or even *sod* (the search for the mystical sense)? All of these were expansions and departures even from Hillel's seven *middot*.

FIRST-CENTURY THEOLOGICAL PRESUPPOSITIONS

Even before the intertestamental period, the concepts of "the one and the many" (later called corporate solidarity), "the now and not-yet" types of fulfillment (later called inaugurated eschatology), and the "patterns" in God's providential working in history, events, personages, and institutions (later called typology or correspondences in historical happenings) were all known in OT days.[3] All of these contribute to what I have termed the OT promise-plan theology.[4]

---

2. David Daube, "Rabbinic Methods of Interpretation and Hellenistic Logic," *HUCA* 22 (1949): 239–76. See my positive discussion of Hillel's seven rules as the way for interpreting the *Peshat*, i.e., the "plain" or "simple" meaning of the text in Walter C. Kaiser, Jr., *Toward an Exegetical Theology* (Grand Rapids: Baker, 1981), 53–55.

3. See Walter C. Kaiser, Jr., *Back Toward the Future: Hints for Interpreting Biblical Prophecy* (Grand Rapids: Baker, 1989; repr., Eugene, OR: Wipf and Stock, 2003). See especially chapter 4, "Go Back to the Past in Order to Understand the Future."

4. See now my *The Promise-Plan of God: A Biblical Theology of the Old and New Testaments* (Grand Rapids: Zondervan, 2008).

Rather than viewing the OT as a series of scattered predictions or prognostications that were eventually to be matched with NT fulfillments after the event happened, promise-plan theology observes that the missing item in such an analysis was the historical *means* by which God kept alive his word of promise in a series of OT fulfillments that joined the first word of announcement with the final fulfillment that came in Jesus the Messiah. Therefore, it often was a matter of "multiple fulfillments" that were all part and parcel of that single goal that led to the ultimate realization of the word of promise in Jesus. For example, five prophets in *four centuries* predicted that "the day of the LORD" (*yom yhwh*) was "near" or "at hand," but it referred to events that occurred and received partial fulfillment in each of their centuries, while each unmistakably saw the near fulfillment as part and parcel of what would happen in the final day's fulfillment by our Lord.

DUAL AUTHOR ISSUES

I am greatly encouraged by Bock's qualifier that despite his approval of *sensus plenior*, he affirms that the duality of having God and the human writers as authors is no problem, "provided what the human author said and whatever more God says through him have a relationship in sense to what the human author originally said." However (as he acknowledges), this is not always what many users of *sensus plenior* mean today. If that tie is cut and a new divine meaning trumps whatever the human author originally intended, why bother with the old revelation?

For example, Bock points to a change in the referent of the *goyim* ("Gentiles/nations") in the Acts 4:25–27 quotation of Psalm 2:1 to now also include the "Jews" in the NT preaching of Peter and John. That may well be, for the word *goyim* normally refers to the other nations beside Israel. But notice that the opposition faced in Psalm 2:3 is not only from the nations/Gentiles, it is directed specifically against both the Father and the Son. (Notice the plural pronouns: "Let us break *their* chains," they say, "and throw off *their* fetters" [italics added]. Therefore the revolt is against the Lord and presumably his Son, for how else can we define the plural pronouns?) So it is not too surprising that Israel would be included in the opposition of the nations/

Gentiles in Acts 4 since now Israel has joined the nations in opposing the Son.

WAYS OF READING SCRIPTURE IN
THE PROGRESS OF REVELATION

To contrast an "exegetical reading" with a "theological reading," however, has both a right and a wrong aspect to it. Here we come to the heart of the matter, for Professor Bock has set before us three main emphases in interpreting the NT use of the OT, each of which fits into various systems of theological endeavor: (1) the NT tells us what an OT text meant even though that meaning may not be evident (or even found) from reading the OT text; (2) the OT determines the meaning and sets the limits for the interpretation; and (3) the NT can develop and complement what the OT meant so long as it does not end up denying what that OT text affirmed. These three views usually correspond to: (1) the Reformed amillennial approach (view 1), (2) the classic dispensational view (view 2), and (3) the views of historic premillenarians and now apparently progressive dispensationalists (view 3). Bock and I are both generally in this third view, which we both argue is the way language works.

Of course, an interpreter must never act as if God has not given the entire canon of the sixty-six books, but that affirmation must not be used as a shortcut to the hard work of exegesis in each immediate context first and prior to asking how this truth or concept grew over the period of the growth of the rest of the canon.

Some appeal to a Christocentric interpretation that claims that an interpretation is not truly Christian until the NT perspective and the message is centered on Jesus. Similarly, Professor Bock likewise uses the *protoevangelium* of Genesis 3:15 to illustrate what he calls the "theological-canonical reading" of that text to point to Jesus himself. Bock asserts that "the human author could not have named Jesus. That understanding is 're-fracted' by the progress of revelation."

On the contrary, the Septuagint (LXX) translation of Genesis 3:15 (third century BC) indicates that a male descendant of the woman would ultimately triumph over "the serpent" (*Hannahash*). In 103 examples of antecedent pronouns appearing in the LXX of Genesis, such pronouns agree with their anteced-ent in every instance except this one example.[5] Here the Greek translators break their own rules of agreement, and instead of making the neuter pronoun agree with the neuter word for "seed" (*sperma*), they make it masculine (*autos*). Even though Jesus' name is not included, the translators' understanding of the provision is unmistakable. What is more, even Eve seems to betray something of the same sense, for when she gives birth to Cain, she exclaims, "I have gotten a man, even the LORD!" (Gen 4:1, my translation of the MT; cf. Luther's rendering). Therefore Eve's instincts were correct, but her timing was way off!

VARIED WAYS THE NT USES THE OLD

Paul's one clear use of allegory is rhetorical and not exegeti-cal. Paul uses an unusual Greek expression when he writes in Galatians 4:24, "all of which things may be put into an allegory"[6] (pers. trans.). The apostle is not advocating allegorical interpre-tation, nor is he attempting to exegete the Genesis passages about Sarah and Hagar. He merely puts the same teaching he has just given into a form that he apparently hopes will help his Jewish audience realize the points he just made, even if he is not exegeting Genesis when he does so.

THREE EXAMPLES OF THE COMPLEX USE OF THE OT IN THE NT

Psalm 2:1–2 in Acts 4:25–26

We have already touched on this alleged problem. But it should be asked once again, why should the book of Acts be given preferential treatment before the context of Psalm 2 (and

---

5. See Ralph A. Martin, "The Earliest Messianic Interpretation of Genesis 3:15," *JBL* 84 (1965): 427.

6. See the especially good discussion by one of my former colleagues, Robert J. Kepple, "An Analysis of Antiochene Exegesis of Galatians 4:24–26," *WTJ* 39 (1977): 239–49.

indeed, the context of whatever else in the OT relates to this context) has been reviewed?

The point I raised above about the plural pronouns of Psalm 2:3 are especially pertinent to this situation. The question is what comes first: the original text and context of the OT or the cognate materials? I stand together with Professor Bock when he concludes: "*As a result, the scope of referents, which appeared to be limited to the kings and rulers of nations, appears to expand, yet within linguistic boundaries of the language used in the psalm's conceptual core*" (emphasis his). He feels the referent has changed, although he cautions us to read "has expanded and been clarified."

Deuteronomy 30:12–14 in Romans 10:6–8

Professor Bock worries—needlessly, I might say—over Paul's use of this OT text: "How does Paul take a text about law and make it a text about Jesus? Or has the text's meaning changed?" No, answers Dr. Bock, both texts focus on the *accessibility* of the word.

What shall we say of Deuteronomy 30:1–10? Is there not a call for repentance here (*shub*, v. 2)? Does not the word of promise (not one of a circumcision of the flesh, but one of a circumcision of the heart) point in the same direction as the one Paul was likewise preaching? Is not the life that is set before Israel by Moses—a call to love the Lord their God with all their heart and soul—made prior to a call for them to also keep his commands (v. 16)?

I think Bock is on better grounds when he too notes that the larger context of Romans 9:30–10:13, as I have in another connection,[7] must be understood here, for the Gentiles had obtained the very righteousness that the Jews were seeking and that Paul was advocating. The Gentiles got it by faith, whereas Israel missed it badly. They thereby failed to obtain this righteousness because they made a law out of righteousness and tried to obtain God's righteousness by their own home-made

---

7. Walter C. Kaiser, Jr., "The Law as God's Gracious Guidance for the Promotion of Holiness," in *Five Views on Law and Gospel*, ed. Stanley N. Gundry (Grand Rapids: Zondervan, 1993): 177–99; esp. 187–88.

substitute for that righteousness, idiosyncratically trying all the time to earn it by works (as if that were possible!). In fact, what Israel stumbled over was the stone laid in Zion, who was none other than Jesus himself. That is why Christ is the end/goal (*telos*) of the law.

I disagree with Drs. Bock and Moo that Paul "replaces the commandment of Deuteronomy 30:11–14 with Christ." I fail to see how "fresh meaning" has come into Paul's preaching when Paul so strenuously advocates that he is preaching "the [same] word of faith" (NASB) found earlier in the writing of Moses (Rom 10:8). Paul didn't want to give "fresh stuff"; no, he wanted to tell "the old, old story" all over again!

Leviticus 26 and 2 Samuel 7:14 in 2 Corinthians 6:16–18

I am not sure I understand what all the fuss is about in this collection of OT texts by Paul. The oft-repeated (some fifty times in the OT and NT) tripartite formula of the promise-plan of God is this: "I will be your God, you will be my people, and I will live with you." The fact that this may also be a fused text is also likely, but there is no harm in that. Likewise, the quote from 2 Samuel 7:14 does indeed point to a regal son of David, but note again that ever since Exodus 4:22–23, Israel too has been called God's "son," his "firstborn," a term used of Messiah (e.g., Col 1:15; and as a plural "firstborn ones" in Heb 12:23).

CONCLUSION

Yes, the meaning of the Bible is stable. Later applications of that meaning can expand the field of referents. But whether there are "fresh meanings" that can be refracted back onto older texts is still an area needing more work lest the grounding of the OT sense become untied and unattached.

RESPONSE TO BOCK

Peter Enns

I read Bock's essay with great interest and found that my own concerns overlapped often with his own. For example, Bock acknowledges that the very phrase "NT *use* of the OT" betrays a contemporary bias. He also sees Christ's fulfillment of the OT in the sense of culminating "a pattern of God's activity in history." Bock also shows historical sensibilities by affirming the necessity of Second Temple evidence for understanding NT hermeneutics, as well as recognizing hermeneutical ambiguities occasionally as a function of translation problems. Most importantly, he consistently reminds readers to resist generalizations in explaining how Scripture works, and rather advocates that biblical behavior be addressed when formulating our belief about Scripture.

These are important affirmations that are joined by several others, many of which I would like to address more fully. But, since space is limited, I should perhaps focus on one general area of disagreement (which has numerous permutations). This concerns the role that OT context plays in "setting the parameters of how the text is used [by the NT authors]." Bock's argument is nuanced (sometimes perhaps too much so), but I question whether Bock has successfully defended his main thesis, often repeated in the essay, that there is "stability" in OT meaning although the referent is "expanded." There are numerous junctures where I find myself parting company with Bock's analysis — indeed, where Bock's analysis does not always match up with affirmations he makes elsewhere.

Bock has two helpful summary sections that can be profitably perused to gain a quick glance at his overall concerns and can serve as a point of departure ("A Few Personal and Hermeneutical Comments" and "Can We Do What the Apostles Did?"). He states that he wishes to provide an approach to the NT use of the OT that is biblical while also having "better potential to defend the stability of meaning to which evangelicals are so committed as a basis for biblical authority." On one level, I understand the point, but on a more important level, it is the study of the NT use of the OT that calls into question the very assumption of "stability of meaning," whether or not evangelicals are committed to it. Bock is more nuanced in the way he presents his case than I have summarized him here. Nevertheless, when he contends that a scriptural meaning has to remain "stable," I find this to be inconsistent with his own repeated appeals elsewhere that we allow scriptural behavior to dictate our theological formulations.

In this same section Bock goes on to say "My thesis will be that the meanings [of the OT and its NT use] are connected and fundamentally one, but not always exactly the same." This raises a concern, namely, the use of ill-defined terms. I do not want to go down the obscurantist road of nullifying Bock's argument by a cheap appeal to "ambiguity of language." All language has by its very nature a certain amount of ambiguity, and my own essay is by no means immune. Still, what is difficult for me is that the "connectedness" and "fundamental oneness" of the two horizons of meaning are not really demonstrated, at least not without Bock making some crucial assumptions in the course of the argument. "Connected," "fundamentally one," or elsewhere "inherent sense" are not really well articulated, especially for those who do not share Bock's commitment to "stability of meaning."

In fact, I will go so far as to suggest that Bock's defense of his understanding of the NT use of the OT, despite his many fine, cogent, and instructive insights, shows marks of an inconsistent analysis and even an unwitting practice of midrashic techniques to demonstrate his point. This sounds much harsher than I intend it to sound, but my main contention is that Bock's thesis cannot be defended without undermining, at least to some degree, the very "connectedness" of the OT and NT contexts that would satisfy evangelicals committed to "stability of meaning."

Perhaps another programmatic statement can be addressed here. In his "personal and hermeneutical comments," Bock states that there is indeed a "freshness" given to the OT by the NT, but this freshness is "in line with the text's inherent 'futureness'" without simply reproducing the original meaning. Moreover, "that 'freshness' is informed by the presence of new factors in the progress of revelation" that were not "obvious at the time of the original production of the text." Finally, it is these added factors that "make a text capable of being read at different exegetical or canonical levels or from different theological perspectives."

There is much here with which I agree, but I am not sure that the difficult hermeneutical issues are adequately addressed. Not all OT texts used by the NT have an "inherent futureness" (e.g., Hos 11:1), and to claim that such a rather well-hidden future orientation supports the notion that the NT interpretation is "in line" with the OT meaning provides little along the way of a hermeneutical "control." The "freshness" of the NT is not so much "informed" by new factors that add a nuance or two; rather, the new factors function to reorient the reader to read the old texts in fresh ways.

This is a bit stronger statement than Bock's, which says that the new factors make the OT text *capable* of being read very differently. There is a slight apologetic tone here—that of protecting the NT against the charge of arbitrary exegesis—but *any* text can be "capable" of being read in multiple ways, provided certain pieces are in place. That is, in fact, the heart of midrashic exegesis. It is not clear to me how these thoughts support the general argument Bock is making.

Perhaps another angle from which to address our differences is to look at the six theological presuppositions Bock highlights early on in his essay. I feel Bock has missed something vital about Second Temple hermeneutics that may have affected the nature of his analysis throughout. The six presuppositions listed are: (1) the Bible is God's Word, (2) the one in the many (corporate solidarity), (3) pattern in history (correspondence or typology), (4) these are the days of fulfillment, (5) now and not yet (the inaugurated fulfillment of Scripture), and (6) Jesus is the

Christ. Bock claims that only the first three are shared by Jews and Christians, but that is not correct. The fourth is a staple of Jewish exegesis at Qumran, which predates the NT, and the fifth (somewhat surprisingly, perhaps) also predates Christianity, a point made by Geerhardus Vos.[1]

Of these six, it is the sixth presupposition that clearly distinguishes Christianity, and it is there that the heart of NT hermeneutics lies. The *manner* in which the Christological dimension is driven home is by means of the other five presuppositions (more or less), which is why a study of Second Temple hermeneutics is so important. But we should not think, "Oh my, there is only one distinguishing factor; I wish there were more." That one distinguishing factor, that Jesus is the Christ and that he died and rose from the dead for the sins of the world, is the central truth around which not only hermeneutical concerns revolve, but, as Christians believe, all of reality. It is *the* distinguishing mark of the faith, and a study of Second Temple hermeneutics brings this to light. Nevertheless, I greatly appreciate Bock's historical sensibilities in drawing our attention to these six presuppositions.

Bock's section on *sensus plenior* is helpful and illustrative, highlighting both his theological and hermeneutical sensibilities while also displaying some degree of inconsistency. He acknowledges that *sensus plenior* is "not a bad" concept, "provided what the human author said and whatever more God says through him have a relationship in sense to what the human author originally said." But this prejudices the issue. The point of studying NT hermeneutics is to see *whether* such a statement is true, or at least to what extent it is true. But to say that *sensus plenior* is fine so long as the NT use has a "relationship in sense" to the OT context almost undoes the appeal to *sensus plenior*, not to mention leaving the matter hanging on a somewhat vague phrase, "relationship in sense."

A similar criticism can be brought to Bock's understanding of "pattern fulfillment." Bock argues that the "sense" of the OT text is "maintained at one level in all fulfillments," although "the

---

1. G. Vos, *The Pauline Eschatology* (Princeton: Princeton Univ. Press, 1930; repr. Grand Rapids: Baker, 1979), 27–28, n. 36. See also Larry R. Helyer, "The Necessity, Problems, and Promise of Second Temple Judaism for Discussions of New Testament Eschatology," *JETS* 47 (December 2004): 597–615.

referent is heightened to a new level of realization in the later [NT] fulfillment." We see here Bock's commitment to holding in tension the fact that (1) the NT moves the OT passage along, so to speak, in ways that do not reproduce the "author's will" (to use Kaiser's phrase), and (2) there must be *some* significant connection between the two meanings. His way of easing this tension is to appeal to concepts such as "pattern fulfillment" and "progress of revelation." I am very much in favor of employing these concepts, but the larger *hermeneutical* issue is by no means solved.

For example, Bock appeals to the "central idea" of Psalm 2, that of the nations rejecting the anointed one, as being preserved in its use in Acts 4. I do not think, however, that it is adequate to say that a fresh reading of the psalm "emerged as the psalm was read by these early Christians," while the central idea remained. Distilling a "central idea" as (presumably) the locus of a stable meaning is not only arbitrary (and somewhat protectionist), but in the case of Psalm 2 it devalues the *radical* nature of the early church's use of the psalm to include *Israelites* as enemies of Yahweh now that Christ has come. I maintain that it is the event of Christ's coming that leads the church to reread the psalm in an expansive and eschatological direction, and thus change the meaning of the psalm from "enemies of God's anointed and God's people, Israel," to "enemies of the Christ, which now includes *Jew and Gentile*." To say that the OT meaning is "stable" surely undercuts the hermeneutical dynamic.

There are other examples where I feel the "stability of meaning" argument to be unhelpful. Although Bock's thesis is that there is a single meaning with a changing referent, in other instances (more than once) he refers to "a change of meaning" (e.g., of Psalm 2 in Acts 4). Likewise, Bock at times claims that the added revelation of the NT provides for more "clarity" on the original OT utterance, or reveals a "depth dimension," but I remain unconvinced that this explains the hermeneutical dynamic. I will concede, however, that clarity and depth are added, provided we understand such clarity and depth as a function of the hermeneutically *determinative* nature of the Christ event for handling the OT.

So I do most certainly believe that Matthew 2:15 lends clarity and depth to Hosea 11:1, but it is not a clarity of what "resides," so to speak, in Hosea's utterance, but an eschatological clarity that results from the last word that God utters in Christ. I think to a certain extent that Bock would agree here, but perhaps I just put it differently than he does.

Finally, another approach Bock takes is to say that at times an "original utterance can *tolerate*" (my emphasis) its heightened NT sense. But I find this unhelpful, since really *any* piece of *midrash* can be deemed tolerably consistent with the OT, provided one comes at the matter with certain hermeneutical assumptions.

Again, there are *many* aspects of Bock's essay that deserve a very patient and lengthy engagement because of their potential to move the church along in its understanding of the NT use of the OT (e.g., his outlining of the "types of usage" of the OT in the NT). But given the space provided and the nature of this volume, I have focused on areas of disagreement. In short, Bock's historical sensibilities are fine-tuned and admirable, but at the end of the day, his argument does less to explain NT hermeneutics than it does to defend an evangelical hermeneutic. As a result, some of Bock's explanations are perhaps more midrashic than he might be willing to admit.

FULLER MEANING, SINGLE GOAL

*A Christotelic Approach to the
New Testament Use of the Old in Its
First-Century Interpretive Environment*

FULLER MEANING, SINGLE GOAL

A Christotelic Approach to the New Testament Use of the Old in Its First-Century Interpretive Environment

Peter Enns

Despite the differences of opinion expressed by the authors of this volume on the topic of the NT use of the OT, we are united in acknowledging one vital theological truth. The NT authors, by citing the OT, are eager to show how the person and work of Christ are a continuation, fulfillment, and climax of the Father's redemptive work that began in the early chapters of Genesis. On page after page of the NT, we see an almost relentless focus on how God's mission to rescue his fallen creation is summed up in his Son's atoning death and victorious resurrection, and how we who are in Christ, the church, both benefit from and participate in his work. The NT authors peel back the curtain of God's drama of redemption to show us that, all along, it was about Christ and his creating of a new humanity, redeemed by his blood and called to serve him in his ongoing ministry of reconciliation to a fallen world.

To grasp this overarching purpose of how the NT writers use the OT is a source of great joy for the Christian. Challenges begin, however, when we move from the principle itself to some of the specifics of how the NT authors demonstrate this principle. Not a few readers of Scripture, going back certainly before the advent of modern interpretation,[1] have noted that the relationship between how a NT author uses the OT and how that OT passage functions in its original context is not always obvious. At times it takes some effort on our part to bring that connection to the surface, and the distance is sometimes considerable indeed. Although there are certainly differences in degree throughout the NT, the distinction between what an OT passage meant originally and how it is used in the NT is not a matter of an isolated incident or two, but a phenomenon that readers confront with some frequency. Biblical scholars, in fact, can be found exerting considerable effort in trying to give an account of it while not always achieving entirely harmonious results, the present volume being an indication of that fact.

The purpose of this essay is to accept the hermeneutical challenge posed by our own Scripture and attempt to give some account of what the NT writers do when they use the OT. In essence, we are asking the NT authors to explain their hermeneutical logic without the benefit of those authors having laid out their thinking processes. What they have given us in great abundance, however, is a catalog of their interpretive behavior; we see the NT writers in action. Our task, then, is to observe how the NT authors went about their interpretive task, to attempt to give some adequate account of some of these phenomena, and then to bring these observations to bear on how we think about the OT and what it means for Christians today to interpret it.

What becomes quickly apparent, however, is that there are important implications of how one explains this biblical phenomenon. One such implication that almost immediately rises to the surface concerns the dual authorship of Scripture. It is not questioned here that Scripture's primary author is God and that he, by his pleasure, works through human authors. The question, rather, is what the relationship is between what God intends to communicate through a given OT author at that particular moment in redemptive history, and how that comports with how NT authors, likewise inspired by God, reflect on those OT passages in light of Christ's coming. Since both are inspired

---

1. John Calvin, to name just one well-known example, wrestled some with these tensions; this is amply summarized in David. L. Puckett, *John Calvin's Exegesis of the Old Testament* (Louisville: Westminster John Knox, 1995), 82–104.

by God, are we to say that there is no difference between the two, or that the differences that do show up are merely superficial? Or are there instances where the two seem to have a chasm between them?

These types of questions surface quickly when we observe the NT use of the OT, and they reflect theological concerns that draw the attention of many evangelical readers of Scripture. For significant disjunction between what an OT passage means in its original context and how it is used by NT authors can be interpreted as a challenge to Scripture's unity, even God's ability to communicate effectively. Hence, various explanations are offered that are geared toward bridging the gap.

The general concern to preserve Scripture's (and God's!) integrity is important, to be sure, but the phenomenon of the NT use of the OT still needs some explaining. And there certainly are legitimate avenues by which this hermeneutical tension can be addressed. For example, what might appear to be an unbearable tension between an OT passage and its use in the NT can sometimes be shown to be less severe by drawing attention to the larger context in which the OT passage is found (to be addressed below).

What is not apparent, however, is whether an appeal to the larger context is consistently, or even normally, at work in the NT. One could even query whether such an appeal is a hermeneutical legitimacy that exists in the *mind of the NT author* or whether it is more in the mind of the modern interpreter seeking to lessen the hermeneutical tension. It seems that much would depend on how we *expect* Scripture to behave; that is, if it is presumed that these kinds of tensions between the OT and how the NT uses the OT are inconsistent with a high view of Scripture, then it would be incumbent upon faithful readers to explore how such tensions could be lessened wherever they appear.

Such a reading strategy will no doubt result in defensible explanations, given the acceptance of certain assumptions and the expenditure of sufficient effort. The results of such methods, however, do not *necessarily* lead to correct, or even compelling, results. The logically prior (and often unasked) question remains, namely, whether our *focus* should be on lessening the hermeneutical tension or whether there is something of positive theological value to be gained by articulating why such tensions occur. This is to ask: How true is it that such tensions are really at odds with an inspired text, in tension with God's character, and so need to be corrected?

THE IMPORTANCE OF SECOND TEMPLE LITERATURE

These and other issues will be raised at various junctures in this essay, and more intentionally in the conclusion. At this point, however, I would like to focus on one particular factor that has influenced my own theological thinking about the NT use of the OT. I do not think it is the only factor worth considering, but, in my view, its implications are not always fronted as much as they could be. Briefly stated, the hermeneutical challenges brought to us by the NT use of the OT cannot be adequately addressed without interacting with the interpretive context in which the NT authors lived, often referred to as the Second Temple period.[2] Moreover, such a historical investigation should have its place as we continue to discuss the many vital issues that are the concern of this volume, namely: Should we model our methodology and exegesis after that of the apostles? Does God speak in "one voice" throughout Scripture, and how does the NT use of the OT affect how we consider such a question? Does typology adequately address what the NT writers do with the OT?

My reason for fronting the issue of the NT hermeneutical context is not an attempt to place historical study "over"

---

2. This refers to the period of time between the return from exile and the rebuilding of the temple in Jerusalem in 516 BC and its destruction at the hands of the Romans in AD 70. The designation "Second Temple" is typically preferred in academic circles to "intertestamental" (which prejudices a Christian perspective) or "postexilic" (a more narrow and historical designation). I prefer "Second Temple" because it better reflects the fact that the NT writers, although standing in the absolutely unique moment in history as God's vessels to record Christ's first coming, were nevertheless living in a particular era marked by well-documented and significant interpretive activity. On this matter, I should also mention that the historical context of the NT encompasses more than what is typically included under the rubric "Second Temple"; namely, Jewish literature. A truly well-rounded discussion would also need to draw attention to Greco-Roman influences. Various schools of NT interpretation have tended to focus on one or the other, but both are relevant. My focus on Second Temple literature should not be misconstrued as an implicit devaluation of the value of Greco-Roman studies, but as an affirmation of the central importance of the Jewish literature for the specific topic of the NT use of the OT.

Scripture somehow. Rather, I simply wish to acknowledge that God himself, in Scripture, has spoken in time and space, and we honor him by taking seriously those contexts in which he, by his wisdom, has chosen to speak. To engage in such historical investigation is not to suggest that God's Word is somehow a slave to historical circumstances, but it is a reminder that the Bible is not a heavenly treatise, hurled down to earth from an Olympian height, or a Platonic ideal kept at a safe distance from the human drama. Rather, God is the Lord of history, and Scripture is God's gracious revelation of himself and his actions *in the concrete, everyday world of ancient Semitic and Hellenistic peoples.* If, therefore, Scripture bears the marks of its common setting, that fact should have no small influence on how we understand Scripture's behavior — in this case, the NT use of the OT.

The great Dutch theologian Herman Bavinck, over one hundred years ago, put the matter well. He wrote that inspiration

> implies the idea that the Holy Spirit, in the inscripturation of the word of God, did not spurn anything human to serve as an organ of the divine. The revelation of God is not abstractly supernatural but has entered into the human fabric, into persons and states of beings, into forms and usages, into history and life. It does not fly high above us but descends into our situation; it has become flesh and blood, like us in all things except sin. Divine revelation is now an ineradicable constituent of this cosmos in which we live and, effecting renewal and restoration, continues its operation. The human has become an instrument of the divine; the natural has become a revelation of the supernatural; the visible has become a sign and seal of the invisible. In the process of inspiration, use has been made of all the gifts and forces resident in human nature.[3]

It is *for this reason* — God's revelation having "entered into the human fabric" — that the study of Scripture as a *historical* phenomenon is neither optional nor peripheral for the church. This is especially the case in recent generations, with our greatly increased understanding of antiquity. Although at

3. Herman Bavinck, *Reformed Dogmatics:* Volume 1: *Prolegomena,* trans. J. Vriend (Grand Rapids: Baker, 2003), 1:442–43.

times challenging, the study of Scripture's historical context is a wonderful, vital, and indispensable responsibility for students of Scripture. Such condescension does not constitute a failing on God's part, nor does it impute a "sinfulness" to Scripture. It simply acknowledges that revelation means that God has spoken in Scripture in time and space, and those factors ought to play a *positive* role in our explanation of biblical phenomena. Through such study, by God's Spirit, we come to learn more deeply and more broadly who God is and what he has done, even if that entails nuancing, correcting, or adjusting our understanding.[4]

If we neglect this vital historical dimension, we run the risk of assuming universal normativity of our own culturally-embedded hermeneutical expectations. Richard Longenecker puts it somewhat forcefully:

> It has become all too common today to hear assertions of a theological nature as to what God must have done or claims of a historical nature as to what must have been the case during the apostolic period of the Church — and to find that such statements are based principally on deductions from what has previously been accepted and/or supported by current analogies alone. The temptation is always with us to mistake hypothesis for evidence or to judge theological and historical formulations by their coherence and widespread acceptance, rather than first of all by their correspondence and exegetical

---

4. For interested readers, I have taken a few stabs at working through this issue, some more direct than others: *Inspiration and Incarnation: Evangelicals and the Problem of the Old Testament* (Grand Rapids: Baker, 2005); "Preliminary Observations on an Incarnational Model of Scripture: Its Viability and Usefulness," *CTJ* (2007): forthcoming; "Exodus, the Problem of Historiography, and Some Theological Reflections," *Act 3 Review* 15/4 (2007): forthcoming; "Bible in Context: The Continuing Vitality of Reformed Biblical Scholarship," *WTJ* 68 (2006): 203–18; "Some Thoughts on Theological Exegesis of the Old Testament: Toward a Viable Model of Biblical Coherence and Relevance," *Reformation and Revival Journal* 14/4 (2005): 81–104; "Apostolic Hermeneutics and an Evangelical Doctrine of Scripture: Moving beyond the Modernist Impasse," *WTJ* 65 (2003): 263–87; "William Henry Green and the Authorship of the Pentateuch: Some Historical Considerations," *JETS* 45 (September 2002): 385–403; "Matthew and Hosea: A Response to John Sailhamer," *WTJ* 63 (2001): 97–105; "The 'Moveable Well' in 1 Cor 10:4: An Extrabiblical Tradition in an Apostolic Text," *BBR* 6 (1996): 23–38; "Creation and Re-creation: Psalm 95 and Its Interpretation in Hebrews 3:7–4:13," *WTJ* 55 (1993): 255–80.

data. History is replete with examples of this sorry condition and its sorry results, and hindsight permits us to recognize it in the past for what it was: a perversion of the truth. But we are "sons and daughters of our parents," composed of the same stuff and subject to the same pressures and temptations. And nowhere do we need to guard against our own inclinations and various pressures more carefully than in our understanding of the New Testament writers' use of Scripture. Neither piety nor speculation—both of which are excellent in their own ways when properly controlled—can substitute for careful historical and exegetical investigation. Nor can traditional views of either the right or left be allowed to stand unscrutinized in the light of recent discoveries.

The Jewish roots of Christianity make it *a priori* likely that the exegetical procedures of the New Testament would resemble, at least to some extent, those of Judaism of the time.[5]

Longenecker's appeal to the importance of historical context is an assumption generally shared by evangelicals, from lay readers who use study Bibles filled with maps, charts, and other historical information, to scholars who regularly produce commentaries, books, and articles aimed at explaining Scripture in context. Few exposed to Mesopotamian creation stories, for instance, would discount their relevance for reading Genesis 1 (even if that relevance is explained in a variety of ways), or Israelite law in the context of other law codes of the ancient world. Likewise, readers of the NT benefit from understanding something of first-century Judaism when reading Matthew's gospel (with its Jewish focus) or when confronting the Judaizers in Galatians. The purpose of being familiar with historical context is that it brings a deeper dimension of understanding and also provides some control to our own interpretations of Scripture. These are basic principles of grammatical-historical exegesis and need little defense for this readership.

By arguing for the importance of Second Temple literature for understanding NT hermeneutical practices, I am simply

5. Richard Longenecker, *Biblical Exegesis in the Apostolic Period*, 2nd ed. (Grand Rapids: Eerdmans, 1999), 185–86.

saying that the principle we bring into biblical studies in general ("historical setting matters") should be applied to the phenomena of the NT use of the OT. If understanding something of ancient grammar and history helps us understand what biblical passages mean, then understanding something of ancient interpretive practices helps us understand how NT authors interpreted their own Scripture. One might refer to this extension of the "grammatical-historical" method as a "hermeneutical-historical" method, since it brings historical questions to bear upon the discussion of the hermeneutical assumptions and practices of the NT authors.

One problem we face, however—at least as I see it—is that an application of grammatical-historical principles to NT hermeneutics shows that the NT authors' engagement of their Scripture was not directed by grammatical-historical principles. By modern conventions, there is often a "disconnect" between what an OT passage means in its context and how it is employed by NT writers. Because such hermeneutical behavior overlaps with that of their Second Temple contemporaries, the importance of studying Second Temple hermeneutical practices becomes, in my view, self-evident.

Engaging the NT use of the OT against its Second Temple backdrop will yield two broad observations. First, as has been routinely discussed (and to which Longenecker refers above), the manner in which the NT authors bring the OT to bear on their writings often reflects *interpretive practices* documented elsewhere in the literature of the Second Temple period. When NT writers cite the OT, we should not presume that the things we take for granted in contemporary interpretation were foremost on their minds (e.g., being bound to an author's intention, allowing historical context to drive interpretation). It is not modern notions that informed their interpretive practices but ancient ones, and it is incumbent upon us to do what we can to uncover those practices.[6]

A good number of what we might consider more problematic uses of the OT in the NT begin to make sense by keeping

---

6. I am not suggesting that modern and ancient conventions are wholly distinct. Nevertheless, contemporary Western interpretive assumptions are the end result of a developmental process that cannot be simply transposed to ancient Semitic or Hellenistic contexts.

one eye open to the interpretive context in which these writers wrote. This is not to say that the Second Temple context provides a blanket explanation for what NT authors did, or that a glance at a Second Temple text will magically open doors. It is, however, to establish the basic *expectation* that the hermeneutical context in which the NT authors wrote cannot help but play an important role in our understanding of their interpretive practices, and therefore what they want to communicate.

Second, the NT authors certainly engaged their Scripture with great energy and purpose of mind, but they were not the first ancient interpreters to do so. The vast literature of Second Temple Judaism, which includes considerable bodies of material like the Pseudepigrapha, Apocrypha, and Dead Sea Scrolls,[7] attests to a high level of Jewish interpretive activity in the century or two before and during which the NT was written. In fact, although it is beyond the scope of this essay, Second Temple texts *from the OT itself* bear witness to a deliberate and creative engagement of earlier texts (e.g., the reinterpretation of Israel's history in 1 and 2 Chronicles vis-à-vis that found in 1–2 Samuel and 1–2 Kings;[8] the interpretation of Jeremiah's seventy years in Daniel 9).

There was, in other words, interpretive activity on the OT long before the NT was written, and the fruit of such interpretive labor came to circulate among interpreters of the time. Throughout Second Temple literature, we see examples of biblical stories

---

7. A proper scope would need to include other ancient texts. For example, the Septuagint (Greek translation of the OT) is at points highly interpretive, as its translators seek to bring the Hebrew OT into a Greek-speaking world. Still, it is not an interpretive text in the same way that the others listed are. Also, the Targums (Aramaic translations of the OT) and later, largely medieval, rabbinic literature (Midrash, Talmud, various commentaries known as Midrashim) are relevant. Even though these texts arise in the centuries following the NT, the exegetical practices and interpretive traditions they contain often reflect a long history of previous interpretative activity. Their later date does not mean we can ignore them, but it does mean they should be handled wisely.

8. One evangelical who has attempted to account for this phenomenon is Raymond B. Dillard, *2 Chronicles* (WBC 15; Waco, TX: Word, 1987); "The Chronicler's Jehoshaphat," *TrinJ* 7 (1986): 17–22; "The Chronicler's Solomon," *WTJ* 43 (1980): 289–300; "The Literary Structure of the Chronicler's Solomon Narrative," *JSOT* 30 (1984): 85–93.

retold by interpreters that reflect established (although by no means universally agreed upon) *interpretive traditions.*[9] Some of these interpretive traditions find their way into the relatively brief corpus of the NT, and so the NT itself at points testifies to the extent to which the results of such earlier interpretive activity came to form commonly accepted ways of understanding certain OT episodes or texts. So, just as the NT shows evidence of being influenced by Second Temple *interpretive practices*, it also shows evidence of being influenced by Second Temple *interpretive traditions* — that is, how passages or episodes *had come to be understood* in the preceding and contemporary Jewish setting.

With respect to these two broad observations, some might object that if Second Temple hermeneutics is so important for understanding NT interpretive practices, why didn't the Spirit give us this information all along? The church has survived for nearly all of its existence without taking this Second Temple, extrabiblical literature into account, so why all of a sudden place such importance on it? And doesn't all this just take the Bible out of the hands of the common people and put it in the hands of a few experts?

Those are good questions, but we need to remember that progress in our understanding of Scripture has been a companion of the church at various stages of its existence and should not be frowned upon, but rather expected. When extrabiblical sources appear and affect our understanding of Scripture, should we not look at them as a gift from God to help us understand more fully what he is saying, even if it means changing or nuancing matters that were previously thought to be beyond dispute? Even if such information was not known to previous generations, are we so settled in our views that we will not allow fresh light on Scripture to be shed? And do we have the right to assume that our forebears would *not* have utilized these data had they been aware of them?

Some of the information we now have in hand was either unavailable to previous generations of Christians or was not as pressing a matter as it is today, now sixty years after the discovery

---

9. A wonderful source for exploring this phenomenon is James L. Kugel, *Traditions of the Bible: A Guide to the Bible as It Was at the Start of the Common Era* (Cambridge, MA: Harvard Univ. Press, 1998).

of the Dead Sea Scrolls. But that does not mean that such influence is an obstacle for Christians to overcome. Rather, it can be thought of as a provision by God to be employed with wisdom *and* enthusiasm. And it is not a matter of wresting the Bible out of the hands of everyday readers and putting it under the control of scholars. For one thing, the heart of the gospel is in no way affected by any of this. Moreover, when contemporary readers pick up an English Bible, particularly one with study notes, they are already benefiting from the work of uniquely trained scholars who have translated it and who help explain it. Biblical scholarship need not be an adversary, and Second Temple literature, like any other extrabiblical source, is a valuable—and I believe God-given—means by which we can calibrate our own efforts to explain Scripture.

When engaging Second Temple literature to address the question of NT hermeneutics, it is also important to be reminded of the diversity of that literature. On the one hand, we must not exaggerate this diversity and thus lose sight of some important unifying factors. What unites such otherwise diverse texts as *Jubilees* (Pseudepigrapha), the *pesher* on Habakkuk (Dead Sea Scrolls), and the Wisdom of Solomon (Apocrypha) is a hermeneutical posture that seeks (1) to mine Scripture (by applying conventional hermeneutical strategies) for hidden, richer meanings in order to hear God speak once again in a community's present circumstances, and (2) to preserve these interpretive traditions for successive generations. These and other valid observations can be made to underscore the commonalities of Second Temple literature.

But if our concern is to understand the NT use of the OT in the context of early Judaism, we must be wary of remaining on the level of generalizations, thus potentially obscuring important issues. This corpus of material is, after all, of a significant size, comprises a wide range of literary genres, spans at least three centuries, and reflects the diverse agendas of their various settings. Each example of Second Temple literature, therefore, has its own character and must be understood on its own terms.

This is similarly true of the writings included in the NT. Though the NT itself is a *collection* of texts, unified in its Christ-centered focus (more below), it also evinces its own degree of hermeneutical variety. It is not helpful, therefore, to think of Second Temple literature and the NT as monolithic entities that stand on opposite sides of a fence, needing coaxing to get to know each other. Rather, *from a hermeneutical point of view* at least, it is better to think of the NT as part of a larger group of texts of Jewish provenance—all of which, despite their real and important differences, *together* make up a distinct but diverse collection of texts we call "Second Temple literature."

If we bring such an attitude to our investigations, we will be in a position to appreciate *similarities and differences* among various Second Temple texts, among various NT texts, and between the NT and Second Temple texts. This will help bring clarity to how any Second Temple author, including NT authors, handled Scripture. Admittedly, the focus of this essay is more on similarities between the NT and other Second Temple texts, and so, certainly, the whole story will not be told here. But by bearing these similarities in mind, we can begin to see more clearly why the NT writers at certain points did what they did, and why they handled their Scripture in ways that do not sit easily with our contemporary conventions.

As I see it, what we find is that the differences between the NT writers and their contemporaries lie not so much in exegetical techniques, where NT authors show themselves to be more "sober" or "restrained" (i.e., more like us). Rather, the central difference is found in their relentless focus on bearing witness to the crucified and risen Christ. Whether for our tastes the NT authors are at times more in harmony with the original meaning of an OT passage or quite distant from it, what provides the grand coherence of the NT is the conviction that Jesus is the climax of God's covenant with Israel. The primary distinction, in other words, is eschatological, that in Christ the last days have arrived and the final stage of God's ancient purposes are being realized. We touch more on this below.

This brings us to one final word of general orientation. The focus of this volume is the NT *use* of the OT, but this is really a subset of a larger issue: the *presence* of the OT in the NT. It is certainly the case that the NT *cites* the OT many times. According to one index,[10] there are about 265 separate OT passages cited in the NT. Some of these passages are cited multiple times, resulting in a total of about 365 instances where the NT actually cites

---

10. Barbara Aland, et al., eds., *The Greek New Testament*, 4th rev. ed. (Stuttgart: Deutsche Bibelgesellschaft, 1993), 887–90.

the OT. For example, in the TNIV Thinline NT (265 pages with only brief annotations and no study notes), there is an average of about one and one-third OT quotations per page (1.38 to be a bit more accurate). That is impressive in and of itself, but to this total must be added allusions to the OT.[11] The book of Hebrews, for example, is replete with OT citations (thirty-seven).

But equally important is how certain OT themes (angels, priesthood, sacrifice, etc.) form the backdrop for significant portions of the book's argument. Likewise, the book of Revelation, which does not appear to contain a single OT citation, is steeped in rich OT apocalyptic imagery. Unless this is understood, the message of the book will elude the reader. Moreover, in addition to citations and allusions, the work of Richard Hays and his students has alerted us to an even deeper and more subtle level at which the OT is found in the NT, what he calls "echoes."[12]

The matter before us, therefore, is more comprehensive than simply how we perceive a NT author "uses" a particular OT text—and one wonders whether NT writers would even have thought of it this way. The OT *permeates* the NT because the NT describes how Christ and his work are the realization of God's purposes throughout Israel's history as recorded in the OT. At times this is seen in direct, explicit, and straightforward ways, while at other times the matter is more subtle and difficult to explain. Either way, the pervasive presence of the OT in the NT should balance any temptation to think of citations of the OT in the NT as a phenomenon to be explained independently from a larger theological program of the NT writers. As C. H. Dodd put it memorably several decades ago, the OT forms the very *substructure* of NT theology.[13]

This observation underscores the vital importance of coming to some account of the NT use of the OT, not just to try to explain what the NT authors do and then ask whether we can follow in their footsteps, but as a way of addressing the very nature of the relationship between the gospel of Jesus Christ and

---

11. *The Greek New Testament*, 891–900, lists well over a thousand OT passages to which the NT alludes.

12. Richard B. Hays, *Echoes of Scripture in the Letters of Paul* (New Haven: Yale Univ. Press, 1989).

13. I am referring to the subtitle of Dodd's *According to the Scriptures: The Substructure of New Testament Theology* (New York: Charles Scribner's Sons, 1953).

the Scripture to which he and the NT writers were constantly appealing. Although the focus of this essay is on the narrower question of the NT use of the OT, the ultimate purpose for engaging this phenomenon is, by way of concrete examples, to give account of this larger question of how the OT forms the substructure of NT theology, or as Paul put it, "Christ ... according to the Scriptures" (1 Cor 15:3, 4).

With these preliminary matters in mind—which I acknowledge have been addressed all too briefly—we now turn to a likewise brief glance at three examples of the NT use of the OT, considered in the context of their Second Temple environment. At the conclusion, I will summarize some of the issues raised by these passages and comment on a number of important and perennial implications.

SOME EXAMPLES

The examples I have chosen are aimed at illustrating what I have laid out above. They are certainly not the only examples available, but are among some that have been of interest to me over the years, for various reasons. Collectively they help illustrate something of how the NT writers adopt both Second Temple exegetical practices and interpretive traditions as they seek to proclaim Christ as the climax of Israel's Scripture. It goes without saying that these passages cannot be treated here with the detailed attention they deserve. The hermeneutical issues they raise, however, are clear enough.

"'And to Your Seed,' Meaning One Person" (Galatians 3:15–29)

A helpful inroad to some of the issues before us is to look at how Paul handles God's promises to Abraham in Galatians 3:15–29 (especially v. 16). This passage is part of Paul's larger argument in Galatians that the "blessing given to Abraham" is also for the "Gentiles through Christ Jesus" (3:14). Gentiles, in other words, are, by faith, heirs to the promises of Abraham, which had heretofore applied to Abraham's biological offspring. What follows in 3:15–29 is Paul's argument for how those promises to Abraham are to be understood as applying to a new people of

God, made up of Jews *and Gentiles*. His argument seems to turn on one word found in those OT passages: "seed" (Hebrew *zera'*, Greek *sperma*).

Paul begins by saying that God's ancient promises of blessing cannot be set aside—they must be fulfilled (v. 15). And to whom were those promises spoken? Paul reminds us: "to Abraham and his seed" (v. 16). Although Paul does not identify precisely the OT passage to which he is referring, there is no doubt that he is alluding to the promises God made to Abraham in Genesis that his seed would be too numerous to count and that the land of Canaan would be given to them. For example:

> The LORD said to Abram after Lot had parted from him, "Look around from where you are, to the north and south, to the east and west. All the land that you see I will give to you and your *offspring* forever. I will make your *offspring* like the dust of the earth, so that if anyone could count the dust, then your *offspring* could be counted" (Gen 13:14–16, emphasis added; see also 12:7; 15:5; 21:12; 24:6–7).

Here, "offspring" is the Hebrew word *zera'*, which is more literally rendered "seed." The word is *singular in form* but can either be *singular or plural in meaning*—a linguistic phenomenon often referred to as a "collective noun" (common English examples include "sheep" and "fish"). What is clear is that, in the context of the promises in Genesis, *zera'* has an undeniably plural meaning. Indeed, that is the very point of the promises, not that Abraham will have *one* offspring, but that there will be too many to count! Even though *zera'* is a singular form, it clearly has a plural meaning in Genesis.

For Paul, however, the singular *form* of "seed" is significant. Now, we can safely dismiss any notion that Paul does not know that *zera'* (or *sperma*, as his Greek OT has it) is a collective noun! Nor does Paul misunderstand the clear meaning of the promises in Genesis, that God would make Abraham's offspring too numerous to count. Rather, the singular form affords Paul an opportunity to seize upon the Abrahamic promise and bring it into conformity with the all-surpassing realization of all the OT promises in the person and work of Christ. After all, we must remember Paul's opponents in Galatia were the Judaizers, who were insisting that Gentiles could only be included as

"Abraham's offspring" (i.e., Christians) by becoming Jews first. These Judaizers, somewhat ironically, understood the promises to Abraham in their original sense; i.e., that it referred to ethnic Israel (specifically, as reckoned through Isaac and Jacob, not through Ishmael or Esau). Paul, however, argues that Abraham's "seed" is not ethnic Israel (plural) but Jesus (singular), the true "seed" of Abraham and the one through whom now Jew *and* Gentile, by faith, are *together* reckoned as Abraham's offspring.

Paul's rendering of "seed" as singular in meaning *because* it is singular in form is a deliberate exegetical decision on his part. This is seen not only in his explicit argumentation in Galatians 3:16, but the fact that Paul reverts to the *collective* sense in 3:29, where he says, "If *you are* of Christ, then *you are* Abraham's seed" (lit. trans.).[14] In contrast to English, Greek makes a distinction between the singular and plural "you." In both cases in verse 29, the "you" is plural: "you are" is the plural Greek verb *este* and the pronoun "you" is the plural Greek *hymeis*. Hence, "all of you—Jew and Gentile together—are Abraham's seed." Paul's theology here is gripping, momentous, nothing less than a grand assimilation of two important OT themes: Israelite exclusivity and Gentile inclusion, themes that find their expression at the very outset of the Abraham narrative:

> The LORD had said to Abram, "Go from your country, your people and your father's household to the land I will show you.
>
> "I will make you into a great nation,
>   and I will bless you;
> I will make your name great,
>   and you will be a blessing.
> I will bless those who bless you,
>   and whoever curses you I will curse;
> and all peoples on earth
>   will be blessed through you." (Gen 12:1–3)

Paul is arguing, against the Judaizers, that Gentiles can now enter God's family *as Gentiles* because of Christ's work. This

---

14. See also Romans 4:13–16, where Paul uses the Greek singular "seed" to refer to *all* of Abraham's offspring, those of the law and those of faith. It seems clear to me that Paul was well aware of his exegetical maneuver in Galatians 3:16.

newly constituted people of God is the ultimate realization of how the nations will be blessed through Abraham. The church, this Jewish-Gentile mixture, in other words, is Abraham's seed (plural), but *only* because Christ is Abraham's seed (singular) first. Jews are no longer reckoned as Abraham's seed by their ethnicity, nor do Gentiles need to become Jewish (through circumcision) before they can be considered heirs of God's promise. Now, the means by which *both* Jew and Gentile are considered descendants of Abraham is through faith in what God has done in the crucifixion and resurrection of Christ.

The theology Paul expresses here is true regardless of his appeal to the flexibility of the collective noun *zera'*. In other words, Paul's theology does not *depend* on his taking *zera'* as a singular in Galatians 3:16 and then as a plural in verse 29. Nevertheless, Paul's handling of the OT promises betrays an exegetical approach that would be deemed inappropriate by contemporary conventions, but hardly so for ancient, Second Temple standards. The fact that *zera'* clearly means multiple, innumerable offspring in Genesis is not Paul's point of departure; it is not what *controls* Paul's exegesis. His concern, rather, is to drive home a controlling theological point, namely, Christ's death and resurrection breaks down ethnic, social, and gender hostilities (v. 28). And he drives this point home through a particularly creative handling of his Scripture, one that seizes on the grammatical flexibility of a collective noun.

Such an exegetical move is hardly characteristic of Paul alone. With respect to *zera'*, there are rabbinic texts that also capitalize on its singular form, even though the only example that comes close to paralleling Paul's handling of the Abraham promise specifically is from a second-century text known as *Seder Olam Rabbah*.[15] But here, too, as with Paul, it is hardly the

---

15. This piece of interpretation seems to have been generated to solve a particular chronological problem (namely, whether the period in Egypt lasted 400 or 430 years). For a quick summary of a complex issue, see David Daube, *The New Testament and Rabbinic Judaism* (Peabody, MA: Hendrickson, 1998), 438–44. Daube is judicious in rehearsing the rabbinic data. Some commentators connect Paul's use of "seed" to speak of Christ with some rabbinic texts that speak of Isaac as the seed and suggest that an Isaac/Jesus typology is at work in Paul. There is, however, no real indication of this in Galatians (or anywhere else in the NT).

case that these rabbinic interpreters are unaware of the collective meaning of *zera'*. In fact, their very existence as a people is dependent on a plural meaning![16] But, similar to Paul's usage (reflecting his training in the Jewish ways of his day), the singular form is exploited as a hook on which to hang an important comment. The difference between these rabbinic texts and Paul is not that Paul, as a follower of Christ, would be somehow more restrained in his exegesis. What makes Paul different is the theology that his creative, rabbinic-like exegesis aims to articulate.

But from an exegetical point of view, what Paul's exegesis here in Galatians shares with ancient interpreters is a creative handling of grammatical ambiguities/flexibilities. In fact, the type of exegetical move displayed here by Paul is far too common a phenomenon to document in the space provided here, other than to say it is a staple of, for example, Qumran exegesis and rabbinic interpretation.[17] What a word means in its context does not necessarily trump what it *could* mean with a bit of prodding.

Such a phenomenon is often referred to as "atomistic" exegesis, meaning particular words or phrases are looked at in isolation, without being informed by the immediate or broader contexts and thus more open to manipulation. Again, it is not the case that these early interpreters did not know what they were doing. Rather, such techniques were simply accepted means of handling texts.[18] And by doing so, these interpreters were in no

---

16. The Targums (traditional Jewish translation of the Bible in Aramaic) seem to go out of their way to add to the Abrahamic promises in Genesis that the promises were to his "*sons*," thus making the plural explicit.

17. Concerning the Dead Sea Scrolls, see Matthias Henze, *Biblical Interpretation at Qumran* (Grand Rapids: Eerdmans, 2005); Maurya P. Horgan, *Pesharim: Qumran Interpretations of Biblical Books* (CBQMS 8; Washington, DC: Catholic Biblical Association of America, 1979). For a more general treatment, see Enns, *Exodus Retold*, 75–83, and various sources and examples in the footnotes. We can also lay to rest any notion that the rabbis observed Paul and followed his lead. Rather, the fact that later rabbinic literature reflects an approach to Scripture seen in Paul demonstrates that *neither* Paul *nor* the rabbis were the point of origin for this type of exegesis. What they display is a hermeneutic that precedes both of them.

18. The staying power of these interpretive traditions is demonstrated in how they have persisted in the subsequent history of interpretation, far removed from the ingenious exegetical activity that originated the tradition. This notion of the

way showing disrespect for God's Word (as we might conclude if people in our time did likewise). They did the things they did *because* they respected God's Word *as both mysterious and as speaking to contemporary circumstances.*

All this is to say that, however true Paul's theology is, the exegesis by which he demonstrates his theology *to a judaizing audience in Galatians* is a product of the Second Temple hermeneutical world in which he lived. In other words, the way in which Paul *uses* the OT here fits quite comfortably in ancient conventions although not in contemporary ones. Bearing this cultural context in mind will help us to understand how Paul could have handled his Scripture so. He is not a fool, unable to perform "proper" exegesis. But neither should we try to mount an argument for how Paul in this passage is, despite clear demonstration to the contrary, consistent with "proper" (modern) interpretive practices.

What is "proper" exegesis for Paul is determined by *his* time, not ours, and this recognition must factor into any contemporary discussion of how we explain the NT use of the OT (and subsequently how we are to be faithful to an apostolic model). The fact that such an exegetical maneuver would not be persuasive today (and in my opinion should not be reproduced, a point to which we will return in the conclusion) should *not* dissuade us from making the necessary observation that Paul's handling of Scripture here in Galatians 3:15–29 is a function of his Second Temple context. Our first task is to understand *what* Paul is doing. Only on the basis of this understanding can we proceed to discuss what it means for us today.

Angels and the Law (Galatians 3:19; Acts 7:53; Hebrews 2:2)

In addition to exegetical *method*, Galatians 3 gives us another issue worthy of our attention: the presence of an extrabiblical interpretive *tradition* in the NT. According to Galatians

---

"afterlife" of these interpretive traditions is succinctly developed in James L. Kugel, *In Potiphar's House: The Interpretive Life of Biblical Texts* (San Francisco: HarperCollins, 1990); *The Ladder of Jacob: Ancient Interpretations of the Biblical Story of Jacob and His Children* (Princeton: Princeton Univ. Press, 2006).

3:19, angels played some role in the giving of the law to Moses on Mount Sinai.

> What, then, was the purpose of the law? It was added because of transgressions until the Seed to whom the promise referred had come. *The law was given through angels* and entrusted to a mediator. (emphasis added)

The mediator, of course, is Moses, but it is curious why the law is said to have been "given through angels." A similar notion is expressed in Luke's record of Stephen's speech against his executioners in Acts 7:53: "And now you have betrayed and murdered him—you who have *received the law that was given through angels* but have not obeyed it" (emphasis added). The anonymous author of Hebrews seems to hold a similar view (Heb 2:2–3):

> For since *the message spoken through angels* was binding, and every violation and disobedience received its just punishment, how shall we escape if we ignore so great a salvation? This salvation, which was first announced by the Lord, was confirmed to us by those who heard him. (emphasis added)

These statements may not appear to be overly significant at first glance, but one simple observation is worth making: the presence of angels at Mount Sinai, through whom the law was given (Gal 3:19; Acts 7:53) or spoken (Heb 2:2), is not something that most of us would say is found on the pages of the relevant OT narratives. If anything, the OT is clear that the law was given by God to Moses directly, without angelic assistance, written by the "finger of God" (Ex 31:18; Deut 9:10) on tablets handed to Moses. There is no word of angels speaking or mediating the law in any way. One issue this raises concerns the historicity of what the NT alludes to, and so is understandably of interest to evangelical interpreters. Is there any sort of connection here between what the NT alludes to and what the OT says happened? Is there, in other words, some justification for what the NT says about "angels and the law"?

To make such a connection, one could appeal to passages where angels are mentioned in connection with Mount Sinai. We see such an incident, for example, in Exodus 3:1–4:17, where the angel of Yahweh (see 3:2) presents himself to Moses in the burning bush. Without intending to erect a straw man, it seems to me that this would be a rather flimsy hook for bearing the weight of the NT evidence. To be sure, it could be part of what led to an interpretive tradition of "angels and the law" for *Second Temple interpreters*, but that is different from arguing that Exodus 3:2 provides *historical* justification for why NT writers would speak of angels involved in the giving of the law. And not only does 3:2 say nothing of the law, but it mentions only *one* angel, the angel of Yahweh, and he quickly collapses into identification with Yahweh himself (3:4), as he does elsewhere in the OT (see Judg 13:3, 20–21, 22–23).

More promising is Deuteronomy 33:2. I find this to be ultimately unconvincing as well, but I feel it is worth addressing here in some detail, as I have come across it occasionally in both written and oral contexts. This passage in the TNIV reads as follows (with the important Hebrew words supplied in parentheses):

> The LORD came from Sinai
>   and dawned over them from Seir;
>   he shone forth from Mount Paran.
> He came with myriads of *holy ones* [*qodesh*]
>   from the south [*mimino*], from his mountain slopes
>   ['*eshdat*].

Perhaps one can see how Deuteronomy 33:2 may present a tempting solution for one trying to find an OT source for the NT tradition. There is a reference to Sinai (line 1), which could suggest the giving of the law. Likewise, the reference to "holy ones" (line 4, Hebrew *qodesh*) could suggest angels. Hence, the combination of "Sinai" and "holy ones" together could imply that angels were somehow present at the giving of the law.

But I do not think the NT authors can be so easily exonerated. Unpacking this issue properly would take considerable space and require a fair amount of interaction with a number of ancient languages, which is more than what is fitting for this volume. Still, the general issue can be laid out somewhat succinctly, and it is perhaps wise to state at the outset what my conclusion is: The NT tradition of "angels and the law" is not supported *by* this OT text, but is the fruit of exegetical activity that has tried to account for a number of difficult elements *in* this text. The main difficulties can be laid out as follows.

To begin with, the Hebrew text of Deuteronomy 33:2 is a bit tricky. First, it seems like all five lines of verse 2 refer to places *from* (Hebrew *min*) *which* the Lord comes: lines 1–3, *from* Sinai, *from* Seir, then *from* Mount Paran. Then in line 5, *from* the south (*mimino*, itself a bit of tricky Hebrew and will be discussed more below). The problem is line 4. Here, too, the Hebrew word *min* is used, thus suggesting another location. Adopting the TNIV translation for the time being for the rest of the verse, it would read woodenly **from** *myriads of holy ones.* That doesn't seem to make much sense, which is one reason why *min* here is translated "with" rather than "from." Although possible in the abstract, this is a bit awkward contextually. But "myriads of holy ones" is not a geographic location, so how can "from" make sense? The fourth line clearly raises questions.

In addition, the word *qodesh* really doesn't seem to mean "holy ones" (i.e., angels). This particular Hebrew root can have a variety of meanings, including holy, holy thing, or holy area (temple), but it is not used anywhere else in the OT to refer to angels, let alone in the singular.[19] A related root, *qadosh*, can mean angels, and this is used in verse 3 (translated "holy ones" in the TNIV), but even there the word clearly refers not to angels but to the Israelites (note the parallelism with "people" in the first half of the verse). It is really pushing matters to see a reference to angels in the fourth line of Deuteronomy 33:2.

There are two other problems with the Hebrew, this time with the fifth line, at the end of verse 2: "*from the south (mimino),* from his *mountain slopes ('eshdat)."* The Hebrew words, *mimino* and *'eshdat,* raise questions.[20] Let's focus for the moment on *'eshdat.* Most English translations consider it a form of the word *'ashed* (or *'eshed*), meaning slope, hence "mountain slopes" in the TNIV. One must admit that this would make perfect sense in the context, since, as we saw, the other lines all have the Lord coming from some mountain. It also fits nicely with *mimino*, which is woodenly translated "from (his) south." The problem with *'eshdat,* however, is lexical: the form as it is found in Deuteronomy 33:2 is not quite the same as what one sees elsewhere in the OT. Normally, the

---

19. It is not a collective noun, like *zera'*, as we saw in the previous example.

20. Technically, *mimino* is made up of *three* words: *min* = from; *yamin* = south; *o* = his. This is a property of Hebrew and does not affect the point I am making here.

plural "slopes of" would be spelled 'ashdot (e.g., Deut 3:17; 4:49), not 'eshdat; a minor difference to some perhaps, but in Hebrew, unlike in horseshoes, close is not close enough. This is why the TNIV note rightly tells us "the meaning of the Hebrew for this phrase is uncertain."

Apparently, the medieval Hebrew scribes who copied the Hebrew texts (and supplied the vowels)[21] had difficulty with this word as well, for the vowels they insert don't really work: the letter shin [sh] is vowelless, thus breaking a rule of Hebrew grammar (it needs a silent shewa). Such an irregularity often signals to us that the Hebrew scribes recognized a problem with the consonants in front of them, and so supplied vowels for what they understood the proper reading to be. (Note that, out of respect for the text, they did not change the consonants!) So, what exactly were they signaling to the reader? By vocalizing it the way they do, they are actually telling us that they consider this to be *two separate words*: 'esh and dat. The first word means "fire" and the second means "law" or "regulation" in several places in Esther, Daniel, and Ezra. It seems that the Masoretes were, for some reason, moved to understand the consonants 'shdt as two separate words, influenced perhaps by how dat was used in these three OT books.[22]

---

21. One factor that makes the study of Hebrew so interesting is that the OT was originally written without vowels. Beginning in the early medieval period, however, rabbis began to devise a system of vocalization in an effort to preserve correct pronunciation and interpretation of their Scripture. These scribes were known as "Masoretes" (from the Hebrew word "hand down"), and their efforts remain to this day: the text from which students today learn their Hebrew is this "Masoretic Text." Their work is also routinely considered to be preservation of ancient traditions rather than innovation.

22. It is also worth noting that at least Esther and Ezra are unambiguously postexilic books, and so already show signs of how Hebrew changed over the centuries: dat is not a word used for law in any other OT book. The dating of Daniel is a controversial matter for some evangelicals, but even those who date Daniel essentially to the sixth century suggest that the book went through stages until it reached its final form some time after the return from exile. This use of dat continued into postbiblical (Mishnaic) Hebrew. Also, this understanding of 'eshdat is followed by Jerome in his translation of the Bible into Latin (Vulgate) around AD 400: "He came with myriads of holy ones, in his right hand a *fiery law*." Even this does not necessarily equate *angels* with the "fiery law" but it does represent an early attempt to account for the Masoretic vocalization. This tradition is also preserved in Targum

What bearing does all this have on the NT tradition of "angels and the law"? It is simply that we would be expecting an awful lot of this one cryptic passage for it to bear the weight of "legitimizing" the NT tradition. Put more directly, if asked "why would the NT think of angels as being involved in the giving of the law?" I would feel a bit disingenuous to offer Deuteronomy 33:2 as a resolution. Even leaving to the side the complexities of the Hebrew and taking a step back from some of the details we have been looking at, the larger picture seems self-evident: Moses is simply saying, "Look out, Canaan. Yahweh is on the move, coming down from the mountains, and he is bringing his holy people with him."

Important for our discussion, too, is the reference to the law in the second half of verse 3 and verse 4:

> At your feet they all bow down,
>   and from you receive *instruction*,
> the *law* that Moses gave us,
>   the *possession* of the assembly of Jacob. (emphasis added)

The "they" who bow down are the "holy ones" in Yahweh's hand, who are the "people" (i.e., Israel) referred to in the first half of verse 3. It is they who receive *instruction* from Yahweh, which is the *law* given by Moses. So, even apart from a particular handling of *'eshdat* in verse 2, law is explicitly referenced in verse 4. Still, there is no reference here, whatsoever, to angels having any part in it.

There is one more piece of important information that should be mentioned at least, and that is how this passage is handled in the Greek OT (known as the Septuagint, or LXX).[23] The reason the LXX is worthy of mention is because the Greek

---

Onkelos, the official Aramaic translation of the Pentateuch in medieval Judaism. The later date precludes our drawing direct connections between it and the NT, but the Targum is hardly following the NT lead on the matter! Rather, it certainly preserves a well-known, perhaps even ancient and honored, piece of Jewish interpretation. Again, the general point is that the NT references to angels and the law are not their invention, nor can they be understood in isolation from the interpretive matrix of Second Temple Judaism.

23. This means "seventy" and is a reference to the legendary explanation of its origin: seventy scribes finishing their work in seventy days.

OT was, by and large, the Bible of the NT writers. Now, this is a bit of an overstatement, since a number of OT citations in the NT seem to correspond more closely to the Hebrew text than to the Greek, and some don't line up with any version in particular. Nevertheless, the LXX's central importance for the NT writers is beyond question, and so we need to see if there is anything we can gain from it to address our specific question of why the NT writers referred to "angels and the law."

If one compares the TNIV of Deuteronomy 33:2 with an English translation of the LXX,[24] one notices some differences (major ones in bold).

"The LORD came from Sinai
and dawned over *us* from Seir;
he *hastened* from Mount Paran.
with myriads of **Kadesh**
on his right hand, **angels with him**.

There are some minor differences ("us" rather than "them"; "hastened" rather than "shone forth"), but there are three major differences. (1) Note how the LXX takes the Hebrew *qodesh* as a place name Kadesh. The difference in vowels is not a major issue here, for the Hebrew text on which the LXX is based had no vowels, as mentioned above, and so the consonants *qdsh* were read as the place name (Greek has no $/q/$ and so uses $/k/$). This fits nicely with the remainder of the passage, which mentions four other place names. (2) Also, what the TNIV translates as "from the south" (Hebrew *mimino*) is here "on his right hand." The fact is that in ancient Near Eastern geography, "right" is one way of saying "south" (facing east, north is left, south is right, west is behind), and so the TNIV's translation is not problematic from a lexical point of view. In fact, it makes better sense of the "*o*", *his*, at the end of the word.

It is not immediately clear, however, why the LXX takes *qdsh* as a place name, in keeping with the general tenor of the

---

24. I will only acknowledge here the added complexity of just *which* "LXX" any particular NT writer would have had access to. The Dead Sea Scrolls have made it particularly clear that the development and state of the LXX during the first century AD is complex. This state of affairs, however, will not affect the general point being made here.

passage to speak of locations from which the Lord came, but then takes *mimino* in a nongeographical way, unless it is to correspond more easily with the next word. The LXX reads that difficult Hebrew *'eshdat*, somewhat inexplicably, as "angels with him." How these two are connected is cloudy indeed, but it likely reflects the Greek translator's attempt to handle a real difficulty.

Why is this important to bring up? Because in the LXX, we have not only the Lord coming from these places, *one of which is Sinai*, but he is coming *with angels*! And since the LXX is so influential for the NT authors, this could easily account for some connection with angels at Mount Sinai, as the NT authors have it. But how the LXX can get from *'eshdat* to "angels with him" is a mystery indeed, and suggests, as is so often the case with the LXX, that its rendering is either evidence of an attempt to explain a real difficulty in the Hebrew, or (more conjecturally) evidence that the Hebrew text upon which the LXX is based is different from the Masoretic Text. [25]

Either way, the simple point must be observed, that the LXX reading is itself evidence of a textual problem with Deuteronomy 33:2. Even if the NT tradition were based on this one verse (which, we must remember, is itself conjectural), then that tradition rests on something that would generate certain theological problems of its own; namely, that either the NT tradition was ultimately based on a Hebrew text not known to us, or is based on the LXX translator's reflections either on a problematic Hebrew verse, or (in my view more likely) his interaction with an interpretive tradition that by his time (a century or two BC) had already come to be commonly known.

I hope I have done sufficient justice to the complexities of these issues surrounding Deuteronomy 33:2–4 without it being too much of a burden. Lest the overall point be obscured, let me state it plainly. The connection between angels and the law is not one found in the pages of the Hebrew OT we have (the Masoretic Text), but seems to be a result of early translators and

---

25. This is a distinct possibility known to us since the discovery of multiple "text types" of the Hebrew OT found among the Dead Sea Scrolls. If this is the case, it would introduce yet another complexity, but one that would not affect the general point to be made below.

interpreters trying to give an account of a difficult bit of Hebrew. I seriously doubt that Paul, Luke, or the anonymous author of Hebrews were cogitating on their OT, trying to ferret out the difficulties of Deuteronomy 33:2. And their words cannot be accounted for *simply* by appealing to the LXX, since the only connection that is *at best* established there is that of angels being *present* at Mount Sinai.

Actually, the only ancient evidence we have for the giving of the *law* being involved is in the Vulgate (although there explicit reference to angels is missing, see n. 22 above) and suggested (somewhat strongly, I would think) by the Masoretic (medieval) vocalization of *'shdt*. It is hard (impossible, actually) to determine who influenced whom, but the simplest explanation is that Jerome, the Christian who translated the Vulgate, was influenced by his own knowledge of the NT as well as his well-known exposure to rabbinic teaching (from whom he learned Hebrew).

The NT texts, however, are influenced by neither the Vulgate nor Masoretes (since both are much later), although I would suggest that the Masoretes are *preserving* an ancient tradition that was likely known already in the first century and of which Luke, Paul, and the writer of Hebrews seem clearly to have been aware. In fact, this tradition must have been very well known for it to have found its way into texts authored by three separate NT writers, and to be mentioned in such a casual manner so as to suggest that their readers would have shared that familiarity. In other words, by remarking that angels were involved in law giving, the NT writers were reflecting a particular and *popular* interpretive tradition that was the product of intense exegetical activity, some of which can be glimpsed in the LXX, Vulgate, and even the vowels of the Masoretic text of the OT. The NT writers simply spoke within the context of this interpretive setting, and neither they nor their audience apparently needed any further explanation.

This raises some issues for us as we consider the question of historicity. If the NT says something about the giving of the law that reflects hermeneutical difficulties rather than historical reality, would this not impugn Scripture's character? Of course, this is a vital question, but in our efforts to safeguard Scripture's integrity (or perhaps better, our understanding of what "Scripture's integrity" entails), we should not be too eager to manufacture explanations. For example, one could argue, if pressed, that the NT authors were given special revelation, that is, knowledge of something that happened at Sinai but which the OT does not record. Hence, even though the OT does not record such an event, such knowledge was revealed to them in the course of their writing Scripture.

This strikes me, however, as wholly conjectural—perhaps even a bit desperate. It is worth noting that the "angels and the law" idea is not presented by the NT authors as anything new or revelatory—the opposite is the case. The reference to angels has a decidedly "matter of fact" or "as we all know" quality about it. In fact, the argument in Acts 7, Galatians 3, and Hebrews 2 assumes that the readers are *quite familiar* with this piece of interpretation. Otherwise, the force of the argument would be lost. One could, I suppose, push the matter back further by saying that this new information was revealed to someone else, not known to us, at some previous time, likewise not known to us, and of which the early church was made aware through apostolic teaching. But at some point one begins to wonder just who might be persuaded by such a line of argumentation, which seems aimed at driving some distance between the NT authors and the interpretive world of which they were a part.

Another line of argumentation by which one could attempt to anchor the NT comments in Deuteronomy 33:2–4 is by saying that the "angels and the law" tradition, although not present in the Sinai narrative, *was* originally present in Deuteronomy 33:2, but was lost due to textual corruption. Admittedly, this is *possible* in the abstract, but one must also admit that this explanation puts an awful lot of stress on what comes down essentially to how one word in the Hebrew is handled: *'eshdat*. It would also require a particular way of reading *mimino* earlier in that same stanza ("in his right hand" instead of "from the south") and also *qodesh* (reading it as "angels" [plural]). Of course, it is still *possible*, but numerous explanations are possible if one is determined enough to find them.

If, however, in order to find an explicit reference in the OT to the angels/law tradition to exonerate the NT authors, one must appeal to a single reference at the end of the Pentateuch in a difficult poetic text, one wonders how strong a case can be made. The case I am making here is that, on the whole, we

should not assume the universal normativity of our own interpretive expectations and then seek explanations that are *possible*
within those conventions; rather, we should give an account of
biblical phenomena that conforms to ancient conventions and
the data we have available.

Let me address further the issue of historicity. If the law /
angels connection originated as an attempt to handle a difficult
and ambiguous piece of Hebrew, one cannot avoid for long the
historical issue such an explanation raises. One way of main-
taining some historical tie here would be to pose a hypothetical
source, analogous to what we find in Judaism's appeal to the
"oral law" (which gives us the Mishnah and Talmud). In that
case, the role of angels at Mount Sinai could be understood as
an *event* well-known through *oral* channels, *even if not recorded
in the OT.* As is taught in Judaism concerning the oral law, not
everything said or done at Sinai is recorded in writing. Some of
it is recorded in Scripture, but some remained on the oral level
and was faithfully transmitted from generation to generation
(perhaps an early hint of which we see in the LXX translation
of Deuteronomy 33:2–3, which can be dated to the first two or
three centuries BC). So, the NT writers in question would simply
be appealing to this nonwritten but no less reliable/authorita-
tive body of (oral) literature.

This is a possible explanation and one that I feel should
be entertained, but this does not mean it is the only or even the
most persuasive one. It seems to be based on an assumption that
the historicity of such an event *must* be concrete in order for it to
be worthy of NT Scripture. In other words, historicity is such a
thoroughly central component of what we consider to be essential
of biblical revelation that, if a NT writer alludes to an otherwise
unattested (or mutedly attested) episode in the OT, its historicity must be assumed, even if the OT itself does not mention it.
Again, it is possible to argue this way, and I am in principle open
to it. Nevertheless, there is a bit of an irony here: in an effort to
protect the NT against the charge of ahistoricity, appeal is made
to a completely hypothetical, extrabiblical, transmission of historical information.

I understand and sympathize with the motive to defend
Scripture's historicity. This is important, but perhaps in this instance we are barking up the wrong tree. Perhaps, when lined

up against what we know of Second Temple practices, a more hermeneutical explanation presents itself as, at least, *plausible* and as worthy of a place at the evangelical discussion table. In my view, the "angels and the law" tradition is more a question of hermeneutical rather than historical interest.

No, this does not put us on the slippery slope of denying or leaving open the window to a denial of the historical nature of the gospel or biblical revelation in general! It is wholly unwarranted logically to argue that, if traditional material is found in one portion of the Bible, the Bible's entire historical witness is thereby impugned. I reject this line of argumentation categorically. The Lord is the Lord of history. Christianity is a historical faith. But this does not mean that we should expect a historical purity such as would not only sever Scripture from the cultural milieu in which it was given, but from the type of historical accounting that we, even in today's world, take for granted all the time (few expect complete objectivity and historical purity in modern historiography).[26]

If we wish to explain how three NT writers can appeal to an undocumented event in the OT, yet speak of it in such a way that presumes its widespread understanding, it may help to broaden our scope a bit. It is worth emphasizing that the "angels and the law" tradition is not the only example of its kind in the NT. There are other examples, no less valuable but that can only be hinted at here, of NT authors referring to episodes involving OT characters or events that are not found in the OT but that the writers presume their audiences to understand. For example: Jannes and Jambres as the names of Pharaoh's magicians (2 Tim 3:8); the reference to the quarrel between Satan and Michael over Moses' body (Jude 9); Noah as a "preacher of righteousness" (2 Peter 2:5); the specific reference to Enoch in Jude 14–15; the reference to Moses' Egyptian education (Acts 7:22); a mobile source of water during the Israelites' wilderness wanderings (1 Cor 10:4).

---

26. A fuller discussion of this issue is not possible here, but any reflections of the nature of historiography with respect to, say, the "angels and law" tradition, would also need to address upfront the numerous *biblical* examples of historiography where degrees of artistry, perspective, and even alteration of events are present, namely, the synoptic passages of Scripture such as Samuel/Kings vis-à-vis Chronicles and the four Gospels. For a brief review of the issues involved, see Enns, *Inspiration and Incarnation*, 59–66.

One difference between the "angels and the law" tradition and these other examples listed here is that the latter all have demonstrably extrabiblical parallels in overtly interpretive literature (i.e., not simply translations like the LXX, although that, too, is by no means devoid of interpretive characteristics).[27] It is possible, however, that *Jubilees*[28] can offer some assistance, since there the revelation given to Moses is mediated through "the angel of the presence." *Jubilees* 1 begins with a declaration that it contains the Lord's recounting to Moses of the law (1:1–4) as well as a recounting of past and future events (vv. 4–6). This goes on for a number of verses, but then in verse 27 we read: "And he [the Lord] said to the angel of the presence, '*Write for Moses* from the first creation until my sanctuary is built in their midst forever and ever. . . .'" Here the angel of the presence does the *writing*. Then in verse 29, that same angel takes *possession of the tablets*. In 2:1, it is the angel who *speaks* to Moses the words he is to record, beginning with creation.

Whether this theme in *Jubilees* reflects in any way a general understanding of angelic mediation of the law is, frankly, impossible to say. But, even though only one angel is mentioned, at least here there is a reference to *concrete angelic activity on Mount Sinai*. Regardless, what is clear to me is that Acts 7, Galatians 3, and Hebrews 2 are better understood within the context of early translations and Second Temple interpretive traditions, rather than as (1) products of their own, private, exegetical ingenuity, (2) special revelation they received of heretofore unknown events, or (3) reflections of an oral body of information that goes back to the events themselves and that was well known but did not make it into the Bible (for some unexplained reason). The presence of interpretive traditions not only in the NT but in Second Temple literature in general is a significant factor in trying to explain this otherwise cryptic reference to angels as giving or speaking the law to Moses.

---

27. A discussion of these interpretive traditions, including extrabiblical references, can be found in ibid., 142–51.

28. *Jubilees*, an account of the events from creation to the building of the tabernacle, is one of the oldest extant pieces of Second Temple literature (early second century BC), and as such, gives us a valuable glimpse into a relatively early stage of biblical interpretation.

"Out of Egypt I Called My Son"
(Matthew 2:15 and Hosea 11:1)

Our previous two examples have touched on the writings of Paul, Luke, and the anonymous author of Hebrews. The second example in particular has highlighted some of the complexities involved concerning the NT use of the OT in the Second Temple period and the degree to which Second Temple interpretive traditions influenced NT writers. One final example, from Matthew's gospel, illustrates in a more direct fashion the Christ-centered focus of the NT writers. The passage we will look at here is one of the more celebrated, if also controversial, in this debate, and much has been written on it. In my view, one reason for the attention Matthew 2:15 receives is that it seems to be such a clear-cut example of a highly theologized, noncontextual, reading of the OT; thus, some effort is spent to disentangle Matthew from the charge of arbitrariness in his exegesis. Matthew's handling of Hosea 11:1, however, reveals his theological depth if we allow his interpretive principles to surface. In other words, Matthew is anything but arbitrary, even if his interpretive approach does not line up with our expectations of responsible exegesis.

It is widely recognized that Matthew's gospel is geared toward a Jewish audience. Hence, Matthew brings the OT into his gospel more times than the other three gospels. He also does so in ways that seem strained to modern eyes. One such example is Matthew's use of Hosea 11:1, which is one of several important OT citations in the early chapters of his gospel by which he ties the story of Jesus to the story of Israel.

> And having been warned in a dream not to go back to Herod, they returned to their country by another route.
>
> When they had gone, an angel of the Lord appeared to Joseph in a dream. "Get up," he said, "take the child and his mother and escape to Egypt. Stay there until I tell you, for Herod is going to search for the child to kill him."
>
> So he got up, took the child and his mother during the night and left for Egypt, where he stayed until the death of Herod. *And so was fulfilled what the Lord had said through the prophet: "Out of Egypt I called my son."* (Matt 2:12–15, emphasis added)

Matthew understands Jesus' trip as a boy to Egypt to escape Herod (and his subsequent return) as a fulfillment of Hosea 11:1. The well-known problem, however, is that even a quick scan of the context of Hosea 11 makes it clear that Hosea himself is not talking about the boy Jesus, nor is he even addressing the issue of a future Messiah. In fact, Hosea 11 is not looking to the future at all but simply alluding to the past.[29]

> When Israel was a child, I loved him,
>> and *out of Egypt I called my son.*
> But the more they were called,
>> the more they went away from me.
> They sacrificed to the Baals
>> and they burned incense to images.
> It was I who taught Ephraim to walk,
>> taking them by the arms;
> but they did not realize
>> it was I who healed them. (Hos 11:1–3, emphasis
>> added)

Hosea's point here is that Israel is God's child, his son, and he loved him, and so he delivered Israel from Egypt. But, in return, the Israelites turned to idolatry. This passage is not *predictive* of Christ's (or anyone else's) coming but *retrospective* of Israel's disobedience and God's deliberating over what he is going to do about it. It is my opinion that it obscures matters to argue that Matthew is observant of or somehow bound to the historical context of Hosea's words, namely, that there actually is something predictive or eschatological in Hosea 11. What drives Matthew to handle Hosea's words is, in my view, something other than a commitment to how Hosea's words functioned in their original setting.

So, why does Matthew handle Hosea this way? Why does he (or perhaps better, how can he) employ a passage that is retrospective of Israel as a nation and treat it as if it is predictive of the boy Jesus, even calling it "fulfillment"? An important factor to keep in

---

29. Not all would accept this initial assessment. For an exchange on this very issue see J. Sailhamer, "Hosea 11:1 and Matthew 2:15," *WTJ* 63 (2001): 87–96; D. McCartney and P. Enns, "Matthew and Hosea: A Response to John Sailhamer," *WTJ* 63 (2001): 97–105.

mind in trying to address this question is that Matthew was writing to a Jewish audience. Such a handling of the OT would not have seemed strange but familiar. Once again, our focus should be on how Matthew's use of the OT would have been heard at *that* time, not in our time. Of course, Jews not believing in Christ would have disagreed with Matthew, but not because their exegetical sensibilities would have been violated. They would have disagreed because they did not share Matthew's faith in Christ.

This leads to a second point. It seems that what drove Matthew's exegesis was not Hosea's own words taken in isolation, but how those words were understood in light of Christ's coming. To put it more forcefully, it is because Matthew *knew* that Jesus was the Christ—writing as he did after Christ's death and resurrection—that he also knew that all Scripture speaks of him. But to say this is not to suggest a superficial rummaging through the OT in search of proof texts to hook his Jewish readers. Rather, Matthew's use of Hosea reflects a deep clarity of theological conviction, but one that can only come in light of the reality of Pentecost.

Although neither I nor anyone else can step into Matthew's head and outline precisely how he understood Hosea, the following suggestion is quite reasonable. It may be that Matthew had in mind not simply this one verse in Hosea 11, but the larger context of that chapter. There were no verse numbers in Matthew's day. Citing one verse may have been a way of saying "that part of Hosea that begins with 'Out of Egypt I called my son.'" If this is true,[30] we may be able to trace out some of Matthew's broader theological underpinnings. The son in Hosea and the Son in Matthew are a study in contrasts. A young *Israel* came out of Egypt, was disobedient, deserved punishment, yet was forgiven by God (see Hos 11:8–11). The boy *Christ* came out of Egypt, led a life of perfect obedience, deserved no punishment, but was crucified—the guiltless for the guilty.

By presenting Jesus this way, Matthew was able to mount an argument for his readers that Jesus fulfilled the ideal that Israel was supposed to have reached but never did. Jesus is the true Israel, God's true Son. Again, this is just one way of putting

---

30. For example, see Dodd, *According to the Scriptures,* as summarized on p. 126.

together Matthew's theological logic, and it is certainly up for debate. What is certain, however, is that Matthew's use of Hosea most definitely had an internal logic that was indeed meaningful to his readers. Our obligation is to try to understand Matthew *as he would have been understood by his original audience*, not as we might be prone to understand him.

Even though both Hosea and Matthew are inspired, Matthew has the final word on how Hosea is to be understood, which can only be seen by looking at the grander scope of God's overall redemptive plan. This is not to drive a wedge between Hosea and God: God inspired Hosea to say what he said for his time. It is, however, to acknowledge that the ultimate meaning of Hosea's words is not exhausted by the circumstances of his moment. Rather, Hosea's words are only truly fulfilled when God says they are, and that happens only when his Son has come to complete Israel's story. Matthew is not reading Hosea "objectively." He did not arrive at his conclusion *from* reading Hosea. Rather, he began with the event by which all else is now to be understood. *It is the reality of the risen Christ that drove him to read Hosea in a new way*: "Now that I see how it all ends, I can see how this part of the OT, too, drives us forward."

As an analogy, it is helpful to think of the process of reading a good novel the first time and the second time. The two readings are not the same experience. Who of us has not said during that second reading, "I didn't see that the first time," or "So *that's* how the pieces fit together." The fact that the OT is not a novel should not diminish the value of the analogy: the first reading of the OT leaves you with hints, suggestions, trajectories, and so on, of how things will play out in the end, but it is not until you get to the end that you begin to see how the pieces fit together. And, in that second reading you also begin to see how parts of the story that seemed wholly unrelated at first now take on a much richer, deeper significance.

If Matthew were to be transported back into Hosea's time and had the opportunity to tell Hosea that his words would be fulfilled in the boy Jesus, and that, furthermore, this Jesus would be crucified and rise again for God's people, I am not sure if Hosea would have known what to make of it. But if Hosea were to go forward to Matthew's day, it would be very different for him. There Hosea would be forced, in light of recent events, to see his words—*precisely because they are inspired by God, the divine author*—in the final *eschatological* context. In a stunning reversal, it is now *Matthew* who would show *Hosea* how his words fit into God's ultimate redemptive goal: the death and resurrection of Christ. And so Hosea's words, which in their original historical context did not speak of Jesus of Nazareth, now do.

Conclusion

Three examples of the NT use of the OT have been considered here. The second example, concerning angelic presence at the giving of the law, is focused on the phenomenon of the presence of interpretive traditions in the NT. The first and third examples pertain more specifically to interpretive methods employed to highlight the Christ-centeredness of the NT authors. Both of these phenomena bring to the surface some important theological issues for us to consider, and we conclude here with some reflections toward that end.

SOME IMPLICATIONS FOR CONTEMPORARY INTERPRETATION

Scripture's "Humiliation" as a Positive Theological Construct

The interpretation of the OT by the NT authors is embedded in their cultural moment. This is not to say that their interpretive comments are wholly determined by their Second Temple context. It is, however, to acknowledge that how the NT authors approached the task of biblical interpretation (their methods) and how they understood certain OT episodes (their traditions) boldly bear the unmistakable stamp of their historical setting. But more important than this bare observation (for it is common sense that any author reflects his or her setting) is the fact that this very process is one that also bears the stamp of God's imprimatur. In other words, the ancient, Second Temple, human feel of the NT authors' interpretive methods and traditions is not something we need to put up with today, work around, or push off to the side. It is, rather, yet another demonstration of how God condescends to the human drama.

To be sure, God is the sovereign Lord over all cultures and all times. He not only steps into the human drama, but he also stands over and behind it. But this makes the matter before us all the more wonderful and amazing. God *could* have set things up any way he pleased. He *could* have done things so differently. But he was pleased to allow the complex matter of, say, the "angels/law" tradition to develop. He was pleased to allow interpretive methods and traditions, so different from what we consider normative today, to be the matrix within which Israel's Scripture was interpreted — in the most pressing moment in human history, the incarnation of the Son of God. It is as if God punctuates the utter humiliation of his own incarnation in Jesus of Nazareth by allowing his Word to take on an analogous humiliation.

If there is any lasting lesson to be learned here, it is memorably articulated by Herman Bavinck. He wrote that a doctrine of Scripture

> is the working out and application of the central fact of revelation: the incarnation of the Word. The Word (Logos) has become flesh (sarx), and the word has become Scripture; these two facts do not only run parallel but are most intimately connected. Christ became flesh, a servant, without form or comeliness, the most despised of human beings; he descended to the nethermost parts of the earth and became obedient even to death on the cross. So also the word, the revelation of God, entered the world of creatureliness, the life and history of humanity, in all the human forms of dream and vision, of investigation and reflection, right down into that which is humanly weak and despised and ignoble.... All this took place in order that the excellency of the power ... of Scripture, may be God's and not ours.[31]

What is so clear for Bavinck is the positive theological value of Scripture's incarnational form. There is a reason why Scripture looks the way it does, with all its bumps and bruises, peaks and valleys, gaps and gashes — it is to exalt *God's* power, not ours. This accent on the Bible's humanity should not be misunderstood as a failure to give the divine authorship of Scripture its due place. Rather, to accent the notion that Scripture reflects

---

31. Bavinck, *Reformed Dogmatics*, 1:434–35 (my emphasis).

the ancient contexts in which it was written is to proclaim as good and powerful what that divine author has actually, by his wisdom, produced. The Spirit's primary authorship is not questioned, nor does Scripture's humiliation imply error.[32] Bavinck's point is simply that the "creatureliness" of Scripture is not an obstacle to be overcome, but *the very means by which Scripture's divinity can be seen.*

In fact, Scripture's divinity can *only* be seen *because* of its humanity—God's chosen means—not by looking past it. And it is not just humanity as a safe theoretical construct. It is a humanity that is "weak and despised and ignoble." *That* is what points us to the divine, just as Christ does in his state of humiliation. To marginalize, or minimize, or somehow get behind the Bible's "creatureliness" to the "real" word of God is, for Bavinck, to strip God of his glory.

The upshot of all this is first of all to acknowledge freely—indeed, enthusiastically—Scripture's humiliation as something God himself has ordained. This does not mean his ways will be plain to us at all times, and it certainly does not mean his ways are our ways. Rather, our focus should be on accepting the Scripture God has given and exploring the richness of its humanity, the depth of its humiliation.

Do *Sensus Plenior* and Typology Adequately Describe the NT Use of the OT?

Embracing Scripture's humiliation, not simply as a factor to be accepted but as a positive theological construct, will have some influence on how we address several important and perennial issues that pertain to the NT use of the OT. Throughout our discussion so far, two related issues have been lurking in the background. Given the nature of the NT use of the OT, as described above, can we say (1) that the OT has a "fuller sense" (*sensus plenior*) than what was envisioned by the OT authors, and/or (2) that the connection between the OT text and its NT interpretation is "typological"? I see these matters as somewhat

---

32. As eloquent as Bavinck is on the incarnational model, he is also careful to guard against misuses of that model as justification for unorthodox views. See, for example, his discussion in *Reformed Dogmatics*, beginning at 1.435.

related. In my view, both terms express true and helpful notions about the NT use of the OT, although bringing these well-known terms into conversation with an incarnational approach to Scripture may add a dimension or two to how these terms are used.

First, with respect to *sensus plenior*, I do feel that this is a helpful theological construct in that it addresses the matter of divine authorship in view of the phenomena we have observed. If we assume (as I do and I presume readers of this volume do as well) that God is the ultimate author of Scripture, then the evidence of the NT use of the OT will bring us to conclude something like "there is a fuller sense for the OT than what God revealed to the OT authors, but that God himself intended to be displayed in Christ."

To put it another way, the original purpose of an OT passage does not exhaust its meaning. Even though that OT author was inspired by God and spoke by his direction to the matters of the day, there is a fuller sense, known to God, that is not understood until it is revealed by the Spirit at Christ's coming, more specifically at Pentecost. Such an explanation does not necessarily raise much of an objection in evangelical circles. But where things begin to get a bit more involved is (1) whether that fuller sense can be understood as a possible *application* of the OT or whether it constitutes a true fuller *meaning*; and, the somewhat related point, (2) whether the "fuller sense" is "consistent with" or "derived from" the text's meaning in its original setting.

As I mentioned at the outset of this essay, the many individual examples of the NT use of the OT defy simplistic categorization. At times, the connection between what an OT author intended and how that is used in the NT is somewhat plainer and straightforward, at other times more subtle, and still at other times the connection between the Old and the New seems virtually impossible to explain. I have chosen examples that I feel are more problematic for some conventional explanations. Regardless, as to the first issue just mentioned, it is hard for me to think that NT authors, in bringing the OT to bear on the gospel, the climax of God's covenant, were only thinking of themselves as "applying" an OT message rather than telling us what that passage in fact really means (albeit in a fuller, Christological, sense).

The distinction between application and meaning is a helpful and important one in certain arenas, to be sure, but I do not think it is of general usefulness when the topic turns to the NT use of the OT. I do not think that Paul in Galatians 3 or Matthew in Matthew 2 was saying, "Here is a possible way of applying the OT to Jesus." Rather, in my view, they were peeling back the curtain and allowing us to see a great mystery, namely, the depths to which Jesus of Nazareth is the climax of Israel's story. The application/meaning distinction may help guard the NT authors against the charge of employing haphazard, subjective, or illegitimate hermeneutics, but what is lost in the process is far too precious. Rather, it seems to me that the NT authors are *subsuming* the OT under the authority of the crucified and risen Christ, the one in whom God's people, and therefore the Scripture that tells their story, now find their coherence.

If I may put it a bit more boldly, it is a failure to reckon with the uncompromising hermeneutical centrality of the person and work of Christ for the NT authors — that is, the eschatological dimension of their recurrent confession that in Christ something "final" has happened — that encourages the dichotomy between "meaning" and "application." How precisely the two horizons relate in specific instances will (and should) always remain topics of inquiry, but to assume that the original and Christological intentions *need* to be aligned (in ways that reflect our own hermeneutical sensitivities) is to get off on a bad start if our task is to understand the NT authors' hermeneutic and would, therefore, marginalize the general thrust of the Bible's own witness.

As for the second, and related, point, the overall hermeneutical phenomenon of the NT use of the OT cannot, in my opinion, be explained by positing a "consistency" between how the OT originally functions and how it is employed in light of the coming of Christ. In this respect, the notion of *sensus plenior* is helpful in alerting contemporary readers that God's Word is not fully understood until the climax of God's covenant with Israel, the person and work of Christ, is revealed. Where it is not helpful, however, is if *sensus plenior* is employed as a theological construct acting as an *alternate* explanation for why the NT behaves as it does; that is, an explanation that does not take into serious consideration the *hermeneutical climate of the NT authors*. Positing a fuller meaning, known to God and revealed in Christ, does not let us off the hook of explaining the hermeneutical activity of the NT authors.

Perhaps a discussion of the related concept, typology, will help illustrate the point. The term is defined in a variety of ways, but it basically refers to persons, events, and institutions in the OT that are legitimate but incomplete expressions of what will only come to a full expression in the person and work of Christ and in the church. Typology is a helpful and time-honored way of expressing how the NT fulfills the OT in broader, thematic ways, and so highlights an important and deep level of coherence between the OT and NT.

Some of these grand themes are well known and hardly need detailed recapitulation here. Christ, in his person and work, is the final temple, prophet, priest, king, and sage. He embodies and brings the law to its completion and ultimate expression. He is the ultimate and final sacrifice, thus rendering the OT sacrificial system obsolete. As God's Son he fulfills what Israel, God's son, was assigned to do but did not complete. He is the second and final Adam, undoing what the first Adam did. Most important, Jesus in the NT does what Yahweh in the OT did.

In all of these ways, Jesus fulfills the trajectories established in the OT. It is true, not *all* OT trajectories find such a fulfillment in Christ,[33] but the broad theological contours of the OT are described as having been fulfilled, that is, having received their ultimate expression, in Christ. But, just as we have seen with *sensus plenior*, typology, although a wholly adequate *theological* description, does not provide an adequate *hermeneutical* explanation for the mechanics of what NT authors do with OT texts. In other words, like *sensus plenior*, typology cannot serve as an alternate explanation for the phenomenon of the NT use of the OT in isolation from the types of data outlined briefly in this essay.

Take, for example, Galatians 3 and the seed/seeds issue. This phenomenon can rightly be explained in part by means of

---

33. For example, Ezekiel's eschatological priest (ch. 44) was to be from the Levite line of Zadok. Christ, the final priest, is from a non-Levite line altogether, the tribe of Judah. I would add that even these OT trajectories that seem to stop short in the NT are not without significant theological value for the church, although a discussion of such matters would take us far beyond the topic at hand.

the theological categories of *sensus plenior* and typology: there is a fuller sense to the Abrahamic promises, and they point to a greater and final articulation in Christ. But one must recognize that this theological explanation does not address the hermeneutical issues involved. To be sure, let us say that in "God's mind," when the Abrahamic promises were uttered, God knew there was more to it (*sensus plenior*) and that it was all heading somewhere (typology), but this does not explain Paul's exegetical logic in Galatians 3. Christ is the final realization of such OT institutions, and broad themes such as temple, priesthood, and kingship are typological, but those examples are very different indeed from the seed/seeds issue.

I would say that the same overarching principle is at work in all of these examples, including the one in Galatians 3, but they work on two very different hermeneutical levels. To put it all another way, Paul's argument in Galatians 3 can be described as an example of *sensus plenior* and typology, but the hermeneutical practices that formed the exegetical "logic" by which those terms are articulated are a function of the historical Second Temple context and must figure into the discussion.

Matthew's use of Hosea 11 is similar. In God's mind, Israel as his son is the incomplete manifestation of what would only come to light in the incarnation of Christ, the true and final Son of God. There is both a fuller and typological sense of Hosea 11 implied in Matthew's use of it. Nevertheless, that identification between Israel and Christ is not something that is derived *from* a reading of Hosea but is only seen in the "fullness of time" when Matthew understands, in retrospect, the deep theological significance of Jesus' life.

The specific hermeneutical problem we as evangelicals face is that, as seen in our examples, the fuller sense and typological trajectory of an OT passage do not so much rise out of the OT passage in question—or at the very least we should say that a "causal" nexus from the OT to NT interpretation is not of the *essence* of the NT use of the OT. Rather, it is only by paying attention to the NT authors at work that these fuller meanings and typological trajectories can begin to be addressed. As glimpsed above, I do not think the ancient author or reader of Genesis thought that the seed promise referred to one person, or that Hosea's comments in chapter 11 led anyone to conclude that the boy Messiah would take a trip to and from Egypt. *God* knew, and we can call this *sensus plenior* and typology, but these designations do not settle the hermeneutical question of the *manner* in which God chose to articulate these matters to a first-century readership, living in the afterglow of the resurrection of the Son of God.

The problem before us, put yet another way, is that the ultimate (trans-exegetical) *theological* coherence between the Testaments, embodied in the person and work of Christ, is expressed *hermeneutically* by methods and traditions of first-century Palestine. One gets the impression, more often than not, that the NT authors were at times mining the OT for opportunities to connect what they knew to be true with Israel's story. The larger question before us, as articulated by Longenecker and Bavinck cited above, is whether we will seize this theological problem as a challenge to be met in furthering our understanding of Scripture, or whether we will deem it fundamentally problematic and, hence, maneuver to alternate explanations.

My concern, from where I stand, is that alternate explanations, at some level, succeed in distancing the NT writers from their hermeneutical environment, on the basis of alleged "higher" theological principles, rather than allowing the witness of Scripture *as a historical phenomenon* to play its proper role in forming the theological principles we appeal to. It is a question, as stated above, of whether Scripture's humiliation will play a positive theological role in evangelical articulations of this phenomenon. To take such a direction could bring temporary discomfort for some but also long-term benefit as we continue to seek to be biblical in our approach to understanding Scripture.

Can the NT Use of the OT Be Adequately Explained by an Appeal to the Broader Context of the Passage Cited?

We have noted above that, as C. H. Dodd has argued, references to the OT by NT authors do at times seem to have more in view than just the specific verse cited. This strikes me as a helpful avenue of approach with respect to Matthew's use of Hosea, as discussed above. Where I would become a bit hesitant, however, is if appeal were made to the larger context as a means of protecting the NT authors against the charge of "illegitimate" interpretation: "I know Matthew's use of Hosea 11 may look odd at first glance, but the larger context of Hosea will show that Matthew is really following the trajectory of the book."[34]

This is unconvincing to me. A look at the broader context (as I have done above briefly with respect to Hosea 11 as a whole) can certainly raise possibilities to explain Matthew's theology, but it leaves unanswered why in the world Matthew would ever think of reading a retrospective passage about Israel as a prospective passage about the Messiah. The answer to that question lies not in a hermeneutical trajectory embedded in the original meaning of Hosea's words, but in a hermeneutical conclusion revealed to Matthew and articulated by means of conventions common to Jewish interpretation of the day.

To put it differently, Matthew's Jewish readers would not, I think, have chided Matthew's use of Hosea on hermeneutical grounds, saying, "You have violated the original sense." And a retort by Matthew, "Not to worry, I am drawing on the broader context to make my point," would not have sufficed. Matthew's understanding of Hosea was Christologically driven, and the means by which he was able to mine Hosea 11 was a hermeneutical standard with which his audience was both familiar and comfortable. So, in this instance, a look at the broader context is revealing, but it neither explains why Matthew did what he did nor why he (apparently) thought it would be appealing to his readers. Those factors are best addressed when we keep before us Matthew's hermeneutical environment.

So, whereas the larger context is a helpful category for understanding Matthew 2:15, it is not a decisive hermeneutical point, nor is it a category that can be applied to every instance of the NT use of the OT. The seed/seeds example from Galatians 3 makes this point self-evident. Paul is most certainly not taking the larger context of the Abrahamic promises into account in his interpretation: the promise is for more offspring than Abraham can count, not one "seed" to come some two thousand years later. The force of Paul's exegesis depends on him *not* appealing

---

34. An argument somewhat similar to this is made by John Sailhamer, referred to in n. 29, although my synopsis here does not address the subtleties of the argument as they deserve. Interested readers are encouraged to read Sailhamer's treatment for a more developed presentation of his thinking.

to the larger context of the OT passage—indeed, not even the
narrow context of the passage itself. Rather, Paul is engaged in
what is often referred to as "atomistic" exegesis, that is, isolat-
ing a word or phrase *from* its context in order to make an interpretive point. What often fuels such atomistic exegesis is some
grammatical peculiarity, ambiguity, or—as in the case of *zera'*—a
grammatical form that simply offers the potentiality of alternate
meaning for Second Temple interpreters.

Now, it is true that Genesis as a whole exhibits a "narrowing" of sorts of the Abrahamic promise: the promise is realized
through Isaac, not Ishmael; through Jacob, not Esau; through
Joseph and his sons, and Judah and Levi begin to take on a certain importance. But this narrowing cannot be used to suggest
that, in the promise to Abraham that his seed will be uncount-
able, there is *actually* embedded a notion that the seed will be
one. A proper accounting of Paul's exegesis cannot rest on such
a tenuous appeal to "larger context," especially since such an
appeal would be every bit as "subjective" or "arbitrary" as Paul
is charged as being, while also obscuring the hermeneutical conventions that actually do explain what Paul is doing. What explains Paul's exegesis in Galatians 3 is not his observance of the
larger structure of Genesis, but his conviction that Jesus is God's
Son, and he employs his rabbinic hermeneutical arsenal to drive
the point home to an audience suited to hear it.

Finally, I should make a brief comment on the "angels and
the law" tradition. The question of larger context is only relevant
when we are attempting to explain an overt piece of exegesis by
a NT author. The "angels and the law" tradition that we see in the
NT, as are the other examples I listed briefly in that section, are
not, in my view, exegetical or interpretive with respect to the NT
authors. Rather, they are interpretive traditions—pieces of interpretation whose point of origin concerned particular passages or
words deemed to require some explanation. Many such interpretive traditions found, for whatever reason, a broader appeal and
so came to be considered legitimate pieces of interpretation for
other ancient commentators on Scripture. In fact, it can be argued
that some of these interpretive traditions came to be so common
that the line between text and interpretation became blurred.
Whether this is the case with the "angels and the law" tradition,
one cannot say (although I am inclined in that direction).

This ancient phenomenon is not at all unlike contemporary examples, of which there are many. We were discussing this phenomenon in one of my classes several years ago, and I asked if anyone could adduce examples in common currency of interpretive traditions coming to be associated with the biblical text, and thus taken as true. One student mentioned, correctly, the issue of Mary riding on a donkey. That is not in the gospels but the image is firmly ingrained in our minds. Another gospel example concerned the wise men. One student raised his hand and said, "Yeah, that's right. I mean, the Bible doesn't even *tell us* what the names of the *three* wise men were." True, the names Caspar, Melchior, and Balthazar are not biblical but part of church tradition,[35] but it *never occurred* to this student that neither is *three* mentioned. For him, "three" simply represented the biblical text, even though this was no less traditional than the names of the wise men. (Not to worry. We had a good laugh and the student has fully recovered.)

This phenomenon of interpretive traditions becoming associated with one's understanding of the Bible is as old as biblical interpretation itself and sufficiently demonstrated in the NT itself. Since the focused issue of this essay is the NT *interpretation* of the OT, it will not do to linger on this dimension of the topic longer than is necessary. Where this issue overlaps with the exegetical examples addressed in this essay, however, is that it illustrates, in its own way, how much the NT reflects the environment in which it was written. Whether this concerns overt exegetical issues or the incorporation of interpretive traditions, the NT behaves in a way that may not sit well with our expectations, at least at first, but that reminds us, as Bavinck (cited earlier) put so well:

> The word, the revelation of God, entered the world of creatureliness, the life and history of humanity, in all the human forms of dream and vision, of investigation and reflection, right down into that which is humanly weak and despised and ignoble.... All this took place in order

---

35. In this sense, Christian interpretation exhibits the same tendency found in the long history of Jewish interpretation: the penchant for naming unnamed biblical characters.

that the excellency of the power ... of Scripture, may be God's and not ours.

Perhaps we expect more of the NT use of the OT than we have the right to. But perhaps the very purpose of this "humiliation" is to remind us, ironically, that the power of Scripture lies solely in God and not in whether it meets our expectations.

Christ as the Hermeneutical Center of the NT Use of the OT

Scripture, as God's Word, is authoritative for the church. That is to say, it has the final word on all matters pertaining to "[God's] own glory, man's salvation, faith and life"[36] and is "useful for teaching, rebuking, correcting and training in righteousness" (2 Tim 3:16). We have also seen that not only does Scripture itself reflect the various cultural moments in which it was written (and no less inspired by the Spirit), but, with the NT use of the OT, the NT authors employed methods and traditions that likewise reflect their cultural moment. In my view, we begin down the wrong path if we assume that Scripture's authority and its cultural qualities are at odds with one another.

Nevertheless, Scripture's enculturedness raises perennial questions, which at some point touch down on the pressing question of whether the NT use of the OT should serve as a model for contemporary interpretation. Many have written eloquently on this important question, and a full answer would begin to approach a book-length treatment. Still, in view of what as been sketched in this essay, it appears to me that we are led to at least a general orientation for addressing this perennial hermeneutical challenge.

Both Matthew's use of Hosea and Paul's treatment of the seed promise in Genesis reveal an important principle at work in the NT use of the OT, namely, that these NT authors were guided in their interpretive work by the eschatological reality of the coming of Christ. The term I prefer to use to describe this eschatological hermeneutic is *Christotelic*. Although I have no strong objection, I prefer this term over "Christological" or "Christocentric," since these are susceptible to a point of view

---

36. *Westminster Confession of Faith* 1.6.

I am not advocating here—needing to "see Christ" in every, or nearly every, OT passage. Such an approach would certainly become artificial if one were to "conclude with Jesus," for example, in every proverb or each of the ten plagues (where is Jesus in the plague of frogs?).

A Christotelic approach is an attempt to look at the centrality of Christ for hermeneutics in a slightly different way. It asks not so much, "How does this OT passage, episode, figure, etc., *lead* to Christ?" To read the OT "Christotelicly" is to read it *already knowing* that Christ is somehow the *end* (*telos*) to which the OT story is heading; in other words, to read the OT in light of the exclamation point of the history of revelation, the death and resurrection of Christ. Revisiting our analogy of reading a novel, it is like reading a story and finally grasping the significance of the climax, and then going back and reading the story in light of the end. It is to ask, "How do earlier elements of the dramatic movement of this book relate to where the book as a whole is going?"

Such an approach, I would argue, is what we find so often with the NT writers as they pore over their Scripture in an effort to demonstrate that what God did in Christ is what gives Israel's entire story its coherence. It is the OT as a whole, particularly in its grand themes, that finds its *telos*, its completion, in Christ, the one in whom God himself determined to punctuate his covenant, the one to whom Scripture bears witness and under whose authority Scripture is now to be understood.

It is important again to stress that the vitality of that OT witness is not thereby eliminated. Think again of the analogy of the first and second readings of a novel. The second, Christotelic, reading can only have its real punch when we understand the OT to be the authentic, revealed, Word of God for its particular moment in redemptive history. To put it another way, by reading the OT witness as actual divine witness (i.e., not reading past it quickly to get to the second reading), we allow the contours of the OT to shape how we hear the final word revealed in God's Son and the NT witness to him.

In this sense, fulfillment is much more than "this OT text must correspond to this NT text." Rather, the utter hermeneutical centrality of Christ's person and work shows us how a "full" understanding of God's ultimate program for the world must await the climax of the story. Again, this does not mean that this knowledge will make every interpretive issue we face magically clear up, but it does intend to assume that we proceed to address those issues according to a hermeneutical template the NT authors seem so intent to work out. This, then, leads to our final point.

Can We Follow the NT Use of the OT as a Model Today (or, What Does it Mean to Follow the NT Example)?

We come to what is really the most pressing issue for Christian interpreters of the OT: How, or to what degree, are we to follow the NT authors? Perhaps the question can be asked a bit differently. I think we all agree that we should put ourselves under NT authority, but the question becomes, "What does this mean, hermeneutically speaking?" In addressing this question, I would like to make two important distinctions, (1) between biblical foundations and Christian proclamation, and (2) between the mechanics of the NT authors and their overarching hermeneutic.

The distinction between reading the OT for biblical foundations and Christian proclamation is simply a restatement of the analogy of the first and second read, but let me touch down here a bit on practical matters. What the NT authors demonstrate is a proclamation of Christ in relationship to the foundational OT witness, but we must not forget that these authors, and presumably their audiences, possessed something that cannot be presumed of all Christian audiences today: a grounding in the OT. For this reason, we must keep in mind that a Christotelic hermeneutic cannot be dismissive of the OT witness—even in places where the OT context is quite distant from the NT author's intention. Rather, even where the NT diverges significantly from the OT, it is only those who are thoroughly grounded in the OT who can recognize this *and*, more importantly, engage responsibly the theological-eschatological importance of such a hermeneutical phenomenon (as we saw, for example, in the seed/seeds example and Matthew's use of Hosea).

Hence, it is important in the life of the church that the OT "on its own terms," so to speak, is taught. And this can take place in numerous settings, including Bible studies, Sunday schools, seminars, and also sermons. This last point may seem out of place in view of the Christotelic hermeneutic I am advocating, but it is largely a concession to how many Christians have lost touch with the OT, even on the level of its basic content. Moreover, many churchgoers in today's world do not go to Bible studies, Sunday school, or attend seminars (a trend that I expect to continue). But they are more likely to attend church regularly. It is for this reason that pastors have the privilege and challenge, in a variety of creative and engaging ways, to teach their people what the OT is about. It may take time to earn the further privilege of bringing these Christians to appreciate more fully how Israel's story is transformed in Christ. And this is not a quick fix, but a process of reunderstanding God's Word, modeled after the NT writers, that may well take considerable time to implement.

The second distinction, between the mechanics of the NT writers and their hermeneutic, brings us to another practical consideration. I will state it plainly, not so much as the final word, but as a plausible, initial, attempt to remain faithful to the NT model: where we follow the NT writers is more in terms of their hermeneutical goal than in terms of their exegetical methods and interpretive traditions.[37] The latter are a function of their cultural moment. Again, that does not mean they can be safely dismissed as irrelevant, for understanding the cultural moment of the NT writers has significant theological payoff (as discussed above). But whereas we do not share the cultural moment of the NT writers, we do share their *eschatological* moment, and it is here that the question of following or not following the NT writers should have its initial focus.

It may be too much to get into here, but I take it as an important biblical proclamation that we, like the NT writers, are living in the last days, the final age, inaugurated by Christ's death and resurrection, which will be consummated at his second coming. The kingdom of God has come but is not yet fully realized. Because we share this same eschatological posture with

---

37. A succinct and helpful articulation of this principle may be seen in D. McCartney, "The New Testament's Use of the Old Testament," in *Inerrancy and Hermeneutic: A Tradition, A Challenge, A Debate*, ed. H. M. Conn (Grand Rapids: Baker, 1988), 101–16.

the NT writers, we also share their eschatological/Christotelic hermeneutic. We, therefore, must model our approach to Scripture after that of the apostles.

This means that they model for us a hermeneutical "attitude," so to speak, that is authoritative for us, even if that authority does not function as a five-step hermeneutical guide. It represents, rather, a frame of mind in which mature believers *expect* their reading of the OT to be ever more conformed to what the NT writers do. This is to say, we, in our interpretation of the OT, are on a pilgrimage of sorts, where our aim is to become as captured by the risen Christ as the NT authors were in their grappling with Israel's story.

As I have said above, such an interpretive posture does not claim to smooth over all difficulties, nor do I think that is what is intended in such an approach. By keeping the hermeneutic of the NT writers before us, we will be more prone to stay on the path they have blazed for us. We will not wonder why they did not do things more as we would have expected. Rather, we will learn to conform our own interpretive expectations to God's Word. This is not a "method," in the strict sense of the word that can be learned in a manual and then applied. God's Word is too rich, deep, and subtle for that. But following the NT authors—or better, committing ourselves to learning more and more just what that means—is indispensable for Christian interpretation of the OT.

RESPONSE TO ENNS

Walter C. Kaiser, Jr.

With the opening lines of Professor Enns's chapter, his emphasis falls right away on the *NT* and the work of "peel[ing] back the curtain of God's drama," rather than finding that this task is to be done in all of God's revelation. Enns observes that "the distance" that occurs between the surface meaning in the OT and how that passage is used in the NT is rather large, providing for a "significant disjunction between what an OT passage means in its original context and how it is used by NT authors." This easily leads to the critical charge that the NT authors fabricated their intentions wherein OT texts mean anything the Christian community claims, despite their plain meaning—a serious charge indeed!

Instead of being troubled by such disconnects in meaning, Enns wonders "whether our *focus* should be on lessening the hermeneutical tension or whether there is something of positive theological value to be gained by articulating why such tensions occur." Enns asks, "How true is it that such tensions are really at odds with an inspired text, in tension with God's character, and so in need to be corrected?" It would appear that he is pleased to leave these tensions in place rather than trying to resolve them exegetically. For him, the surface meaning only demonstrates that God has spoken in time and space, but this is not the same as the full divine meaning contained therein. This divine meaning apparently remains hidden in, around, and under the verse(s) until Christ and the NT authors unpack it!

This surely gives a new meaning to "paradox theology." It also voids the doctrine of the concursus of the divine and the human writers of Scripture, for the two senses seem to share little in common. Moreover, for the Reformers and throughout the history of the church, never was the *regula fidei* imposed on a text to deny or to supersede its *sensus literalis*.

SIGNIFICANCE OF SECOND TEMPLE LITERATURE

Enns believes that the NT authors' use of the OT reflects the *"interpretive practices* documented elsewhere in the literature of the Second Temple period." To do less or otherwise would be to adopt modern notions of interpretation. But it is precisely at this point that the debate must be joined, for it must be questioned whether OT scholars found it necessary to use the *interpretive practices* of Mesopotamia, Egypt, Anatolia, and the like when they too engaged in Near Eastern cognate studies. Indeed, what commonly agreed upon interpretive practices (matching such Second Temple methods as *pesher* or *midrash*) could be suggested by OT scholars for interpreting the parallel ancient texts from the Ancient Near East? In fact, there were outright rejections of some of these materials from being included in the canon, such as the Apocrypha and Pseudepigrapha.

Much of Enns's strategy for using Second Temple interpretive practices rests on what he has explained more fully elsewhere as the "incarnational analogy"—Christ's taking on flesh is understood to be analogous to Scripture's own "incarnation" (i.e., its taking on human dimensions integrated with its divine origins). But this analogy cannot be made to fit in every way possible, as Enns himself recognizes. Therefore, what can be included in a checklist for those human "incarnational" features found in the divinely initiated Scriptures?

What is missing from Enns's *Inspiration and Incarnation*[1] is an example of *pagan interpretive practices* that serves as evidence of an incarnational interpretive practice, unique to a particular cultural era. All else reflects a common sense approach to

---

1. Peter Enns, *Inspiration and Incarnation: Evangelicals and the Problem of the Old Testament* (Grand Rapids: Baker, 2005), 17–21.

speaking and interpreting, stemming from the common grace of the *imago Dei*.

SOME EXAMPLES

Seed Meaning "One" (Galatians 3:15–29)

In Enns's treatment of Galatians 3:15–29, his point seems to be twofold: (1) the blessings to Abraham found in Genesis 12–17 were only for "Abraham's biological offspring," while Paul opens it up to the Gentiles as well; and (2) the argument turns on the word "seed," which Paul interprets as "Christ," who is himself Abraham's biological offspring.

What is surprising here is that Abraham was directly told that "all peoples on earth will be blessed through [him]" (Gen 12:3b). Thus, it is incorrect to claim, as Enns does, that only "Abraham's biological offspring" were originally understood to benefit from this blessing, until Paul opened it up for the Gentiles. It must not be thought from Genesis 12:3 that the Gentiles would rise up to "bless themselves," as if the Niphal form of the verb was to be rendered as a *reflexive* instead of a *passive*. In the five patriarchal texts where this aspect of Abraham's blessing appears, three of them (12:3; 18:18; 28:14) use the Niphal form of the verb and only two use the Hithpael (22:18; 26:4).[2] Betil Albrektson concludes that this is a clear reference to a divine plan in which Abraham had been chosen to be God's instrument for reaching all the nations of the earth—Gentiles obviously included![3]

Enns complicates his understanding of this text by retreating to what the Judaizers limited the "seed" of Abraham to mean—ethnic Israel. But Paul and the writer of Genesis knew

---

2. For the most definitive discussion of the passive meaning of these verbs ever presented, see O. T. Allis, "The Blessing of Abraham," *Princeton Theological Review* 25 (1927): 263–98. See especially p. 281, where he lists possible examples of the passive meaning also for the Hithpael. To this day, no one has answered Allis's arguments.

3. Bertil Albrektson, *History and the Gods* (Lund, Sweden: Gleerup, 1967), 79. See also my *Mission in the Old Testament: Israel as a Light to the Nations* (Grand Rapids: Baker, 2000), 15–21.

that "seed" was a collective word that had a singular focus in the one who would crush the head of "the Serpent" (Gen 3:15), yet with a plural reference that embraced all who would believe as Abraham did—Jew or Gentile! Why, then, is it necessary to scour all the rabbinic texts to find just one second-century AD text (*Sedem Olam Rabbah*) to parallel Paul's meaning in its so-called singular manifestation? As Enns correctly observes, "*neither* Paul *nor* the rabbis were the point of origin for this type of exegesis. What they display is a hermeneutic that precedes both of them." Exactly so—that is what the OT claimed originally on both counts. I enthusiastically agree with Enns on this point.

Sadly, our agreement is short-lived. For Enns goes on to claim, "What a word means in its context does not necessarily trump what it *could* mean with a bit of prodding." Enns's allowance for "atomistic exegesis" in the NT ought to be demeaned and avoided with a passion.

On the matter of Christ being indicated by the word "seed" in Genesis 3:15, note that the one who is identified by the pronoun "he" (*hu'*) is the one who would crush the head of the Serpent. True, we are not told that his name would be "Jesus" or even that he would be the "Messiah." But there is no mistaking the fact that Eve assumed that her first male offspring would be the person who would end all the trouble resulting from the fall.[4]

Angels and the Law (Galatians 3:19; Acts 7:53; Hebrews 2:2)

I am not sure much can be made out of these verses for the discussion of the NT use of the OT and their possible introduction of the fact that angels played a role in giving the law on Mount Sinai. Enns has given us a wonderful study, but in the end I am not able to conclude much more than he did. None of the suggestions made in the history of interpretation yield any sense of probability, much less assurance we are on the right track. The translation of Deuteronomy 33:2 is difficult—an assessment that even antedates the Masoretes and all textual traditions we now possess. It is at best only "conjectural" that

---

4. On this text, see my response to Darrell Bock.

the angelic transmission of the law can be traced back to this verse in Deuteronomy.

Enns introduces this problem because it raises the question of the historicity of the text and what should be considered historical reality in that text. But as they say in law, "hard cases make bad law." So also here—hard texts make bad hermeneutical rules and principles.

"Out of Egypt I Called My Son" (Hosea 11:1 and Matthew 2:15)

Enns is not the only evangelical who has highlighted this use of the OT, for it really does appear *at first reading* that Hosea had no intention of predicting anything about the Messiah, much less his escape (or entrance) into Egypt. The verse seems to be a straightforward reference to the historic exodus of Israel from Egypt. So what was fulfilled in Matthew?

Matthew appeals to this OT text at the point in the narrative when the holy family is *entering*, not exiting, Egypt (Matt 2:15). Therefore the connection should not be sought in parallel exits of Israel and Jesus from Egypt. The emphasis rather should be on the words, "I called *my son*" (emphasis added).

Should we say with Enns that, whereas the "original historical context did not speak of Jesus of Nazareth, now [it] do[es]"—after Matthew retrojected his meaning to that effect on the unsuspecting Hosea? Is that not what we call eisegesis? If Jesus of Nazareth was not found originally in Hosea 11:1, did all readers of Hosea need to wait until Matthew uncovered God's hidden message for the first time in the days of Herod? But if Enns's *sensus plenior* argument here is wrong (and I must graciously say I think it is), what alternative do we have for understanding how these words were fulfilled?

I would offer this alternative. First, Hosea 11:1 begins covenantally with, "When Israel was a child, I [God] *loved* him." Another covenantal expression that is similar to Hosea's use of the word "loved" is found in the prophet Amos: "You only have I *chosen* of all the families of the earth" (Amos 3:2). In accord with that same sense for "loving" and "choosing" Israel when he was still just a "child" (*na'ar*), Hosea goes on to call that same "child"

(Israel), "my son." The technical use of that term began all the way back in Exodus 4:22 — "Israel is my firstborn son." Both the terms "firstborn" (which means one who is first in rank and in preeminence, not necessarily one who is chronologically first in birth order, since Jacob/Israel was actually born after Esau) and "son" lend themselves to a collective type of understanding and are used to refer simultaneously to "the one and the many" (as in corporate solidarity).

It is in this sense that the divinely inspired Hosea deliberately chose to use two singular nouns to represent the whole nation, while also realizing from antecedent Scripture that there was a coming Man of Promise who would appear under the similar reference, "my son" (e.g., 2 Sam 7:14; Pss 2:7; 89:27; Prov 30:4). Thus, when Israel was delivered by God as they crossed the Red Sea, there was in that crowd one who was the next installment in that promised line of messianic progenitors. Should anything have happened to all Israel, and in particular to that next "son" in the line of "sons" leading up to Jesus, the rest of revelation along with Christmas and Easter would have been cancelled.[5] "My son" is the key technical term for understanding this passage.

WHAT ABOUT *SENSUS PLENIOR* AND TYPOLOGY?

Enns argues that the NT has a "fuller sense" (*sensus plenior*) than what the OT authors envisioned in their writings. Apparently God purposely intended this fuller sense to be displayed later on, but where he hid this meaning, Professor Enns forgot to tell us. It certainly was not in the *sensus literalis*, that is, in the grammar, syntax, and meaning of the words in the text. So where is it hiding? If it is between the lines, as it were, then it is not "inspired," for Paul teaches that "all scripture/writings (*graphe*) are inspired" (2 Tim. 3:16, pers. trans.).

But Enns does know that this fuller sense is not equal to a possible *application* of the OT text, but it is itself "a true fuller *meaning.*" He also knows that the fuller sense, contrary to what

5. See my "fuller" treatment on Hosea 11:1 and Matthew 2:15 in *Uses of the Old Testament in the New* (Chicago: Moody Press, 1985; repr. Eugene, OR.: Wipf and Stock, 2001), 47–53.

Darrell Bock advocates, is not necessarily "consistent with" or "derived from the text's meaning in its original setting." In fact, Enns argues, "to assume that the original [meaning of an OT passage] and Christological intentions *need* to be aligned (in ways that reflect our own [modern] hermeneutical sensitivities) is to get off on a bad start if our task is to understand the NT authors' hermeneutic." That surely leaves the OT text as the orphan text with a lesser revelatory value than the NT. It is not clear why Enns even bothers with the OT, for it contributes very little, if anything, to the deeper or fuller meaning that comes with the appearance of Jesus and the NT. Enns's view opens up a clear rupture between the *sensus literalis* and the meaning derived by NT authors using Second Temple interpretive methods.

WILL THE LARGER CONTEXT OF THE OT EXPLAIN THE NT USE OF THE OT?

Enns agrees with C. H. Dodd that going beyond just the specific verse cited in the OT to the larger context can be helpful. At the same time, Enns argues that such a method should not be used to protect the NT authors against the charge of an "illegitimate" interpretation. Then why try? Even though he rejects the thought advocated by many in his same tradition that nearly every passage must "see Christ," he does believe in a "Christotelic" reading of the Bible. To read the Bible this way is to read it *"already knowing* that Christ is somehow the *end* (*telos*) to which the OT story is heading." But if it is not there in the first place, how can the story be used to show this "end" was anticipated?

CAN WE TODAY REPEAT THE NT'S MODEL OF USING THE OT?

Dr. Enns does not wish to be dismissive of the OT, even where the OT context is quite distant from the NT author's intention. But it still is not clear why we would not be dismissive of it since the really important material comes from the newly imported data in the NT. Enns argues we should make the NT the Bible of our day and read the rest of the Bible through those new eyeglasses, as should all who wish to come to the Savior as well. This will end up, I am afraid, making the NT a canon within a canon and demeaning God's older revelation to a historical curiosity only.

RESPONSE TO ENNS

Darrell L. Bock

There is much I like about Enns's essay. It stresses the relevance of reading the NT text with sensitivity to how texts were being read in the first century. It recognizes that those who were interpreting were not doing exegesis in the narrow sense, but reading texts in light of considerations of the whole of God's promise. It also is clear on how Christ himself serves as a source of revelation.

PRELIMINARY NOTES

Yet the chasm this essay posits between what a text meant and what it means appears to be overstated. The essay's classification says much here — "Fuller Meaning, Single Goal." There is nary a word about any connection to what was originally said. My point is that the connections exist between what was said and what is said, and they can be articulated with more than saying that the goal was Christotelic. Many of the texts the NT uses were being read in a messianic or eschatological sense before Jesus Christ came onto the scene. This means that some readings are as *eschatotelic*, if I may coin a term, as they are Christotelic (in many cases, the sacred texts used were perceived to be about the end, yet with no reference to the Messiah explicitly). I also think that the essay underestimates the importance of reading history in a parallel or typological manner, something that does clearly impact many texts, including some of the ones Enns discusses.

SECOND TEMPLE LITERATURE

I find myself in substantial agreement with what Enns affirms about the importance of Second Temple literature. This literature represents an attempt to make sense of and synthesize what the sacred texts of Judaism affirmed. Some of these syntheses the early Jesus movement took up and developed, since they shared the Jewish heritage these texts reflect. I cannot say it any better than Enns does when he states, "If we neglect this vital historical dimension, we run the risk of assuming universal normativity of our own culturally-embedded hermeneutical expectations"; or, "The purpose of being familiar with historical context is that it brings a deeper dimension of understanding and also provides some control to our own interpretations of Scripture. These are basic principles of grammatical-historical exegesis and need little defense for this readership."

I react, however, when Enns says this:

> One problem we face, however—at least as I see it—is that an application of grammatical-historical principles to NT hermeneutics shows that the NT authors' engagement of their Scripture was not directed by grammatical-historical principles. By modern conventions, there is often a "disconnect" between what an OT passage means in its context and how it is employed by NT writers.

The unqualified nature of this statement is a problem. I would say that the engagement was not *merely* or *exclusively* grammatical-historical in its application, but that parameters for what is said are very much tied to these kinds of considerations. I agree with Enns that interpretive practices and traditions are also at work here and are important to consider, since they often do reflect the wider synthetic kind of reading I see at work in many texts.

Another summary statement that gets my reaction is this one: "Whether for our tastes the NT authors are at times more in harmony with the original meaning of an OT passage or quite distant from it, what provides the grand coherence of the NT is the conviction that Jesus is the climax of God's covenant with Israel." The sentence suggests that some applications are distant from the original utterance. For Enns, as long as the statement coheres in Christ as an eschatological figure, then there is no problem—only "tension."

However, we must not forget that these texts were trying to persuade people coming out of Judaism that Jesus did fulfill their promises. If there is quite a distance between the original meaning and its fulfillment, then those to whom the texts are presented will argue that such claims do not amount to a fulfillment, or even have the possibility of being such, since there is no connection between what was said and what is said. My point here, in part, is that such texts often were read eschatologically in Judaism, but not always messianically. The early church often developed these texts in a messianic direction or made connections to the Messiah, *in line with previous expectation*, yet in ways *that also saw patterns of how God acts when he saves*. Such *combinations of elements* mean there is a tighter connection between these original texts and the early church's appeal to them than Enns's language suggests.

THE EXAMPLES

Enns's examples provide help to make my point. Enns's discussion on "seed" is surely right: that (1) in the Pentateuch, "seed" led ultimately to the nation of Israel being like the sands of the sea; and that (2) Paul knew of both the corporate and singular meanings of the term. However, there are elements of Paul's understanding of this concept, tied as it is to being God's children, that Enns does not develop. In Romans 9, Paul makes clear not only that he understands the promise's corporate element but that it operates in a manner where the many come out of the one. The promise runs through "one seed" of Abraham (Isaac and Jacob) and not through another "seed" of Abraham (Ishmael or Esau).

In this way, we see a "pattern." The many come through the one. So just as the children of Abraham became the nation of Israel, so now the children of God's new eschatological people come through the chosen seed of Abraham, the Christ, to become the eschatological people of God, and in a way that includes Gentiles who are incorporated in that seed. I suspect that this kind of theological underpinning and synthesis is at the core of Paul's argument in Galatians 3. It is such theologizing that belongs to methods so common in the Second Temple period. This would not only be common to the period, it also would reflect a reading that Jews of the time could potentially appreciate because the idea that the end is like the original period of salvation is a frequent theme of Jewish eschatological readings (e.g., new creation, exodus, and day of the Lord themes work with such patterns).

A final point here is that such a reading is a far cry from the "atomistic" rabbinic readings to which Paul's handling is often compared and to which Enns alludes when he says, "Such a phenomenon is often referred to as 'atomistic' exegesis, meaning particular words or phrases are looked at in isolation, without being informed by the immediate or broader contexts and thus more open to manipulation." My own take is that there is a larger context and a method of reading being applied here that makes this reading the opposite of an atomistic reading. Paul is not making too much of an exaggerated detail. He is highlighting the detail to make a comprehensive theological point that a consideration of the larger context of hope allows one to make.

The same kind of consideration applies to Enns's second example from Galatians 3:19, Acts 7:53, and Hebrews 2:2. Much of what Enns says here is again helpful. The Pentateuch sets forth the idea that God gave the law (Ex 31:18; Deut 9:10). The discussion surrounding Deuteronomy 33:2 is complex. However, the injection of the presence of holy ones here is important. It shows that this event took place with some sense of angelic association according to this text. Note how Enns concludes here: "I would feel a bit disingenuous to offer Deuteronomy 33:2 as a resolution."

One thing that Enns does not consider is whether Deuteronomy 33:2 could be *part* of a resolution. To my mind, there is a first-century belief that is important here: namely, that no one ever has seen God (John 1:18a). It seems that by the first century for many Jews, God was so holy that being directly present with him was not a readily received idea. Angels were seen as adequate "representatives" of him. So what I am arguing here is that a reading of the tradition of angels and the law fits both with the kind of thing to which Deuteronomy 33:2 alludes, as well as to a developed theological theme that was a part of the first-century landscape (as Enns well notes but does not clearly emphasize, as seen in *Jubilees* 1:27, 29; 2:1). It may well be the fact that the LXX reading of Deuteronomy 33:2 reflects such a theological conclusion as well.

Paul's point would then emerge as a result of both the kind of thing a first-century reading of Deuteronomy 33 suggested, as well as a general theological understanding of how God's activity came to be seen. Such additional options show that the situation may be more complicated than either choosing between an original reading or saying it simply came from somewhere else in a meaning distant from the original sense. For in Paul's claim, the idea also would be present that God is represented through angelic activity; it is just that this presence is more indirect than the direct way God is involved in the revelation of Jesus.[1]

As Enns closes out this example, he points to four ways a text can work:

> Regardless, what is clear to me is that Acts 7, Galatians 3, and Hebrews 2 are better understood within [(4)] the context of early translations and Second Temple interpretative traditions, rather than as (1) products of their own, private, exegetical ingenuity, (2) special revelation they received of heretofore unknown events, or (3) reflections of an oral body of information that goes back to the events themselves and that was well known but did not make it into the Bible (for some unexplained reason). (The bracketed (4) is my additional numbering to his sentence.)

To these options I add a fifth, which may be a mere difference of emphasis with him, but one that I think occupies a key role in many such texts. It is this: (5) deductions made within a worldview moved by canonical teaching and elements (what we often call even today, "doing theology").

My observation about his final example, Hosea 11, is similar to the other discussions. I agree with Enns that Hosea 11:1 is about the past. Yet there is an eschatological element in the near

---

1. I will also note that as a result of his handling here, Enns makes more out of this example in terms of method and historicity than I am willing to see. The other examples he cites do illustrate a point I share with him, namely, that traditions and sources are used in the NT that do not reflect details of the Jewish Scripture.

context, as Hosea 11:8–9 holds out the promise that Israel will not be destroyed by God's judgment. Now if we combine this future hope with the idea that salvation at the end is like the way it was at the start (theological pattern), then Matthew's reading becomes theologically comprehensible, using themes that made sense at the time. Enns's conclusion here — "What drives Matthew to handle Hosea's words is, in my view, something other than a commitment to how Hosea's words functioned in their original setting" — becomes an overstatement because something from Hosea's context (as well as something that fits basic Jewish beliefs and hermeneutical concerns) can be seen to be at play.

In sum, there is more at work here in the development of NT readings than merely a Christological principle. The examples Enns presents have mostly appealed to themes already extant in Jewish readings outside of Christology to make sense of what the NT is doing. These are cases of fuller meaning, yes, but not merely for one goal. Rather, the meaning read in a reflective context of theology done in light of the whole of the revelation of promise is a key player that allows us to describe and appreciate the readings the NT authors give.

AN ANALYSIS OF THREE VIEWS ON THE NEW TESTAMENT USE OF THE OLD TESTAMENT

Kenneth Berding

The issues discussed in this volume are complex. One of the goals of this book has been to take a topic that is usually only discussed among biblical scholars and make it accessible to a broader audience of those who are aware of the difficulties discussed on these pages but are not sure how to get started in answering them. The goal of this final chapter is to bring the issues and their proposed resolutions into sharper focus.

My coeditor, Jonathan Lunde, opened the book employing the metaphor of five key issues orbiting one central question. That central question is the relationship between the intended meanings of the OT authors and those derived from those texts by NT authors. The five orbiting issues, each of which has been addressed by our three authors in their essays, clarify the differences between our authors. The approaches of each author to the five "orbiting questions" will here be reviewed. The close of the chapter will draw attention to one benefit of each view, one potential problem with each view, and one probing question for each of our contributors.

A SUMMARY OF CONTRIBUTORS' RESPONSES TO THE FIVE ORBITING QUESTIONS

Sensus Plenior

Each contributor was asked to comment on whether there is a "fuller" meaning to the utterance of an OT prophet than the prophet understood. In other words, is there more meaning that God (the divine author) intended to communicate in an OT prophet's words that goes beyond what the OT prophet himself could access but which a NT author brings to the surface?

Walter Kaiser rejects the notion of *sensus plenior*. Only "that which stands written in the text" should be considered Scripture. Thus, the only meanings that are accessible are those "discoverable by the rules of language and exegesis." Meaning is "unchanging." The only thing that changes is the "significance," that is, the application of the same meaning to "new situations, persons, institutions" and the like. Kaiser rejects the notion that certain NT passages suggest *sensus plenior*, including 1 Peter 1:10–12, 2 Peter 1:19–21, and John 11:49–52. He asserts that there is a "generic wholeness" of the "divine promise-plan of God" that is found throughout the OT of which the prophets would have been aware. Furthermore, the prophets were "divinely enabled" to see both near fulfillments and distant fulfillments. Thus, the "boundaries" of meaning for the NT authors were already delineated by the OT literary and biblical-theological contexts. Because OT texts have "divine authority," the NT does not change the meaning that is already resident in OT texts.

Darrell Bock is willing to employ the term *sensus plenior* in a limited sense, acknowledging that God looked ahead and saw the various contexts and referents of what he had in mind "even if the prophet did not." Bock argues that there is a "central idea" that is "stable" in OT texts that are reused in the NT. This "basic principle" or "subject matter" is what connects an OT text and its employment by a NT author. Though the original meaning does not change, there are new "contexts" in which the meaning is employed, and thus new "referents" to which it applies. Furthermore, because of the passing of time and progress of revelation, there is a perspective formed in later contexts that allows a "fresh understanding" of an earlier text to emerge. The reason *we* are often perplexed by the way the NT authors use OT texts is because NT authors are not only reading on an "exegetical level," they are also reading on a "canonical level" and thus are taking into account the broader "themes" to which a particular OT text is connected.

Peter Enns affirms that *sensus plenior* "is a helpful theological construct" because it addresses head-on the issue of an

OT text having both a human and a divine author, with God as "the ultimate author." Thus, "the original purpose of an OT passage does not exhaust its meaning." As a result, sometimes (though not always) there is a "disconnect" between what an OT prophet intended in his day and the understanding a NT author offers when he uses an OT passage. But our "focus" becomes misdirected if we feel obliged to find explanations for the "hermeneutical tension" that we experience when we discover that NT authors have sometimes incorporated into their texts new meanings of OT texts. The NT authors are not constrained by "grammatical-historical principles" since they are participants in an interpretive climate that differs from our own day and age. Rather, the NT writers are constrained by the singular conviction that "Christ is somehow the *end* (*telos*) to which the OT story is heading."

Typology

Each author was asked to comment on whether typology is a valid category and, if so, how it should be understood.

Kaiser accepts the validity of typology, namely, that there are repeatable patterns in the OT that find NT fulfillment. Furthermore, it is within the central "promise-plan of God" that such typology is most likely to occur. But Kaiser maintains that the vital test for anyone who claims to have found a type is the issue of "divine designation," that is, a "needed divine indication that it was a type." Any prediction, including a type, "must be seen ahead of time and not added after an alleged fulfillment takes place."

Bock makes "typological patterns in history" a focal-point of his understanding of the NT use of the OT. He suggests that as God's revelatory activity progresses and expands into new contexts, "the force of earlier passages in God's plan becomes clearer." Though some typological patterns are inherently predictive, in other cases "the pattern is not anticipated or looked for until the fulfillment makes the pattern apparent." This latter case "is still a prophetic category because God designed the correspondence," even if the prophet himself could not always see that his words would eventually function typologically. Bock's emphasis on such patterns of fulfillment often plays a key role in how he resolves difficult NT uses of the OT.

Enns affirms the validity of typology as "a helpful and time-honored way of expressing how the NT fulfills the OT." He values the study of broad theological patterns of the OT in light of the fact "that it was all heading somewhere." But Enns questions whether typology constitutes "an adequate *hermeneutical* explanation" for what the NT authors actually do with the OT. According to Enns, it is not the presence of typology that *explains* the behavior of the NT authors vis-à-vis the OT; it is the fact that the NT authors are participants in the interpretive environment of Second Temple hermeneutics that explains their interpretive practices.

Context

Each author was asked to address the issue of how the NT authors view the *contexts* of the passages they use. In other words, do the NT authors draw on the broader contexts of the passages they employ or do they atomistically pull verses out of their contexts?

In Kaiser's treatment of specific passages, he models the idea that NT authors using OT texts would have drawn on the literary contexts surrounding the OT texts they employ. But Kaiser also emphasizes the importance of allowing any given OT passage to be informed by "the divine revelation found in the books that *preceded* the selected text." That is, when a NT author uses an OT text, he is drawing both on ideas that are found in the immediate literary context and also on "the antecedent scriptural development of words, phrases, concepts, events, and expectations" that this OT passage has already drawn upon.

Bock rejects atomistic readings and argues that the NT authors are aware of "two sets of contexts," the "exegetical" context and the "canonical" context. Regarding the exegetical context, Bock works with the assumption that the NT authors have the literary context in mind when they choose to utilize a particular verse, thus encouraging their readers to make connections with the ideas in the surrounding verses. But without minimizing in any way the immediate literary contexts, the decisive "context" for understanding what the NT writers are doing with the OT is often the "canonical context." The end result is that readings of the OT by the NT authors become "the product of a kind of grand synthetic reading ... in light of the progress of revelation."

Enns asserts that sometimes the NT authors read the OT contextually and sometimes they do not. But he rejects the idea that an appeal to context is the way to resolve the purported tension between what a passage seems to say in its OT context and how a NT author uses it. Since Enns believes that the NT authors fully participate in a wide range of interpretive practices common in the Second Temple period, he merely has to ask on a case-by-case basis which method(s) a NT author is utilizing. Thus, in one passage, Galatians 3, Enns can assert that Paul engages in "atomistic exegesis" of the seed/seeds promise to Abraham, but in a different passage that Matthew may be working under the assumption that his readers will tie into "the larger context of that chapter" when he cites a single clause from Hosea 11:1 in Matthew 2:15.

Exegetical Methods

Each of our contributors was asked to comment on the relationship of NT interpretive methods to the methods of other Second Temple interpreters. Specifically, to what extent do the NT authors share in the interpretive environment, assumptions, and methods of their contemporaries who also utilize or interpret the OT?

Kaiser argues against appealing to purported parallels between extrabiblical interpretation and the interpretive activities of the NT authors. "One would be hard-pressed to find any convincing apologetic value for validating the messianic or doctrinal claims" of the NT authors by appealing to such extrabiblical interpretive approaches as *midrash*, *pesher*, or allegory. In other words, the NT authors would lose the potential to persuade others of the truth of their message—and indeed would lose their own "confidence and hope"—if they in fact employed the "novel and unique" style of interpretation found, say, among the rabbis.

Bock argues that the NT authors do share in the interpretive assumptions and methods of their contemporaries in a number of ways while still diverging from them in other ways. He lists six presuppositions that guide the NT authors, but argues that only "the first three were shared with Judaism, whereas the last three were not." Of those shared with Judaism, two in particular show up regularly in Bock's explanations of particular texts: (1) "the one in the many" and (2) "pattern in history."[1] Thus, though he considers such parallels to be "crucial underpinnings" for understanding how NT authors use the OT and therefore encourages careful study of such extrabiblical literature, he resists any appeal to Jewish methods that involves a rupture in the essential unity between OT and NT meanings.

Enns spends a large portion of his essay emphasizing the importance of Second Temple literature for understanding what the NT authors are doing with the OT. In his view, their "hermeneutical behavior overlaps with that of their Second Temple contemporaries." No wedge should be driven between the activity of the NT authors and that of their contemporaries. Thus, Paul "is a product of the Second Temple hermeneutical world in which he lived." This is true both in regard to the NT authors' "interpretive practices" and in regard to "interpretive traditions" that make an appearance in the NT. What distinguishes NT interpretation from other Second Temple interpreters is not the *method* of the NT authors; what distinguishes their interpretation is the NT authors' inspired conviction that the OT all points to *Christ*.

Replication

Our final question concerns whether we should model our exegesis after that of the apostles. Can we do what they did when we interpret the Bible? Surprisingly, given the frequent variety of their responses to the other questions, all our authors responded "yes" in one way or another to this question. Their reasoning, though, differed in each case.

Kaiser says that we "certainly may follow in the steps of the NT writers when they use the OT." We may do this, he reasons, since the NT authors "argue most carefully" when citing the OT, taking into account not only the immediate context of a text they

---

1. I refer you also back to the description of these in the introductory chapter (pp. 37–39).

employ, but also "all the divine revelation found in the books that *preceded* the selected text." Stated differently, since the NT authors' method of OT interpretation is grammatical and historical, "we need only observe the methods [they] used and follow them in each new situation we face in our day."

Bock contends that we read the Bible the way the apostles did "even when we claim we do not." What he means is that all interpreters of Scripture necessarily find themselves working within theological categories that reflect their understanding of the way broad scriptural themes fit together. His plea, though, is that any "theological-canonical" reading engaged by us be "done within the framework of the theological grid the Scriptures give us." In our own endeavor to properly interpret the Bible, then, "the apostles are the witnesses and become our hermeneutical guides."

Enns argues that we should follow the lead of the NT writers, but "more in terms of their hermeneutical goal than in terms of their exegetical methods and interpretive traditions." Since our own generation has on the whole lost contact with the basic framework of the OT, and in light of the fact that we live in a time and culture in which people generally hold to different assumptions of how texts should be interpreted, we cannot simply assume that we will be able to follow the methods of the apostles. But we should aim to develop "a frame of mind" in which we "*expect* [our] readings of the OT to be ever more conformed to what the NT writers do."

Readers of this volume, however, should not suppose that everyone who studies the subject of the use of the OT in the NT will answer "yes" to the question of whether we can model our exegesis after the pattern of the apostles. Since contrary views on this issue have been discussed in the first chapter by Jonathan Lunde, they will not be repeated here.

A SUMMARY OF ANSWERS TO THE FIVE ORBITING QUESTIONS

At the risk of oversimplification, I have included a chart here to allow our readers to clearly see the similarities and differences between each of our three contributors.

	KAISER	BOCK	ENNS
Sensus plenior?	No, the prophets knew where their prophecies were heading.	Yes, but only in the limited sense of acknowledging that the OT writers could not always see fulfillments that emerge later.	Yes, because Christ-as-*telos* holds it all together. This, however, is not the way to resolve the "hermeneutical tension."
Typology?	Yes, but it must be seen ahead of time and possess "divine indication" that it is a type.	Yes, and fundamental for resolving difficult cases; can be either prospective or retrospective.	Yes, but again not the way to resolve the hermeneutical tension.
Context?	Yes, both the immediate literary context and the antecedent "promise-plan" context are important.	Yes, the immediate "exegetical context" is drawn upon but the "canonical context" is the key.	Sometimes yes and sometimes no.
Use of Second Temple exegetical methods?	No, such comparisons are misguided.	Sometimes yes, but constrained by the NT authors' commitment to a canonical reading.	Yes, and this is the central issue in the discussion.
Replication?	Yes, because the NT authors are careful interpreters just as we should be.	Yes, but particularly in terms of their overall appeal to canonical themes.	Yes, but less in terms of their exegetical methods and more in terms of their "Christotelic" goal.

ONE BENEFIT OF EACH VIEW, ONE POTENTIAL PROBLEM WITH EACH VIEW, AND ONE PROBING QUESTION FOR EACH CONTRIBUTOR

I will conclude this chapter with a brief description of one *benefit* of each view, one *potential problem* with each view, and one *probing question* for each of our contributors. Each comment will be limited to two sentences and will focus on issues that have not received lengthy discussion in the *responses* sections of the book. Consequently, it is hoped that this book will conclude with a certain amount of open-endedness and thereby underscore that there is still much work to be done in sorting out the difficult question of how the NT authors use the OT.

Benefits

Single meaning, unified referents. One benefit of adopting the view defended by Kaiser is that it is the approach that most directly satisfies the inclination of many readers that there *should* be a direct connection between a "prophecy" and its "fulfillment." Interpreters of the OT can accord full weight to the intended meaning of the OT authors.

Single meaning, multiple contexts and referents. One benefit of adopting the view defended by Bock is that readers of the Bible who hold this view will regularly find themselves making connections with the grand themes of Scripture. Passages will not be viewed in isolation; they will necessarily be connected to the movement of themes from one biblical context to the next in light of the progress of revelation.

Fuller meaning, single goal. One benefit of adopting the view defended by Enns is that the interpreter of the NT does not have to feel he or she is explaining away the most apparent interpretation of a NT text to make it fit with the OT. The interpreter of a NT passage can vigorously pursue the intended meaning of a NT text in its own literary context without necessarily having to worry about how such an interpretation might *agree* with an OT author's intention.

Potential Problems

Single meaning, unified referents. One problem with adopting the view defended by Kaiser is the possibility that interpreters may find themselves presuming upon the conscious intention of an OT author ideas that cannot readily be shown from the immediate context to be in his mind. This is especially important in those texts (and contexts) that do not themselves clearly indicate that the necessary "antecedent" theology is in the author's mind.

Single meaning, multiple contexts and referents. One problem with adopting the view defended by Bock is similar to the one highlighted above for Kaiser, but concerns the NT context. Interpreters adopting this approach may at times have to *assume* that certain canonical-theological themes are in a NT author's mind, even when those themes are not explicit in the immediate NT context. Such an assumption, of course, runs the risk that meanings that are not in fact present may get imported into the text being considered.

Fuller meaning, single goal. One problem with adopting the view defended by Enns is that an interpreter may be left with the nagging sense that there *ought* to be a true continuity of meaning each time a NT author uses an OT text. Though Enns would likely say that such an impulse is a function of our own cultural and historical setting, it is still the case that the felt need for legitimization is widespread among Christians.

One Probing Question

For Kaiser. Are there no positive benefits of comparing the assumptions and methods of other Second Temple interpreters with the assumptions and methods of NT authors, particularly when there are many *apparent* parallels?

For Bock. Is it legitimate to extract a principle formulated in the discipline of *linguistics*, that is, the separation of the *sense* of a word from its *referent*, and apply such a distinction to the NT use of the OT? Since such an analogy is fundamental to Bock's approach, it seems that a defense needs to be made of the legitimacy of using a linguistic micro-distinction to explain the macro-movement of theological concepts from one end of the canon to the other.

For Enns. Is Christ-as-*telos* the *only* way that OT passages connect to the NT? If Enns grants that there are other trajectories along which an OT idea can reach the NT, how do those other bridges connect with the "Christotelic" movement of the OT?

CONCLUSION

It is hoped that readers of this book have come to appreciate how much there is to be learned from each of the three approaches defended, regardless of which perspective they currently find most persuasive. It is also hoped that this volume will be an encouragement for Christians of our generation to think more intentionally about broad connections between the OT and the NT. This is something each of our authors is deeply concerned about. Finally, it is hoped that this dialogue will play at least a small role in encouraging more students of the Bible to enter into this complex area of study known as the NT use of the OT.

SCRIPTURE INDEX

Page numbers in **bold** indicate a more extensive treatment of a biblical passage.

SUBJECT INDEX